This is far and away the best parenting  book ... have
read hundreds of them. *Imperfect Paren*... ...
it's not for eggheads; it's for real par... ...
Matthews's message reassures anyone w... ...
one: Building a relationship with your child will bring you the
confidence to face any parenting challenge, and your love for each other
will just keep on growing. Your child will thank you.

—**TERRIE MOFFITT, PHD,** NANNERL O. KEOHANE UNIVERSITY PROFESSOR,
DUKE UNIVERSITY, DURHAM, NC, UNITED STATES; COAUTHOR OF
THE ORIGINS OF YOU: HOW CHILDHOOD SHAPES LATER LIFE

Imperfect Parenting is brimming with life-changing insights. Dona
Matthews, with compassionate and incisive expertise, distills the latest
research into understandable tips and tools that can help any parent. But
perhaps more important, she outlines a new approach to parenting that
will make us more effective as parents and strengthen our relationships with
our children. Dr. Matthews does this by combating the punishingly perfec-
tionistic culture around parenting today that tells us that, unless we've
checked every box on the "good parenting checklist," we have failed. *Imperfect Parenting* instead empowers parents to embrace imperfection constructively, and approach every challenge with renewed confidence and hope.

—**TRACY DENNIS-TIWARY, PHD,** PROFESSOR OF PSYCHOLOGY,
THE CITY UNIVERSITY OF NEW YORK, NEW YORK, NY, UNITED STATES;
AUTHOR OF *FUTURE TENSE: WHY ANXIETY IS GOOD FOR YOU
(EVEN THOUGH IT FEELS BAD)*

Imperfect Parenting is a treasure, filled with cutting-edge parenting advice backed by solid research and Dona Matthews's many years of experience supporting families. This book shows how parents and everyone involved in a child's life can build or rebuild a strong relationship, which is the ultimate foundation of optimal emotional health.

—**MONA DELAHOOKE, PHD,** AUTHOR OF *BRAIN-BODY PARENTING: HOW TO STOP MANAGING BEHAVIOR AND START RAISING JOYFUL, RESILIENT KIDS* AND *BEYOND BEHAVIORS: USING BRAIN SCIENCE AND COMPASSION TO UNDERSTAND AND SOLVE CHILDREN'S BEHAVIORAL CHALLENGES*

Imperfect Parenting covers a wealth of practical information, from advice for healthy eating and sleep to suggestions for how parents can engage with the cognitive, academic, social, and emotional aspects of their children's development. It is written in a warm, caring way with supportive tips for parents in taking care of themselves as well as their child. Insights from the author's clinical practice are well integrated with research-based conclusions. The book affirms the message that responsive, loving care is more important for children's development than any specific parenting dos or don'ts.

—**JENNIFER LANSFORD, PHD,** RESEARCH PROFESSOR, CENTER FOR CHILD AND FAMILY POLICY, DUKE UNIVERSITY, DURHAM, NC, UNITED STATES

Dona Matthews tackles both difficult and mundane problems of parenting with loving yet practical guidance that is grounded in evidence. I would recommend this book to new parents, those feeling overwhelmed by daily struggles with offspring, and teachers who wonder how classroom behaviors relate to what children may be experiencing at home.

—**RENA F. SUBOTNIK, PHD,** DIRECTOR, APA CENTER FOR PSYCHOLOGY IN SCHOOLS AND EDUCATION, WASHINGTON, DC, UNITED STATES

All parents, both new and experienced, will benefit from reading this compassionate guide to the art and science of parenting. Dona Matthews uses stories and case studies to illuminate the research behind building successful, protective relationships with children. *Imperfect Parenting* is a highly relatable and ultimately forgiving handbook that gives us permission to learn from our mistakes as we help our children develop into the best versions of themselves.

—**NANCY STEINHAUER,** PRINCIPAL, THE MABIN SCHOOL, CANADA'S FIRST INDEPENDENT ASHOKA CHANGEMAKER SCHOOL, TORONTO, ON, CANADA; COAUTHOR OF *PUSHING THE LIMITS: HOW SCHOOLS CAN PREPARE OUR CHILDREN TODAY FOR THE CHALLENGES OF TOMORROW*

Dona Matthews shows how parents who learn to respect their children's uniqueness, and relate to them with understanding and compassion, form strong connections that support them in becoming themselves. She describes how neuroscience and psychology inform the relationship skills that lead to easier and happier family relationships, as they support children's diversity and growth.

—**NICOLE A. TETREAULT, PHD,** NEUROSCIENTIST; AUTHOR OF *INSIGHT INTO A BRIGHT MIND: A NEUROSCIENTIST'S PERSONAL STORIES OF UNIQUE THINKING*

IMPERFECT PARENTING

IMPERFECT PARENTING

HOW TO BUILD A RELATIONSHIP WITH YOUR CHILD TO WEATHER ANY STORM

Dona Matthews *PHD*

 AMERICAN PSYCHOLOGICAL ASSOCIATION

Published by
APA LifeTools
750 First Street, NE
Washington, DC 20002
https://www.apa.org

Order Department
https://www.apa.org/pubs/books
order@apa.org

In the U.K., Europe, Africa, and the Middle East, copies may be ordered from Eurospan
https://www.eurospanbookstore.com/apa
info@eurospangroup.com

Typeset in Sabon by Circle Graphics, Inc., Reisterstown, MD

Printer: Gasch Printing, Odenton, MD
Cover Designer: Mark Karis

Library of Congress Cataloging-in-Publication Data

Names: Matthews, Dona J., 1951- author.
Title: Imperfect parenting : how to build a relationship with your child to
    weather any storm / by Dona Matthews.
Description: Washington, DC : American Psychological Association, [2022] |
    Includes bibliographical references and index.
Identifiers: LCCN 2021036897 (print) | LCCN 2021036898 (ebook) |
    ISBN 9781433837562 (paperback) | ISBN 9781433837579 (ebook)
Subjects: LCSH: Parenting. | Parent and child. | Parents--Psychology.
Classification: LCC HQ755.8 .M383 2022 (print) | LCC HQ755.8 (ebook) |
    DDC 649/.1--dc23
LC record available at https://lccn.loc.gov/2021036897
LC ebook record available at https://lccn.loc.gov/2021036898

https://doi.org/10.1037/0000274-000

Printed in the United States of America

10 9 8 7 6 5 4 3 2 1

CONTENTS

ACKNOWLEDGMENTS

This is one of those books that's built on countless interactions and experiences over all the years of a life. And it's thanks to the insightful observations of Susan Herman, development editor for the American Psychological Association's (APA) LifeTools series, that I was challenged to plumb the depths of my life experience—both personal and professional—and make connections to the knowledge and understanding I've been acquiring for all these decades. Susan enabled me to write the book I'd wanted to write for a long time (but hadn't yet fully imagined) and to deeply enjoy the process. She responded to an earlier version of the manuscript by asking for more stories about parents and kids, fewer lists, and less academic language. She envisioned a livelier book than I could've written without her. If you enjoy this book, it's thanks to her.

I want to acknowledge here all the parents, children, students, and colleagues I've known through the years, all those whose lives have touched mine in one way or another. I have learned something from each one of you.

My first contact at APA Books was Emily Ekle, editorial acquisitions director, academic and professional books. Her enthusiasm for my original concept motivated me to complete the manuscript that later became this book.

Linda McCarter, acquisitions editor at APA Books, has steered the book through the process. Her warmth, intelligence, and positive attitude have encouraged me to do my best work. She leads a team of professionals who exemplify much of what I write about here—so much more is achieved with constructive support than with negativity. Linda and her colleagues at APA Books have shown me how that is just as true in writing as parenting.

I've been working with my agent, Beverley Slopen, for a long time now and am grateful for her insistence that I learn to write with more warmth and authenticity (and less of a detached academic voice), her wise and ready counsel at every step along the way, and her friendship. She has helped me navigate the treacherous shoals of the world of publishing and has always steered me well.

In a wonderful example of another principle I discuss in this book, I want to thank my daughter, Robin Spano, for her writing help along the way. She helped me bring alive some of the families and situations I discuss here, in a happy example of all the surprising ways we can learn from our kids if only we let that happen.

I want to dedicate this book to my husband, Stephen Gross, whose absolute certainty that I had something important to say encouraged me to stay with the writing process through many years and many obstacles. Stephen insisted that I pull together the themes and discoveries I've made along the way of my professional journey in a coherent package that supports parents and nurtures children's best development. That's the book I've tried to write, and if I've succeeded at all, Stephen deserves much of the credit.

And finally, enlivening my world in so many ways, I want to acknowledge my children, their partners, and my wonderfully surprising grandchildren, each one of whom makes my world richer, brighter, and more meaningful: Ashley Gross, Kai Kwa, Sasha Kwa, and Riley Kwa; Alex Gross and Simon Papa-Gross; Erin Kawalecki, James Kawalecki, Theo Kawalecki, Zoe Kawalecki, and Jackson Kawalecki; and Robin Spano, Keith Whybrow, and Devon Whybrow.

IMPERFECT
PARENTING

INTRODUCTION

Your 2-year-old rejects most of the foods you offer. At first, you figure, What's new? Don't all toddlers throw their food on the floor at some point? Then, after a hair-raising late night in the emergency room, you have your child tested for food allergies. You learn that you'll need to find healthy alternatives for an entire category of foods that have, until now, been go-to options in your family's diet. Plus, you will have to come up with a way to kindly yet unequivocally communicate with caregivers, friends, preschool staff, and your child's grandparents about what your child can and cannot eat.

Your 11-year-old slips noiselessly from their online learning environment into watching a live-streamed game before settling for a few hours into their multiplayer digital universe. Distance learning in sixth grade has gone surprisingly well so far, and your child has turned in every assignment on time this week. So why not allow a little mind candy today? you ask yourself as you glance over your child's shoulder. The game includes a constant scroll of real-time chatter. Trying not to look too closely, you wonder, Is that chatter age appropriate? Probably not. Could my child be learning how to talk like an online troll right now? What rewards can I offer that will pry my child away from the screen?

Your 14-year-old sends you the text from school that you never, ever wanted to see. Classrooms are on lockdown due to "police activity in the area." Your heart stops. Is it someone robbing the corner store and making their getaway nearby? Not that that's good, but it is better than some alternative scenarios. Finally, a new message comes through: "All clear." Everyone is safe. Your child doesn't want to talk for much of the afternoon, but the next day is full of questions, anger, and fear. The incident is reported on local news sites, and discussion quickly spreads online. What can you possibly say or do to help your child feel confident or, at the least, clearheaded enough to go back to school?

Your 22-year-old moves back home with you after university, informing you they need a break. "I've been going to school for 17 years straight and need time to think about what I want to do with my life," they tell you. "That's too big a decision to make lightly." They spend the next 3 months going out every evening, going to bed late, getting up late, then lounging around the house until their friends are available again while you and your partner continue to earn the money that keeps it all happening, as well as doing the shopping, cooking, and cleaning that keeps the household running. How much longer should you support your child in this lifestyle? Are you doing more harm than good by enabling this dependence—which verges on freeloading—at this stage of their life?

At this time of widespread stress and rapid change in so many dimensions of our lives, you may feel at a loss for the right tools to give your child what they need to know. As illustrated in these stories, some of the lessons you'll have to teach are different from the ones you learned in your own childhood. Other lessons are the same but wear different faces. For example, telephone etiquette is still important; however, your child won't likely be calling their friend's house number and politely speaking to the family member who happens to pick up. Likewise, respecting other people's dinner and sleep time still matters. But are there time boundaries on texting or social media messaging? Most people silence their notifications when they don't want to be disturbed—don't they?

You may be surprised to learn that good parenting, at its heart, is as simple and old-fashioned as the relationship you build with your child. That's true across all ages, stages, and situations, whether you're a new parent of a healthy young baby in a two-parent family, someone contemplating fostering a child in care with your same-sex partner, a single parent with a teenager and serious financial pressures, or the parent of someone on the autism spectrum or with gifted learning needs. Perhaps this simple truth—that your relationship with your child matters more than anything else you might give them or teach them—is more important now than ever. By "now," I'm referring to late 2020 and early 2021, when I did the bulk of this writing. Families' experiences during the COVID-19 pandemic have heightened the need for parents to adopt the attitudes, knowledge, and skills I discuss in the book. However, I believe the same principle will remain true over time.

You may be wondering about complicated issues such as "How can I allergy proof, bully proof, or bulletproof my child?" or "How can I always know the right way to react, the right moral lessons to teach my child?" or "How can I possibly be a perfect parent under these circumstances?" The answer is: "You can't, and that is all right."

What you can do to keep your child safe and help them thrive is pay attention to how you are with yourself and then to how you are with your child. In this book, I provide a set of attitudes, habits, values, and practices that can help you reduce your stress and feel empowered to solve your problems or energized to find the help you might need to do that. As you realize that being a good parent is all about cultivating a certain way of being with your child, your questions about what exactly to do in every possible situation will become less important. You'll feel more in control and more confident in areas of your life that might have felt out of control at times.

Using stories taken from the lives of families I've worked with over the past 3 decades and grounded in current findings about human development, positive psychology, neuroscience, and mindfulness, I explain how the most important things you can do as a parent are to cultivate a healthy mindset about being a parent and build a relationship of love and respect for your child. I illustrate how nobody gets it right all the time and that that's just fine. Each of us is learning and growing along with our children.

Through the ways you respond to problems, setbacks, failures, and adversity, you can be a model of coping and resilience that will help your child build the skills they need to manage the problems they encounter in their own lives, now and in the future. You won't be perfect. Nobody ever is. What matters most is your attitude to the imperfections and snags you experience. A transformative special education teacher used to reassure his students—who had spent most of their lives until then messing up, failing, and having problems—"Practice makes better. Perfect is boring."[1]

You'll see a social justice thread running through this book. This comes from observing the benefits to children and parents when they make healthy connections with diverse others and from a philosophical and practical belief that we each do better when we all do better, that when one person is suffering and excluded, we are each diminished. This does not mean I prioritize the problems of those who are experiencing deprivation and obvious hardship, because nested in my commitment to social justice is an appreciation that the problems experienced by those with apparent advantages—health, fame, fortune, or something else—are also real problems and worthy of consideration. Every person deserves respect and kindness, no matter their age, background, or circumstance.

HOW DOES CHILDHOOD SHAPE ADULTHOOD?

When thinking about how you are as a parent and how you want to be, it can help to know something about current research findings on the factors most conducive to your child's optimal development into adulthood. *The Origins of You: How Childhood Shapes Later Life*[2] is one of the sources of findings and perspectives that I share in this book. Written by four renowned developmental scientists, it reports on 40 years of research with over 4,000 children, starting at birth and checking back with these children in a comprehensive fashion every few years into their mid-40s. It includes results from three major studies: the Dunedin Multidisciplinary Health and Development Study, in Dunedin, New Zealand; the Environmental Risk Study, which follows twins born in England and Wales; and the National Institute of Child and Human Development Study of Early Child Care and Youth Development, which included children growing up in 10 different locations in the United States, across a variety of race, socioeconomic circumstances, and family situations.

The Origins of You is a treasure trove of information on child and adolescent development, with important implications for parents. The authors address big questions such as the relative impact of genetic inheritance and environmental influences on life success, violence, and depression in adulthood; the strengths and problems of day care; and the ways young people are affected by bullying, cannabis use, and the neighborhoods in which they grow up.

The authors emphasized that genetic and environmental factors are probabilistic and not deterministic. That is, there are far too many complex interacting variables to say with certainty that any one thing—parenting style, abuse, neighborhood violence, divorce, genetic markers—will lead to any particular outcome. It is useful to know how one parenting approach generally leads to happier outcomes, but that doesn't mean that's the only approach that works or that a dramatically different approach will necessarily lead to problems. Their findings show that when risk factors are compounded, the probability of problems increases, but even then, some children prove resilient.

Some of the most important findings in *The Origins of You* concern protective factors that increase children's and adolescents' resilience in the context of life stressors. For example, the authors found that attachment security in infancy works to buffer and prevent many of life's most problematic outcomes right through into middle adulthood. A baby who is securely attached to an adult—typically but not always a parent—trusts that adult to keep them safe. They've learned that the parent will soothe them in times of distress; feed them when they're hungry; and keep them clean, safe, and warm. A securely attached infant shows distress when separated from the object of attachment—usually a parent—and joy when that person returns. As the baby gets a bit older, they generalize that feeling of trust to other people. A securely attached child is more likely to be calm, trusting, sociable, and engaged in learning. They react better to stress and are better able to manage their emotions.

Knowing this about attachment security has obvious implications for parents of infants—love your baby with all your heart and be as present and available as possible—but it doesn't mean there's no hope for a child whose early attachment experience was insecure or intermittent. The probabilistic (not deterministic) approach to understanding development means there are usually other supports a caring adult can provide along the way to increase a child's chances of making it through to a healthy and happy adulthood. Wherever you are now is the right place to start putting these findings about optimal approaches into practice.

The Origins of You concludes on a note of optimism, reminding the reader that development is open ended and that understanding what impacts a child's development helps us identify effective interventions when things go wrong. The authors and their colleagues are continuing to collect data as the study participants approach their 5th decade, with emerging data showing what leads some people to age more slowly—or quickly—than others.

Throughout this book, I share current research findings, including those reported in *The Origins of You*, because they lead to recommendations for supporting your child as they grow into an adult. At the same time, I want to emphasize that nothing about children's development is written in stone. Your personality, your child's temperament, your family's situation, your cultural background and values, and everything else that makes you *you* are all important factors in figuring out how best to parent your child. You might learn something from the research findings, but what's most important is that you look for your own best way based on your unique set of circumstances.

WHAT YOU'LL LEARN IN THIS BOOK

The decisions you make as a parent are important, but underlying what you do on a daily basis—informing it, molding it—is who you are in relationship to your child. When you invest your attention and energy in building a relationship with your child, you don't have to know in advance how to react to every problem, and you don't have to punish yourself for wrong decisions you might have made in the past. Instead, you can have confidence to face any challenge, reach out for support without feeling you're a failure, repair mistakes or hurts you may have caused, and keep on growing. Your love for your child also grows, gaining dimension over time as they develop through ages and stages. Regardless of how your child ends up living their life, you can feel good knowing they have essential relationship skills that will stand them in good stead in every dimension of their life because you modeled those skills through your own attitudes and actions.

In the first chapter, I ask you to think about who you are as a parent, the idea of good-enough parenting, and what kind of temperament your child has. I discuss ways your parenting style and your child's temperament might interact and ways you might think about fine tuning your style to better match their temperament without putting a burden of perfection on yourself.

In Chapter 2, my focus is on how children, teenagers, and adults make mistakes, fix them, and grow. I address the role played by your attitude in dealing successfully with challenging circumstances your child presents—such as toddler tantrums, childhood disobedience, and adolescent rule breaking—and discuss the roles of punishment and consequences in healthy parenting.

In Chapter 3, I share the research on mindfulness, describing its applications to your life as a parent and a human being. I illustrate how mindfulness can help you cope with problems your child may exhibit, such as stuttering, social anxiety, and truancy. Mindfulness can help you achieve self-acceptance and the calm patience that allow you to bypass your anxiety so you can deal most effectively with problems your life presents, including problems you might have with your child.

Chapter 4 is about taking good care of yourself. It may sound trite, but you can't take good care of others if you're not taking good care of yourself. In this chapter, I discuss the important roles of sleep, nutrition, and balance as they affect you and your child.

In Chapter 5, I address the ways each of us is unique. I describe some of the research on the way the brain grows and changes over time. Each person has a complex combination of interacting genetic and environmental factors, leading to the infinite spectrum of individuality we experience all around us. This explains why what works for most parents with most kids might not work in your situation.

The focus of Chapter 6 is on learning across the lifespan. I review how intelligence develops and how it builds over time in areas of interest, with opportunities to learn. I illustrate how you can keep getting smarter as long as you're breathing, no matter what your child or anyone else might tell you.

Chapter 7 is all about creativity. I share some definitions of creativity you might not have encountered, as well as techniques for becoming more creative. I show you how you can nurture your creativity and give your child opportunities for creative self-expression.

Chapter 8 is perhaps the heart of this book; at least, it is where my focus is most explicitly on matters of the heart as they affect the practical details of your life and parenting. In this chapter, I describe why and how to choose love, positivity, caring, and connection. I discuss empathy, emotional self-control, friendships, happiness, and self-confidence, focusing on how they enrich your life as well as your child's and that of everyone else with whom you come into contact.

Chapter 9 is about wisdom. It's about being the adult in the room—not perfect, but wise. I discuss ways of dealing with tough topics such as bullying, divorce, your child's fear of death, and tragic events in the news. I describe how showing up is enormously important and how dealing with these tough topics builds on many of the other topics we've covered, such as self-care and mindfulness.

In the final chapter of this book, my emphasis is on how we are all in this together. I talk about the importance of listening, collaborating, and looking for ways you and your child can make a difference and contribute to your community. Participating in making the world a little bit better not only supports your well-being in a number of ways, but also, the healthier your community, your country, and our planet, the greater the chances are that you and your child will thrive.

In each chapter, I talk about the big themes first, then break down how these themes can play out when your child is at different stages. I've included sections for the ages you might expect: birth through 5, 6 to 10, and adolescence—11 to 18. I also include advice for parenting your child through their young adulthood, from 19 to 24. If your child is neurotypical, they are, in some ways, all grown up by the time they reach this age range. However, that doesn't mean you've fulfilled your parenting role and can get on with your life with no worries about the kids. This is a time when they have to make some serious life-changing decisions. If your child feels that you support and respect them, that goes a long way toward them making the best possible decisions, decisions that can impact the rest of their life. For that, they need your calm, caring wisdom as much now as they ever did.

Throughout the book, I use as examples parenting scenarios taken from real life and real families I have worked with in my role as a helping professional. I have been careful to change details in each case to protect individuals' privacy while preserving the essence of the scene or the relationship depicted. Sometimes, even when the circumstances are different, we can see and hear our own reactions as they are enacted in others' stories, and we can use others' examples to imagine what we might do differently in the future.

NOTES ON WRITING STYLE

You may have already noticed that I talk about "your child," rather than children and adolescents in the plural or more generically, even though, in addition to parents and grandparents, I'm also writing for teachers, counselors, and others who work with children and adolescents, whether or not they're parents themselves. In my work with kids over the years, I have learned that it's all about the one-on-one relationship you have, one child at a time.

On another writing style note, I use the pronoun "they" to talk about individual children, rather than alternating "he" and "she" or using "he/she." I like "they" because I find it less of a distraction from the message I'm trying to convey and also because it better reflects my commitment to social justice and inclusion. "They" includes everyone, and I like that.

WHO ARE YOU AS A PARENT?

Somebody's got to be crazy about that kid. That's number one.
First, last, and always.

—Urie Bronfenbrenner,
The Ecology of Human Development

Good parenting starts with love and devotion, and if that were the only thing you knew about being a parent, you'd have a head start on the game. If you're already crazy about your child or adolescent, most of what's in this book will feel familiar, whether or not you've already thought about it this way. If you're not yet crazy about your kid, I'll give you some practical ideas for building a strong and healthy relationship that will help both of you weather the storms that life brings today and tomorrow. And if sometimes you're crazy about them, but sometimes you have a hard time feeling anything but exhaustion, anxiety, or irritation, I'll give you some ideas for managing that, too.

PARENTING STYLES

Like every other parent, you bring your own personality, background, values, and circumstances into your approach to your child and to being a parent. Similarly, each child is a unique blend of genetic and environmental influences. And therefore, your way of parenting your child is unique to you. It depends on numerous interacting influences and demands, all of which change over time and each of which makes your approach distinctly different than that of others. That being said, it can be useful to think about how your parenting might fit into one of several different parenting style categories.

One of the most widely used approaches specifies four styles of parenting: permissive, authoritarian, authoritative, and neglectful.[1,2] Few parents fit neatly into one of these styles. Most of us reflect some combination of styles, sometimes changing in response to changing circumstances and experiences. The case of Elizabeth and Sara helps to illustrate this. As with all the stories about people I use in this book, some details (including names) have been changed to ensure confidentiality.

Case Study: Elizabeth and Sara

Elizabeth was happy when she learned she was pregnant. She enjoyed setting up the baby's room, and she and her husband, Neil, looked forward to sharing their lives with a baby. Elizabeth was even happier when one of her best friends, Sara, learned she was also pregnant and her baby would be born soon after Elizabeth's.

The two friends went to prenatal classes together and read most of the same books on parenting. Observing unruly behavior in other people's children, they affirmed that their children would have regular bedtimes and learn to be polite and well-behaved.

And then reality hit. Elizabeth's baby cried long and loud and often and refused to be comforted. When she or Neil put Ezra to bed, he wailed until he exhausted himself and fell into a short, restless sleep. When he woke, he whimpered briefly, then quickly ramped it up to ear-piercing roars. Elizabeth and Neil ignored these cries and trusted Ezra would eventually learn to sleep on their schedule, as the books on sleep training reassured them would happen. Every morning, they argued about whose turn it was to get the baby, each of them believing they already did more than their share of parenting duties.

Then Sara's baby was born. Little Suzy was just as demanding as Ezra, and the friends started attending the same mom-and-baby drop-in group. The group leader gave advice on sleep training and advised the new moms not to let their babies manipulate them into extra cuddles. That made good sense to Elizabeth, so she and Neil continued their practice of letting Ezra cry it out.

Sara felt guilty about breaking the rules, but she didn't have the heart to let her baby cry alone. Sara felt that Suzy was just trying to make her needs heard and that she would stop crying when she felt soothed and understood. Sara and Roy rocked Suzy to sleep two or three times a day. They cuddled her and sang to her until she fell asleep, cherishing the moments when she was calm and happy, and rather than resenting her demands, they felt compassion for her suffering when she was crying.

As time went by, Sara worked around baby Suzy's schedule and helped her learn to manage her rages. She and Roy didn't punish her for her tantrums, believing she needed love and guidance to learn how to behave within acceptable limits. Instead of time-outs, they gave her time-ins—extra cuddles and conversation—when she was overwhelmed or out of control. By the time Suzy was 4, there was increasingly more sunshine and less turbulence in their family life.

Things went from bad to worse for Elizabeth, though, as Ezra got old enough to say "No!" and fought to have his needs met with roars and fists and feet and teeth. There were daily meltdowns and punishments until Ezra's day care provider told Elizabeth they would not be able to manage him unless something changed, and that the family needed professional help. Elizabeth was outraged, but as she thought about it, she was glad to hear there might be help available. She realized she and Neil were at the end of their ropes with each other and with Ezra.

In presenting the story of these two friends who had vastly different experiences with their young children, you've probably guessed that I left out a lot of details. And you're right. I wanted to highlight two different approaches to parenting infants and toddlers and hint at two different possible outcomes, but the picture of sunny child versus stormy child does oversimplify things a bit. First, there are more factors that make the two children different than the number of hours each was held during the night. And who knows whether Suzy will stay mellow or whether Ezra won't eventually learn to get along with others. Second, there were more factors besides their responses to nighttime crying that made the parents different from one another. And third, though I've shown one set of parents as making a choice that was a better fit for their child's needs, this doesn't necessarily mean that they felt successful all the time, and the other set of parents felt like failures all the time.

For example, Sara found that working around Suzy's schedule was nearly impossible, and there were a lot of difficult conversations about whether she needed to downshift her career temporarily to accommodate the baby's needs or whether Roy should do so or whether they needed another solution altogether to the work conundrum. It hurt to miss deadlines, and Sara did end up downshifting her career until Suzy went to kindergarten, which necessitated some real changes in the family's finances, as well as sacrifices to Sara's career ambitions. Sara and Roy felt less than perfect fairly often.

Though I painted Elizabeth and Neil's experience as negative in some ways, it turns out that they actually did feel success, at least as far as Ezra's sleep was concerned. After sticking to their sleep training plan for several trying months, Ezra's nighttime sleep periods stretched longer, and his daytime nap schedule became consistent too. Elizabeth and Neil were proud of how well they had partnered to give him predictable routines that told him, "Now is sleep time." It was just that this new issue—the tantrums and hurting other kids at child care—seemed beyond a formulaic solution. And that was all the more frustrating because their sleep plan had (eventually) worked. It had buoyed their confidence, and now, they felt defeated over something that they "should" have been able to deal with.

Suffice it to say, parents' temperaments, backgrounds, situations, and values affect their parenting, and before going further, you might want to think about your own parenting style.

Quiz: What Is Your Parenting Style?

For each of these questions, choose the answer that best describes how you think or feel. There are no **wrong** answers or trick questions; this is about helping you think about your own approach to parenting.

1. What are your top parenting priorities?
   (a) Love, kindness, and respect are the most important things I can give my child.
   (b) Structure, security, and discipline are my most important parenting responsibilities.
   (c) Love and kindness are essential but so are security and structure.
   (d) My priorities don't make much difference to my child. Kids grow up to be who they were meant to be, regardless.
2. How do you react to a disobedient child?
   (a) A disobedient child needs patience and understanding.
   (b) A disobedient child needs consequences.
   (c) A disobedient child provides a learning opportunity for the parent, as well as the child.
   (d) A disobedient child is annoying.
3. How do you handle disrespect?
   (a) Disrespect is just a passing phase. I ignore it.
   (b) I don't tolerate disrespect. It's my job to teach my child respect for their parents and others in authority.

(continues)

Quiz: What Is Your Parenting Style? (*Continued*)

    (c) When my child is disrespectful, I listen, take into account any worries they might have, and before dealing with it, consider whether they might be hungry, tired, cold, or something else.

    (d) Disrespect is a form of disobedience. It's annoying, and I try to tune it out.

4. What is your view on punishment?

    (a) Punishment is never useful.

    (b) When my child disobeys or misbehaves, I impose the appropriate punishment. It's in my child's best interest to know they can't get away with bad behavior.

    (c) I impose consequences as needed, but I never punish my child.

    (d) Thinking about and enforcing a punishment is usually more trouble than it's worth. Being a parent is not my only job.

5. What is your position on household rules?

    (a) I don't like rules myself, so I don't set very many of them for my child.

    (b) Children feel more secure when their parents can be depended on to set and enforce the rules.

    (c) Household rules are a chance for collaborative problem solving with my child.

    (d) I set rules sometimes—about bedtimes and kitchen cleanup, for example—but nobody seems to follow them.

6. How do you react to rule breaking?

    (a) When my child breaks a rule, I usually pretend to act tough for a few minutes, then give my child a hug. I want them to know they're loved.

    (b) Just as it's my job to set the rules, it's my job to enforce them.

    (c) When my child breaks a rule, we work together to figure out appropriate consequences.

    (d) I'm usually too busy to notice when rules get broken, so I don't spend a lot of time on enforcement.

Quiz: What Is Your Parenting Style? (*Continued*)

7. What is your position on household chores?
   (a) My child has chores, but when they don't do them, I try not to nag.
   (b) My children are responsible for doing their chores. That's not negotiable in my house. Privileges such as screen time or playtime come after chores, not before.
   (c) I'm somewhat flexible about enforcing chores. I like to see them done on time, but I understand there are times that other things should come first.
   (d) Chores get done at my house only when I go on a rampage.
8. Do you ever bribe your child to get them to comply with you?
   (a) Bribes are one of the best ways to get my child to do what I want them to do, except I prefer to call them "incentives."
   (b) I expect good behavior, so I punish my child for bad behavior. I don't bribe them to be good.
   (c) I'm not averse to bribery when necessary, although I try to encourage good behavior for its own sake whenever possible.
   (d) Bribery is one of the most important tools in my parenting toolbox. It alternates with punishment, depending on my mood.

Answers: Your Parenting Style

Add together the number of times you answered each of (a), (b), (c), or (d). Where there was more than one right answer for you, include all of them in your tally.

PARENT AS FRIEND: PERMISSIVE PARENTING STYLE

Parents who choose (a) most of the time fit most closely into the permissive style. They love their child but prefer not to set and enforce rules. Instead, they trust that with love and understanding, in a spirit of harmony at home, their child will find their own best way.

THE BOSS: AUTHORITARIAN PARENTING STYLE

Parents who choose mostly (b) see themselves as an authority figure in their home and fit best into the authoritarian style. They provide structure and security and generally don't accept challenges to their rules. In the case study described earlier, Elizabeth and Neil could be described as authoritarian parents, at least for the first few years of Ezra's life.

THE FIRM BUT UNDERSTANDING PARENT: AUTHORITATIVE PARENTING STYLE

Parents who choose (c) most often can be seen as authoritative in their parenting style. They believe that children need love, kindness, and respect, but they also see the value of reliable rules and guidance. They use positive reinforcement and reasoning rather than punishment, providing emotional support and comfort, as well as high expectations. Like Sara and Roy in the earlier story, they listen to their child's concerns, seeing misbehavior as opportunities for learning, both for themselves and their child.

THE UNINVOLVED PARENT: NEGLECTFUL PARENTING STYLE

Parents who generally answer (d) are most closely aligned with the neglectful parenting style. They're somewhat disconnected from their children and provide neither dependable warmth nor much by way of security and structure. Their lack of involvement can result from one or more causes, including too many competing responsibilities; childhood trauma; problems with health, whether psychological or physical; addiction; or other serious concerns.

Best Long-Term Outcomes: Authoritative Parenting Style

According to most studies, children's long-term development goes better when their parents' behavior falls mostly into the authoritative style.[3,4] Although loving your child is the single most important factor in their doing well over the long term—and you can love your child no matter what your parenting style—your parenting style matters too. A child with at least one authoritative parent is more likely than others to demonstrate emotional strengths, including independence and self-reliance; social strengths that lead to positive relationships; and cognitive strengths, including academic success. They are less likely to show signs of being depressed or anxious, or to be antisocial, delinquent, or involved with drugs.

The characteristic that appears to be most important to the success of the authoritative style is psychological flexibility. A parent who approaches issues with their child in a rigid way may be successful at controlling or managing the child's behavior in the short term, but the child is less likely to thrive in the long term. Parents experiencing more stress—whether because of internal anxiety or because of external stressors such as poverty or family disruption—are less likely to respond to their child in a psychologically flexible and authoritative way. Much of my emphasis in this book is on ways to reduce your experience of stress, both to enjoy your own life more and also to free your attention for establishing a strong and healthy relationship with your child.

Some critics have observed that this approach to parenting styles is culturally biased and that the authoritative style reflects the values of White middle-class parents. Using our story from earlier, it seems that Sara has a flexible job that allows her to start and stop tasks at different times during the day. This, in turn, frees her to be responsive to her baby's needs. Many parents don't have control over their work schedules, so they need to rely on other caregivers to provide that extra cuddle when it's needed. If you imagine Sara and Roy as White, the reality is that while they might catch criticism about their child or their parenting style from time to time, they are probably free from fears that their child will one day be perceived as a threat, either by a stranger who spots them in the neighborhood or by a police officer. So, they may not have to expend as much energy as a parent of color expends worrying about how others will perceive their child.

Taking these criticisms into account, a more nuanced understanding of parenting styles recognizes that parenting happens in a particular cultural context and is mediated by the parent's background and values. What works best in one situation may not work best in another, and each parent must craft their own approach to parenting. This can vary across situations or change over time as a family moves neighborhoods or the child grows into an adolescent.

Regardless of culture, the optimal approach is a warm and psychologically flexible version of authoritative parenting, where a parent is both emotionally responsive to their child and also demanding, and where the parent adapts their demands both to their cultural values and their child's changing needs. If it needs to be a grandparent or a next-door neighbor who provides the child with a steady dose of warmth and high expectations, that is all right too. I speak of any adult who serves in a parental role as a parent. Across a variety of measures, children of flexibly authoritative parents score better on assessments of empathy, confidence, kindness, and conscientiousness. They do better than others at problem solving and are better liked both by peers and adults. They do better at school and are more likely to grow into adults who thrive.

Authoritative Parenting Style by Age

THE EARLY YEARS: BIRTH TO 5

From birth to 5, your child needs you to be fully engaged and hands-on in every dimension of their lives—food, sleep, and activities. You're the one creating the environment and making the rules, so that might appear to suggest a more autocratic style. But as the stories of Elizabeth and Sara illustrate, a flexibly authoritative approach

24

works best even during this period. Sara was responsive to Suzy's needs even then and took a strong but gentle role in gradually shaping Suzy's behavior so that by the time she was ready to start school, she had learned how to behave in a way that allowed her to make friends and thrive at learning tasks. As time went by and things got worse, Elizabeth did get professional help to understand Ezra's needs more deeply and learn new ways to respond to him. Although it took a lot of time and effort to learn new parenting habits, Elizabeth's story illustrates how a parent can pivot from one style to another at any time they realize things could be going better.

CHILDHOOD: 6 TO 10

If you've been flexibly authoritative with your child in the early years, they move into the world of friendships and school with some confidence, skills, and coping mechanisms that support their continued thriving. And if you haven't been authoritative before now or if your child was in someone else's care until now, your child will still benefit if you begin now to adopt the elements of that style that work for you. Perhaps you find some areas in which you can be more flexible, more responsive to their preferences. As they move through the childhood years, an authoritative parent gives their child increasing responsibility and freedom, matching their increasing competence with increasing opportunities to make decisions that matter to them. That can be difficult for a parent because there are times when their child may make the wrong decision. One of your jobs is learning when to let that happen, in the interest of your child's independence and confidence, and when you need to intervene for their safety.

ADOLESCENCE: 11 TO 18

The benefits of an authoritative parenting style become apparent when your child is an early adolescent. If you've been mostly authoritative until now, then when everything in your child's body and world is changing, they enter this period with the coping skills and decision-making skills that stand them in good stead. And as with each of the other stages, if you haven't always been an authoritative parent, it's not too late to learn how to provide flexibility in how you respond to your child while giving them the support they still need. (I talk a lot more about how to do that in later chapters of this book.) Through this period from 11 to 18, an authoritative parent further strengthens the relationship with their child, giving them increasing autonomy, becoming increasingly reactive and available and decreasingly proactive in making and enforcing rules.

Young Adulthood: 19 to 24

Even into their mid-20s, your child still benefits from your taking an authoritative approach. At this stage, that means being available when they have issues or problems and also staying alert to possible concerns, ready to intervene if you're needed but only when they want your support. Even if your young adult is living in your home, an authoritative parent is no longer setting rules but rather working together with them to establish harmonious cohabiting practices, such as kitchen cleanup and other chores. Things will go better if you've been an authoritative parent all along, but even in this final stage of parenting, you can still learn to be flexibly responsive and available only as needed.

GOOD-ENOUGH PARENTING

Perfection is rarely attainable, and in some situations—like parenting— it's better to strive for being good enough. This applies to yourself as a parent and also to your aspirations for your child. Today, at a time of rapid global change and increasing widespread anxiety, when parents have so many legitimate worries, it's more important than ever that you and your child learn how to relax into being good enough.

I'm not advocating a laissez-faire disinterested attitude—quite the reverse, in fact. I am suggesting you find a way to take good care of yourself and enjoy being with your child without worrying too much about doing everything the way you or others think you should do it. One way of thinking about this is to settle into being a "good-enough" parent: securely attached to your beloved child and keeping them safe, warm, and fed but not aiming for parenting perfection.

The idea of the "good-enough" parent came from a pediatrician's observation in 1953 that mothers who aimed for perfection were getting in the way of their child's best development.[5] The good-enough mother, D. W. Winnicott argued, is totally available to her baby during infancy, but as time goes by, she slowly begins to attend to her own needs and interests, as well as to the child's. In this way, the child learns over time to deal with frustrations and delays and begins to take ownership of their own experience. (The same can apply to a father, of course, but in 1953, mothers were usually the parents most closely involved in parenting, especially in the early years.)

In 1987, in *A Good Enough Parent*, Bruno Bettelheim recommended that parents support their children in becoming their truest, best selves, not the children the parents want them to be.[6] Like Winnicott, he wrote about the problems with perfectionism: "Efforts to attain [perfection] typically interfere with that lenient response to the imperfections of others, including those of one's child, which alone make good human relations possible."[7] I love that concept— our aim as parents should be kind and loving patience with ourselves and others as we make the inevitable mistakes that go along with living a life and attempting to manage conflicting needs and desires.

One of Bettelheim's arguments for a good-enough approach to parenting is that those who strive for perfection are inclined to blame themselves or others when things don't go well. He observed that blame never helps but rather causes more problems within families, sometimes to the point of putting marriages and other coparenting relationships in jeopardy.

In the first several weeks and months of your baby's life, they need someone to meet their needs preemptively, if possible, and with some urgency. Being reliably loved and fed and kept clean and warm and protected helps them feel safe enough in the world to begin to explore and reach out into the world with confident curiosity. As your child gets older, however, they need you to begin to attend to your own needs again, as well as to theirs. By releasing the pressures on yourself to be a perfect parent and deciding instead to be good enough, you and your child are freed to enjoy each other and to thrive.

IS YOUR CHILD FRIENDLY AND OPTIMISTIC? OR FIERCE AND FEISTY?

As I hinted earlier, in parenting your child, you're working not only with your own personality, cultural environment, and preferred parenting style but also with your child's unique personality and temperament. Your child may be easy to be around—curious, calm, and friendly—or they might be moody, negative, and challenging. Probably they're somewhere in between or variable over time. Many differences in personality and attitude reflect a child's life experience, including family and cultural influences, but some of the differences are innate, resulting from genetic factors such as temperament.

Temperament: What Is It?

There are many different approaches to defining temperament, but there is a consensus that it includes these nine factors[8]:

- **Activity level.** Right from birth, people vary in their energy level and restlessness. Some are naturally calm, some have a

28

high level of energy they must learn to channel, and others need to find ways to get motivated.

- **Regularity.** Regularity applies to bodily functions such as sleep patterns, bowel habits, and appetite. As with each of the factors that combine to describe a person's temperament, there is wide variability in children's regularity right from birth.
- **Approach and withdrawal.** People vary in how they respond to meeting a new person, engaging in a new activity, or going to a new location. Some welcome new situations with enthusiasm; others are slow, hesitant, or even fearful.
- **Adaptability.** Some people react enthusiastically to new people and situations. Others resist change, preferring stability and predictability.
- **Sensitivity.** Some people are highly sensitive to sounds, flavors, textures, and other sensory stimuli. Others don't notice or perceive them as acutely.
- **Intensity of reaction.** People vary in how intensely they respond to stimuli and situations, whether positively or negatively.
- **Quality of mood.** Some people are born with pleasant, optimistic temperaments, and others are born with more negative and critical attitudes.
- **Attention span and persistence.** The ability to stay focused on a challenging task comes more easily to some than to others right from birth.
- **Distractibility.** Some people can be easily distracted; others are better able to ignore disturbances, including ambient sounds, smells, and other environmental factors.

Temperament and Your Child's Experience of the World

As you might realize in reading through the list of temperament components, your child's temperament has a profound effect on their life experience. If your child needs to take some time before they feel comfortable at a birthday party, say, or on the first day of school, they will experience entering those situations very differently than a child who draws energy from noisy social situations.

There are many perspectives on temperament. According to one of the most widely used approaches, the three major categories are *easy*, *slow to warm up*, and *difficult*. About 40% of babies can be classified as having an easy temperament: They adapt quickly and well to new situations, react mildly, are regular in their routines, and have a generally positive mood. About 10% have a slow-to-warm-up temperament: They withdraw from new situations, have a low level of activity, and show a lot of negativity. They don't like to be pushed into things and are frequently thought of as shy or sensitive. About 10% of babies are born with a difficult temperament. They withdraw from new situations, have intense reactions, have a hard time establishing routines, and exhibit a generally negative mood. Finally, about 40% of children can't easily be categorized because of their unique temperament factors.[9]

Your child's temperament is neither your fault if they're difficult nor to your credit if they're easy. It's just something they were born with, one of the only psychological factors recognized pretty universally as genetic in origin. In the stories of Elizabeth and Sara, both their children were born with difficult temperaments. And as those stories illustrate, a parent's response to their child's temperament makes all the difference in the extent to which a child with a difficult temperament can thrive. Regardless of your child's innate temperament, however, your parenting style makes a difference in helping your child find the assets in their temperament and reduce the potential liabilities.

Before considering more deeply the intersection between parenting style and temperament, I should mention that there are times when a child gives every indication of having a difficult temperament but is, in fact, dealing with a physical or neurological problem— a chronic disease,[10] for example, or food allergies, a hearing problem, attention-deficit/hyperactivity disorder, or autism spectrum disorder. What appears to be a difficult temperament can be a medical problem that you and your child need help with, so if you have a child that is easily distressed and hard to comfort, talk to your pediatrician or family doctor about the situation and investigate other options and possibilities.

The Orchid and the Dandelion: Understanding Difficult Children

One way of thinking about children's variations in temperaments is to contrast the easy child, whose approach to people and life makes it easy to think you're a great parent, and the difficult child, whose basic temperament means you're going to be working overtime for many years just to keep things on an even keel. Most children fall somewhere in between, and only about 10% are truly difficult. It's worth spending a bit of time thinking about that 10%, partly because their parents need extra support and partly because most children show some elements of a difficult temperament some of the time.

In *The Orchid and the Dandelion: Why Some Children Struggle and How All Can Thrive*,[11] Thomas Boyce shared a lifetime of collaborative research that was driven partly by the dramatically different adult lives led by his sister and himself. Boyce—a renowned pediatrician and epidemiologist—and his sister were best friends as children. He built a rich life for himself, both personally and professionally, while she—as intellectually gifted as him or more so, he wrote—died of a suicidal drug overdose in her 50s, after decades of suffering from mental health issues.

Boyce distinguished between *dandelion children*, those who show a remarkable capacity for thriving in almost every circumstance, and *orchid children*, who are "exquisitely sensitive to their environments, especially vulnerable under conditions of adversity but unusually vital, creative, and successful within supportive environments."[12] On the continuum from pure dandelion to pure orchid, Boyce sees himself as more of a dandelion, with some orchid sensibilities. He described his sister as being closer to pure orchid and unable to overcome the hardships they both endured in late childhood and adolescence.

Orchid children have a tender responsivity that causes them to absorb their circumstances. They are often the person who appears to most need help in a family that isn't working well for any of its members. They might be the most obviously dysfunctional one, the apparent failure, the troubled one when in reality, the whole family system needs help. Orchid children are also a source of insight and creativity. Boyce wrote,

> The same extraordinary, biologically embedded sensitivities that render such children so unduly susceptible to the hazards and adversities of life make them also more receptive to the gifts and promises of life. . . . Orchids are not broken dandelions but a different, more subtle kind of flower.[13]

Sensitivity is important, and so is availability. Boyce wrote that there is no substitute for a parent's reliably available time, affection, and attention. He said when it comes to children's need for a parent's attention, quality time is important but that quality can never substitute for quantity.

In *The Orchid and the Dandelion*, Boyce reported on research he and his colleagues have been conducting for decades. He shared findings that shed light not only on the nature of the dandelion–orchid experience but also on best practices for parents, teachers, mental health professionals, and policy makers. One especially fascinating set of findings shows that highly stress-reactive children (orchids) become either the sickest or the most successful of children and ado-lescents, depending on the emotional health of their families. Orchid children do worse than others in harsh environments and do better than others—across a variety of cognitive, academic, and health measures—in supportive environments. If you're the parent of an orchid and want that child to thrive, you have a special burden of responsibility to create a positive atmosphere at home.

Boyce suggested that orchid children are not so much vulnerable as they are unusually susceptible to family conditions. He reviewed research on nonhuman primates and rats, showing that, as with humans, between 10% and 20% of each animal population shows an orchid-like sensitivity. When the orchid offspring in the animal studies are reared by nurturing mothers, they thrive. When orchid offspring have mothers who are anxious, disinterested, or neglectful, the young ones don't do well at all.

Teachers also play a significant role in an impressionable child's life, especially in preschool and kindergarten. A young orchid child who experiences an informal and accepting atmosphere where each child feels welcome and valued is likelier to thrive in the long term. In another example of the interaction between parenting and teaching styles and temperament, a highly sensitive child whose teacher is authoritarian and cold or who praises only those who fit within a narrow framework of expectations is likelier to experience depres-sion and other serious problems impacting their physical and mental health and academic success as years go by. Dandelion children are also affected by the quality of their early years' teachers, but the differ-ences in long-term outcomes aren't nearly as dramatic.

"Spirited," Not Difficult

Although children with difficult temperaments are, by definition, demanding, negative, and easily irritated, each has their own unique personality and their own specific needs. As babies, those with a difficult temperament usually cry more than others, and their cry can be distinctively loud and piercing right from the beginning. When Elizabeth's son (in the story at the beginning of the chapter) was born, the nurses in the hospital told her they always knew when Ezra was crying: His wailing lasted longer and was louder and more frequent than any of the other babies in their care.

With unpredictable patterns of sleeping and eating and angry or fearful reactions to changes and new experiences, children with difficult temperaments can be enormously challenging to parent. Even more discouraging, perhaps, is that difficult children don't grow out of the innate factors that lead to their negativity.

Although you can't change your child's temperament, Thomas Boyce's research demonstrates that your parenting style can make a big difference in whether your child is able to capitalize on the strengths associated with their temperament. And the more difficult they are, the truer that is.

Language is always important in framing people's attitudes, and there are good reasons to think about those with difficult temperaments as "spirited" rather than difficult. In *Raising Your Spirited Child*,[14] Mary Sheedy Kurcinka wrote about an activity she does with parents in her Spirited Child classes. She gives each parent three index cards and asks them to write on each card a word that describes their child on a bad day. She collects the cards, shuffles them, and then makes a list for the group. Some typical words are "destructive," "obnoxious," "defiant," "exhausting," "explosive," "whiny," and "stubborn."

Kurcinka directs the participants to work in pairs, taking turns saying "My child is . . ." and then reading aloud from the list of negative attributes. Some parents cannot complete the exercise. They are overcome with emotion, in a state that Kurcinka labeled the "red zone," a place where negative emotions overwhelm thoughtful reasoning and empathy. In the red zone, the fight-or-flight response prevents a parent from seeing the child's vulnerability, their inherent sensitivity and goodness. The parent sees only an adversary.

Kurcinka's work with parents shows that by changing the words you use to think about your child, you can soothe your own frightened or angry reactions, change your perceptions of your child, and move into an emotional zone where thoughtful, responsive parenting becomes possible. It's only in that healthier "green zone" that you can help your child become the wonderful person you hope they are.

A Spirited Child Activity to Try

Here's an exercise you might enjoy and that might be beneficial for you and your child. The more their temperament tends to the difficult end of the spectrum, the more powerful it can be.

When you're in a calm, reflective mood, make a list of your child's behaviors and attributes that drive you crazy. Put them in the most judgmental language possible—aggressive, argumentative, obstinate, exhausting, and so forth. And then spend some time reframing each of those descriptors, looking for what is good and strong and valuable underlying the behavior. It won't be easy, but with some thoughtful attention to the way you perceive your child's more problematic attributes, you can change a habit of negativity and judgment into one of positivity, optimism, and proud affection.

For example, if you're tempted to see your child as aggressive, try to see them as committed to achieving their aims. Remind yourself that that's a great attribute going forward into adulthood. When they're argumentative, look at them as independent minded, another valuable attribute for creativity and life success. Instead of seeing your child as defiant, perhaps you can enjoy their feistiness, the spirited nature that helps them find their own voice and forge their own path in the world. Instead of destructive, perhaps your child pulls things apart to understand how they work. Instead of exhausting, try to think of your child as bountifully energetic, an attribute most of us would like more of. Instead of thinking of your child as explosive, look for the passionate sensitivity that motivates the explosions, and that can motivate creativity as time goes by. If your child appears inflexible, perhaps they feel strongly about meeting high standards, and that's a good thing when applied to certain kinds of work. A child who seems obnoxious might be anxiously trying to ensure they're loved unconditionally, needing your reassurance and not your censure. Instead of stubbornness, maybe there's an underlying strength of character, a cardinal virtue in my books.

The positive language works to calm your system. It helps you feel more confident, hopeful, and competent, even when your child is at their most demanding and difficult. Yes, you still need to help your child shape their socially unacceptable actions into behavior that will allow them to thrive, but you are much better able to do that from a position of loving acceptance than from a place of angry opposition. In many ways, that's the essence of good-enough parenting and the authoritative parenting style.

When a stranger comments on your child's behavior or suggests they have a difficult temperament, you might say something such as, "Yes, they're very spirited," or "I prefer to think of them as spirited." When someone closer to you—a family member or friend—makes a comment indicating they see your child as difficult, you might acknowledge the challenges you and your child experience and then share your way of reframing the behavior as reflecting an internal reality for the child. For example, you're at the local children's museum with a friend and your 9-year-old son. It's time to leave, and your son starts crying and shouting, "No! I don't want to go home!" After helping him through his tantrum—more on that in a later chapter—and getting him out of the museum, you can tell your friend, "Drew has an intense curiosity and loves to learn new things. It was very hard for him to leave the museum. I got caught up in the experience myself and forgot to prepare him ahead of time that it was going to be time to leave." Remind yourself that each of us experiences things differently, that it's neither good nor bad to be intensely reactive or calm.

The couples I introduced in the first section of this chapter— Elizabeth and Neil and Sara and Roy—were dealing with children with difficult temperaments, kids we can think of as spirited or orchids. After Elizabeth acknowledged that she needed help, she found Zara, a therapist who used the Kurcinka method. Zara helped Elizabeth and Neil reframe their approach and implement many of the suggestions at the end of the chapter. She also helped Elizabeth understand and manage her own sensitivities so she wasn't so easily triggered by Ezra's challenges. Habits and attitudes aren't easy to change, so it took time, effort, and perseverance, but eventually, Ezra's behavior problems settled down. He will always be highly sensitive, but over the next few years, he became a happier, more loving, and more curious little boy.

TAKING IT INTO THE COMMUNITY: POSITIVE CONNECTIONS

Just as authoritative parenting and accepting less than perfection in yourself work to make you more accepting of your child's unique temperament and personality, living in a friendly neighborhood strengthens your parenting and supports your child's development. I am not suggesting you should move from where you live to somewhere "better." Rather, I am asking you to think about how connected and supported you feel in your community and whether there might be ways you can either reach out to your "village" or be a better neighbor to someone else. On both a small scale and a larger one, people do better when they feel welcome and accepted rather than judged. They also do better when they are friendly and welcoming to their neighbors.

According to the research findings reported in *The Origins of You*[15] (which I mentioned in the Introduction), positive neighborhood connections increase a young person's resilience and decrease their likelihood of engaging in self-harm, as well as aggressive and antisocial actions. One of the mechanisms of this is the way a neighborhood acts to support or undermine effective parenting.

In large studies of children's development over time, the biggest factors predicting aggression and antisocial behavior in childhood and adolescence were levels of poverty and deprivation, on the one hand, and parental warmth and structure, on the other hand. Boys growing up in economically deprived communities were more likely to become aggressive and antisocial, but that was less likely to happen when their parents provided both warmth and monitoring, which was more likely to happen in a friendly, connected community.

Whether your community is dealing with social disconnection (which can happen even in the wealthiest neighborhood), drug abuse, effects of systemic racism such as bad air quality, or something else, one good way to increase the chances your child will grow into a successful adult is to strengthen the social connections in your neighborhood.

Collective efficacy is a term sometimes used to describe the impact of communities on children's and adolescents' development, as well as adults' health and well-being. According to the authors of *The Origins of You*, collective efficacy is "the combination of informal social control and social cohesion, and thus the willingness of community members to look out for each other and intervene when trouble arises, especially on behalf of the community's youths."[16] Research in Chicago shows collective efficacy lacking in some luxury high-rises but as strong in some of the poorest African American neighborhoods, especially those led by a strong church. In assessing collective efficacy, the researchers looked for whether neighbors could be counted on to intervene when children were misbehaving (e.g., skipping school, spraying graffiti, disrespecting adults). They also asked whether people saw their neighbors as trustworthy and sharing their values.

Where there was a greater sense of collective efficacy, young children were less likely to behave in antisocial ways. As the kids got older, there was a steeper decline in antisocial behavior. The researchers concluded that supportive parenting acted as a protective factor for kids in disadvantaged neighborhoods and that collective efficacy was a protective factor for supportive parenting. Their findings have important implications for parents, as well as for legislators and policy makers.

KEY TAKEAWAYS: HOW TO BE A GOOD-ENOUGH PARENT FOR YOUR CHILD

- **Be warm, demanding, and flexible.** Authoritative parenting means providing reliable rules and guidance, as well as responsivity to your child's changing needs and your own changing circumstances.
- **Accept and affirm your child's unique personality.** Regardless of your child's temperament, accept them the way they are and don't try to change them. Sensitive children discern the slightest nuances of their parents' judgments, whether spoken or not, and they respond deeply to those opinions.
- **Provide the comfort of the ordinary.** All children benefit from routines they can trust, and reliable routines are particularly important for orchid or spirited children, who can be alarmed—yes, really, alarmed—by new foods, new people, new smells. Regular family schedules—meals, chores, bedtimes—provide a sense of control and trust in a world that often feels chaotic and unpredictable. This may get less important as your child gets older, but routines they can trust continue to provide a sense of security.

- **Look for ways to strengthen collective efficacy.** Establish and maintain connections with your neighbors. Support neighborhood businesses and coffee shops. Be good to the children in your neighborhood, and support them in learning prosocial behavior. Do that kindly, never harshly, understanding that you gently stepping into a parenting role can make a difference in their development.

CHAPTER 2

HOW HUMAN BEINGS MAKE MISTAKES, FIX THEM, AND GROW

> *The best thing parents can do is to teach their children to love challenges, be intrigued by mistakes, enjoy effort, and keep on learning.*
>
> —Carol Dweck, *Mindset*

Do you know anyone who loves challenges and is intrigued by their mistakes, who actually welcomes setbacks and failures as opportunities to learn what they can do differently or better? I've occasionally met people like that and found them a pleasure to work with or spend time with. There's no judgment when anyone slips up, just an acknowledgment of what might be learned from the situation. We're going to come back to this idea of welcoming mistakes, which Carol Dweck has identified as one of the main characteristics of what she calls a "growth mindset."[1] But first, I'd like to talk about some situations where this idea might be relevant.

EXAMPLES OF MISTAKES PEOPLE MAKE

What's the best way to respond when your child is doing something they shouldn't do? The answer to that depends on a lot of different variables—your child's age, their personality, how frequently and severely they're pushing the limits, the circumstances of your life, and lots more. Imagine you're the parent in each of these situations. How would you respond?

Three-year-old Xandra shoves her little brother aside so she can grab a toy away from him, one she'd been playing with before. Her brother, Dante, falls over.

- Response 1. You take the toy away from Xandra, saying, "You know it's not okay to push and grab." You pick Dante up and give him a hug, asking if he's okay, and then return the toy to him. You give Xandra a time-out, telling her she should think about how she'll do better next time.
- Response 2. You calmly ask for the toy back from Xandra and give it to Dante. You gently explain your problem with her behavior—it's not nice to shove and grab—and ask that she apologize. You stay firm on the need for an apology, not allowing her to do anything else until she has apologized to Dante.
- Response 3. You think about whether there's something Xandra needs—maybe a reassuring snuggle. Maybe she's overtired or hungry; maybe she's feeling jealous of the attention her baby brother gets. Once you think you've identified and met that need, you ask, "Instead of shoving your brother and taking his toy, is there a better way to get what you want?"

Four-year-old Geraldo is pouring milk from a glass into a cup and back again. For the third time, you ask him to stop. Milk spills everywhere.

- Response 1. You roar at Geraldo, asking why he wasn't careful and reminding him you'd asked him three times to stop doing it. You give him a time-out so he can think about what he's done wrong, and then you clean up the mess.
- Response 2. You calmly tell Geraldo he can't have any more milk today. Then you clean up the mess and proceed with the day.
- Response 3. You breathe in and out deeply and say to Geraldo, "Whoops. What do we do next?"

You walk into the living room and see that 9-year-old Molly has spread books, games, art supplies, and puzzle pieces everywhere. The place is a mess. It wouldn't be so bad, except that you have to be on a video call soon, and your office is also the living room.

- Response 1. You yell, telling Molly she knows better than this, that this is not only the family living room but also your office. You demand she clean it up immediately—no screens, no dinner, no anything until it's done.
- Response 2. You firmly but gently give Molly a time-out and clean up the mess yourself, putting it all into boxes that she won't get access to for 24 hours.
- Response 3. You say, "My goodness. You have a big job ahead of you. You know what's next, right?"

You hear from your son's school that 14-year-old Deon has attended fewer than half the days in the last 6 weeks. You ask him about it. He admits he's been skipping school and, after a bit more conversation, tells you he's been spending time with some friends at a downtown mall.

- Response 1. You shout at him and tell him you had trusted him, and now you can't possibly do that. You tell him you (or a family member) will escort him to the school door every morning for the next 2 weeks, and someone will be there to pick him up at the end of the school day. You confiscate his electronics and tell him he has no screen privileges until he's proven he is reliable.
- Response 2. You ground him for 2 weeks. After school each day, he has to come home or to your workplace; tell you about his day, class by class; and spend the rest of the day and the evening at home.

- Response 3. You ask him what's going on in his life and try to understand why school is so problematic or why his friends or the mall are so attractive to him.

Your 21-year-old daughter, Amanda, has been fired from another job for her bad attitude. She doesn't want to go to college—there is nothing she's interested in studying or training for. She lives at home with you and informs you she's going to take a few months off before she looks for work again.

- Response 1. You explode. You tell Amanda you'd like to take a few months off, too, but you can't afford to do that. "If you are not going to school or working, forget it," you tell her. "I am not supporting you while you laze around doing nothing."
- Response 2. You tell her she's an adult, and she'll have to pull her weight. If she's not working, she'll be responsible for the household shopping, cooking, laundry, and cleaning.
- Response 3. You welcome this as a chance to help Amanda figure out what she wants to do next. You ask her to think about what she likes doing and how she'd use her time, hour by hour through the day, if she weren't at work. You collaborate on designing a daily schedule that involves some contribution to household maintenance, as well as some kind of part-time learning or training and some kind of community service. You also help her find career counseling resources; most towns, cities, and colleges have services that help young people figure this out.

You miss an important deadline at work, and your boss tells you they'll replace you if it happens again. Your kids have been sick, and you've been doing more than your share of staying home with them.

- Response 1. You blame your partner for your precarious job situation. If they were carrying their weight in the family, this wouldn't have happened.
- Response 2. You say nothing to your boss, your partner, or your kids, vowing to do better next time.
- Response 3. You acknowledge to yourself that something has to change. You talk to your boss about your family situation and ask if you can work something out that allows you to take care of both family and work. You discuss the same thing with your partner.

I'll come back to these scenarios later. In the meantime, I'd like to share a perspective on handling mistakes and misdemeanors that I and many others have found transformative, a perspective that might be useful in responding to the mistakes in the situations I outlined.

MINDSETS

Carol Dweck's groundbreaking book, *Mindset*, was published in 2006. Dweck, a developmental psychologist, was already well known for her work on motivation and attribution theory—how people's beliefs influence their decisions, actions, and lives. In *Mindset*, she synthesized 4 decades of research and identified two distinct approaches people take to situations they encounter and to their own abilities. She called these approaches the "fixed mindset" and the "growth mindset" and showed how mindsets have a dramatic effect on people's lives.

If you hold a *fixed mindset* perspective, you believe that intelligence and other abilities are fixed at birth. In other words, you believe people are born with a certain amount of intelligence, creativity, musicality, and athleticism, and that level is permanent. Those with a *growth mindset*, however, see ability as changing with motivation and effort. They believe that abilities develop incrementally, with appropriate opportunities to learn.

Dweck's findings about growth mindset are consistent with the evidence on the brain's plasticity, which shows that the brain develops actively and changes in response to environmental influences, starting before birth and holding true across the lifespan. The opportunities an infant has to interact with their world affect their developing intelligence. The same can be said for a young child's engagement with the environment, holding true through adolescence and even into late adulthood. Even for children with profound developmental delays and adults in the early stages of dementia, mindset findings and neuroplasticity research come together to show that a surprising amount of learning is almost always possible.

Conflicting Views on Whether Mindsets Are Helpful

Mindset became a runaway bestseller shortly after publication. Carol Dweck's TED Talk was viewed many millions of times. Educators and psychologists began using the idea in all kinds of ways. Companies sprang up selling tools and materials that were advertised as based on mindsets. And then, there was the predictable pushback. People began to criticize the concept. Replication studies yielded less-than-promising results. Like other ideas adopted too widely and too quickly and therefore subject to misunderstanding and misapplication, the mindsets idea became a victim of its own success. In the recent edition of *Mindsets*, Dweck wrote about these misunderstandings as "false growth mindset." She discussed the importance of attending to the nuances and avoiding a superficial application of a simplified version of mindset theory.

To address the controversies, Dweck collaborated with David Yaeger, a professor at the University of Texas at Austin.[2] They devised a randomized controlled study to examine the efficacy of teaching mindsets to over 12,000 ninth-graders from a nationally representative sample of public schools in the United States. They found that even short and inexpensive mindset interventions can work, especially with low-achieving students, but that context is critical. Schools with climates that celebrated academic success and curiosity saw the largest gains, including an 8% reduction in student failure. Both high- and low-achieving ninth-graders who experienced two 25-minute mindset interventions chose more challenging math courses in 10th grade. These findings were replicated in a Norwegian study that included over 6,500 students.

In my work with graduate students, teachers, parents, and children, as well as in my own life, I've seen extraordinary evidence of the benefits of working toward a growth mindset. As the conflicting perspectives and research findings suggest, context and nuance matter. It helps a lot if the whole culture you're in supports progress and celebrates small "wins." The idea of a growth mindset is simple but profound, and it's worth spending a bit of time thinking about what's involved.

Mindsets Are Specific to Certain Areas of Life

You might have a growth mindset about cooking or sports—seeing these as talents that develop over time with effort and learning opportunities—but believe that mathematical intelligence is fixed. You might realize that people can develop their vocabulary but think that social or emotional intelligence is fixed. The research findings—and my professional and personal experience—show that mindsets apply to each domain of competence or skill and that wherever you hold a growth mindset, you will be happier and more successful in that area than if you held a fixed mindset in that area.

Mindsets and Children's Intelligence

From the perspective of a fixed mindset, some children can be categorized as inherently smart or gifted. From the standpoint of a growth mindset, however, giftedness develops over time when circumstances support that. Parents and teachers who encourage a child's continued engagement in the learning process, independently of where that child starts out on an intelligence test scale, are working from a growth mindset and fostering gifted-level development in that child. This is an important realization for all parents, educators, and children, but it has a particularly meaningful focus for those interested in social justice. Applying the growth mindset to education means that children who live in challenging circumstances and come from marginalized backgrounds get the support they need to benefit from high-challenge academic opportunities.

Don't Tell Your Child They're Smart

One of the surprising conclusions from the research on mindsets is the importance of avoiding the standard ways we often praise children and instead giving them the right kind of praise. Dweck wrote, "Praising children's intelligence harms their motivation and it harms their performance."[3] If you want your child to think of their abilities through a growth mindset lens and not as fixed, don't tell them how smart they are, how beautiful, how creative, or anything else they might see as being out of their control. Instead, praise them for how well they're doing on the basis of their diligence, persistence, and effort. Praise them for their sustained commitment to a practice schedule or the learning strategies they're applying. Ask about their goals and objectives, and help them see how their efforts are helping them get there. Put the emphasis on their agency, not on something over which they feel no control.

Focus on Effort, Not Speed

When I ask a group of parents or teachers how they might identify a particularly capable student, I usually get fixed mindset responses such as, "Smart kids are fast thinkers," or "They learn really quickly." That kind of response gives me a chance to discuss ability from the standpoint of a growth mindset: High-level accomplishment requires hard work over time, as well as motivation. Those who prize speed can undercut the thoughtfulness that goes into long-term achievement. As Einstein said, "It's not that I'm so smart, it's just that I stay with problems longer." When someone learns something quickly, it means they already understand some of the foundational principles. Or it can mean they're processing the material more superficially. It does not mean that they're innately smarter than someone who spends more time on the learning.

Welcome Failure as a Learning Opportunity

Risk-taking and attitudes toward failure are distinguishing features of fixed and growth mindsets. If a person holding a fixed mindset doesn't do well on an activity or a test, they feel embarrassed or humiliated and sometimes decide they don't have what it takes to succeed in that area ("I just can't do math" or "I'm no good at sports"). They see a setback as showing up their incompetence, so they do their best to avoid challenges. Those with a growth mindset, however, perceive failure as an opportunity to learn what they still need to work on, so they're much likelier to take on higher level coursework and other challenges.

Don't Set a Limit on Your Child's Potential

Scott Barry Kaufman included a chapter on mindsets in his 2013 book, *Ungifted: Intelligence Redefined: The Truth About Talent,*

Practice, Creativity, and the Many Paths to Greatness.[4] He described a study in which Carol Dweck and her colleagues found that teachers with a fixed mindset were

> significantly more likely to diagnose a student as having low ability based upon a single, initially poor, performance. They were also more likely to comfort students for their low ability, saying things like "It's okay—not everyone can be good at math," which did in fact reduce student engagement with school subjects.[5]

In *Mindset*, Dweck wrote, "An assessment at one point in time has little value for understanding someone's ability, let alone their potential to succeed in future."[6] If a test-taker has a fixed mindset, they will believe their test result is a statement about their potential, not just a snapshot of a moment in time. Those with a growth mindset recognize that we can't possibly measure someone's potential because future achievement depends far too much on factors such as motivation, drive, effort, and persistence. So, a test-taker with a growth mindset knows that no matter the result they get on the test they took today, it doesn't necessarily predict how well they'll do in the future.

You can sometimes predict whether your child will enjoy an activity or do well on it according to their past or present performance, but you can't predict what will engage their curiosity and mind in the longer term or what they will take to a high level. That means don't set any limits on what you think your child is capable of, but rather, encourage them to follow their interests with optimism and enthusiasm. When they don't do well at something, the best kind of comfort you can offer is to ask what they need to do better next time.

Take, for example, 8-year-old Dian, who has always been fascinated with numbers, and their relationships with each other. By the age of 4, she was figuring out complex addition and subtraction questions, and before she was 6, she was doing two-digit multiplication for entertainment.

Dian sailed through math classes at school, always getting top grades, until she reached Grade 3 when her teacher required the students to explain their work. Dian tried hard, but she just couldn't do it. The basic processes had become so automatic for her that they'd become obvious. She'd always get the right answer, but she couldn't say how she'd got there. Her marks plummeted, and her frustration grew, and by the middle of the school year, she was close to failing and described herself as hating math. The teacher was sympathetic to Dian's frustration and consoled her by saying that sometimes people start out fast at something but then slow down when they get a bit older and that nobody is good at everything.

While it is true that sometimes people speed up or slow down in their ability to master different areas of learning and that nobody is good at everything, Dweck would argue for a different response to Dian's frustration. Her teacher might work out a compromise where if Dian were able to get to the right answer and tried to show her reasoning on one question, that would be enough. Maybe the teacher could invest some one-on-one time with Dian to help her get over this hurdle and learn how to figure out her reasoning as a piece of detective work that Dian might actually enjoy. Maybe a tutor could be found to help Dian, someone who was good at numbers and also able to explain how they were figuring things out. One way or another, someone with a growth mindset would look at Dian's frustration as an opportunity to explore work-arounds, not as a sign she wasn't good at math anymore.

Avoid Labeling Your Child, Even With Positive Labels

Dweck's research shows that it's best to avoid labels as much as possible. If intelligence, creativity, and athleticism are not fixed but rather develop, it doesn't make sense to label your child, even informally and positively, as "the smart one in the family" or "the athlete." As Dweck wrote in *Mindset*, "Telling children they're smart, in the end, made them feel dumber and act dumber, but claim they were smarter. I don't think this is what we're aiming for when we put positive labels on people."[7]

By labeling a child, we unintentionally support them, their parents, and their teachers in a fixed mindset. A label conveys permanence and too often becomes part of a person's identity ("I am learning disabled," "I am autistic," "I am gifted"), which carries corrosive repercussions over time. In the course of Dweck's research, she observed that telling kids they were smart led them to take on a fixed mindset and then to fear failure because not doing well at something shows they aren't really so smart. Kids in her studies who were told they were gifted avoided taking harder classes and didn't do as well as those who were told that hard work builds intelligence. On the basis of their long-term research, Dweck and her colleagues recommended that parents and teachers avoid the gifted label and instead encourage a growth mindset, showing kids that the harder they work, the smarter they get.

"You Aren't a Failure Until You Start to Blame"

Dweck described basketball coach John Wooden as a great example of growth mindset in action. He was a legend in college basketball, both as a player and as a coach, with an outstanding winning record: His team won the national championship 10 out of 12 years when he was head coach at UCLA. He is remembered for many things, one of which was his surprising attitude to failure. He realized that getting something wrong was the best motivator for learning and so welcomed the players' and team's setbacks. He also encouraged his players—many of whom came from disadvantaged backgrounds—to see past any limits that others might set for them: "Things turn out best for people who make the best of the way things turn out," he said.

Wooden reacted with anger to anyone's attempt to blame someone or something for any kind of setback. He reprimanded players who missed shots if they complained about another player interfering with their aim. He didn't allow players who were late for practice to blame bus schedules or heavy traffic. He objected to grumbling about the referee if his team lost a game. He accepted the inevitability of losses and mistakes, but he did not accept anyone using blame to deflect them. He was famous for telling his players, "You aren't a failure until you start to blame."

Using John Wooden's story, Dweck made the case in *Mindset* that setbacks should be welcomed as learning opportunities and are wasted when they're not owned. Those who learn from their failures take on tougher challenges, look at problems more constructively, and are more resilient. By working through the obstacles they encounter, those with a growth mindset achieve higher levels of success than they would otherwise have thought possible.

PUNISHMENT, TIME-OUTS, AND CONSEQUENCES

Before returning to the mistake scenarios I outlined at the beginning of the chapter, I'd like to discuss some of the options parents often use when responding to problems they experience with their children and teenagers.

Many adults believe in punishment, whether that's defined as spanking or its more widely accepted cousins—shouting, time-outs, and loss of privileges. "Kids need consequences for bad behavior," parents often tell me. I know what they're talking about, but the problem is that solid research has found that kids don't learn anything good from punishment. Consequences are sometimes used as punishments, but they aren't necessarily the same thing, as I discuss in the next section. The essential difference between punishments (which are not effective in the long term and can be harmful) and beneficial consequences is your attitude toward the child's misdemeanor and your child.

When I was a child, my mother read an article that suggested she count to 10 when she was angry. I remember her counting aloud with her teeth clenched to prevent herself from boiling over when one of her six active children behaved irresponsibly or worse. The counting worked to put us on alert that she was mad, but by the time she got to 10, she'd usually be laughing at herself—here she was, a grown woman, following the trendy advice of a magazine—and she'd be unlikely to come down too hard on the offending child. In retrospect, I think that was perfect. She managed to communicate her displeasure, and we were aware that next time we did whatever we'd done, things could get bad, so we'd be wise to behave differently in the future, but nobody was embarrassed or hurt in any way; in fact, everyone felt better, not worse. The lesson was learned, and a healthy atmosphere was preserved.

Your child needs you to respond to aggressive, oppositional, or destructive behavior, but the research on child development shows that angry punishment doesn't work well.[8,9] Punishment might get your child to comply with your demands, but that compliance will be expensive. Your child will feel worse about themselves, their bad feelings will go underground into simmering resentment, or both. No matter the age of your child, punishment may seem to bring you a short-term victory, but it's a lose–lose proposition in the end.

Look for Natural or Logical Consequences

The best way to change a person's behavior is to let them suffer the natural consequences of that behavior. If you don't do the laundry or expect someone else to take care of it, you won't have clean clothes to wear. And if your child insists on leaving their raincoat at home on a wet day, they'll get wet and uncomfortable. Just like you with no clean laundry, your child will have no one but themself to blame for their misery and will be considerably more likely to comply in the future with your suggestion that they take a raincoat.

Like natural consequences, logical consequences happen as a result of someone's actions, but unlike natural consequences, they're imposed by someone else. In both kinds of consequences, the person is experiencing some type of trouble that connects in some reasonable way to their misbehavior, increasing the likelihood they'll make better choices in the future.

There are several reasons natural and logical consequences work better than more punitive responses to misbehavior. To begin with, they make sense in a way that punishments never do. They're therefore easier to accept and more effective as teaching tools. Because logical consequences focus on the deed rather than the perpetrator, they don't shame your child the way other punishments do; humiliation breeds resentment and retaliation rather than learning. Logical consequences also help your child realize they have control over their behavior and its consequences, an important realization.

Natural and logical consequences are great when they make sense in a situation, but they aren't always appropriate. Sometimes your child has made an innocent mistake and doesn't need any kind of punishment or consequence, just a hug and a discussion about what happened. On the other end of the spectrum, sometimes the problems are too big to think about imposing consequences, in which case you may need professional help.

Also, someone has to invent the consequence. If you and your child are both tired, irritable, or out of sorts, it may be beyond your reach at the moment to generate something appropriate. Another problem with imposing consequences is that some parents can't resist the temptation to save their child from the difficult experience. In the raincoat situation, for example, most parents have a hard time letting a young child get drenched when they refuse to wear a raincoat. Finally, there are times when the natural consequence of a certain misbehavior is completely inappropriate or far too dangerous— think running into the road, consuming household cleaning products, or refusing to wear a seat belt.

A final note on consequences: They don't always show immediate effects. Most people don't change their ways instantly, so if you like the idea of using consequences, give it time, and you will probably notice your child taking more and more responsibility for their behavior.

Time-Outs: Please Don't Use Them

Most parents know they shouldn't hit their child, and they don't do that. Fewer parents, but still most, know they shouldn't shame their kids, ridicule them, or yell at them because emotional punishments lead to self-doubts and anger rather than contrition and improvement. But the same adults—the ones who know not to spank or shame their child—can sometimes think it's okay to banish their child for misbehavior, giving them a certain amount of time away from social contact in which to calm down and/or become sorry for what they did.

I know there are lots of reasons to think time-outs are great. When you give your child a time-out, the misbehavior is stopped in its tracks. Not only can your child calm down with a time-out, but you can also calm down yourself. Time-outs appear to be logical: If your child's behavior is noisy, aggressive, or antisocial, what could be a better consequence than sending them away from others? You hope the time-out will give your child time to think about what they did wrong and feel sorry about it. And of course, time-outs are nonviolent, infinitely better than spanking, yelling, or shaming kids.

However, time-outs don't work the way you might think they do.[10,11] Instead of teaching your child to do better, time-outs are more likely to lead to humiliation, fear of abandonment, reduced self-esteem and confidence, erosion of their trust in you, and a negative home atmosphere. No matter how you might view it, your child experiences a time-out as a humiliation. That means that during the time-out, they'll either conclude they're not a good person and feel bad about themself and less confident, or they'll feel unfairly treated and get angry. The sense of injustice may lead to further bad behavior, of course, but that's probably better in the long run than sad, dejected good behavior. When you send your child away from you, you remind them of their vulnerability and the fact that they need you. If your child is sensitive or even mildly anxious, this can trigger real fears that you might abandon them.

Time-outs may appear appropriate to you, but they can be quite damaging. If your child behaves badly on purpose, it usually indicates they're feeling bad about themself already. If their misbehavior is unintentional, they'll feel misunderstood and unfairly treated if you give them a time-out. In either case, a time-out makes them feel worse about themself. When you give your child a time-out, you're telling them you want to spend time with them only when they're complying with your rules about how a child should behave. Their feelings about being bad don't disappear. They come to the surface sooner or later in a distorted or magnified form.

When you give your child a time-out, as when you punish them in other ways, you're establishing a climate of fear where the powerful person gets to make the rules, and the powerless one has to obey. Yes, you must make rules for your kids, and your kids have to follow those rules, but there are ways to do it that don't erode healthy self-concept and confidence.

One of the big reasons not to banish a child is that they don't have the neurological tools needed to handle overwhelming feelings.

They aren't capable of the necessary depth of insight until puberty, and even then, it's not reliable until they're in their early 20s. Sending them for a time-out will only make them feel lonelier, unfairly treated, and angry.

Time-outs are far more appropriate for adults than for children, and in fact, you might find time-outs a good solution for yourself if you tend to yell first and reflect later. You can't always absent yourself, though, so think about it ahead of time, and identify one or more coping mechanisms such as the counting-to-ten technique that my mother used, something you'll have ready to use as needed so you don't give in to your desire to banish your child. (I address coping mechanisms more fully in the next chapter, Chapter 3.)

RESPONDING TO MISTAKES AND MISBEHAVIOR BY AGE

The Early Years: Birth to 5

At the beginning of this chapter, I posed two problems parents might encounter in their child's first 5 years. The first scenario involved 3-year-old Xandra, who had shoved her brother Dante to the ground and grabbed a toy from him that she'd been playing with. I gave three possible response options: taking the toy away from Xandra, hugging Dante, and giving Xandra a time-out; calmly giving Dante back the toy and explaining the problem to Xandra, insisting she apologize; and contemplating Xandra's hidden needs before talking to her about better ways to get what she wants.

In the second situation, Geraldo was pouring milk back and forth from a glass to a cup. You asked him three times to stop, and milk spilled everywhere. The response options were roaring at Geraldo and giving him a time-out before cleaning up the mess yourself; calmly telling him he'd get no more milk today before you cleaned up the mess; and calmly saying to Geraldo, "Whoops. What do we do next?"

Until 3 or 4 years old and sometimes a little longer, you can expect to be dealing with a lot of mistakes, misbehavior, and aggression. Your child is not being bad, but there's a lot they're still learning about. They have little or no impulse control, and they don't yet have the insight or communication skills to tell you what's wrong or what they'd like you to do. Sometimes they see misbehavior or aggression as the best way to get your attention.

Open disobedience in young children is usually a message that they're not getting what they want. This isn't conscious, and they don't distinguish between reasonable desires such as hunger, thirst, or human warmth and unreasonable demands such as another child's toy, one more cookie, or not being put into a car seat. Most parents know their little one is more likely to lash out or misbehave when they're not feeling well, they're hungry, they're tired, or they're worried about something. And really, who can blame them for using what seems in the moment to be the only means at their disposal to voice the seriousness of their complaints and their frustration at being so powerless?

Punishing your young child—whether shouting at them, giving them a time-out, or something else—will only make things worse. If you act out of impatience or anger, it will make your child feel even more frustrated, and it will also show them it's okay to be impatient and angry. That's probably not the outcome you're hoping for.

Your child's misbehavior or defiance gives you a chance to help them acquire better coping mechanisms for dealing with difficult feelings. If you can channel a growth mindset and work on learning to welcome your little one's acts of disobedience or aggression as opportunities to discover what they need, you'll retain your sense of perspective and behave with as much calm wisdom as possible. It may not make immediate sense, but the more you're able to welcome acts of blatant disregard for your demands, the less frequently you'll experience them.

In both the Xandra and Geraldo scenarios, the third option is most consistent with the research on growth mindsets, child development, and punishment. The ideal response is to find a way to welcome the misbehavior as an opportunity to help both you and your child learn something about taking care of the child's needs. You want to address any underlying needs—food, a snuggle, curiosity—and help the child meet those needs in a more acceptable way in the future. In the interest of their long-term development and your household harmony, you don't want to frighten them or make them feel worse about themselves.

With Xandra, after taking care of any underlying needs, you might want to discuss the acceptable options in a situation like the one in which she found herself. You could try role-playing the situation with different ideas for resolution, such as finding something to trade with her brother, asking him for it nicely, suggesting a time-share, or doing something else until he's finished with it. Communicate with your manner and words that you love her and know she'll do better next time. You might say, "Everyone makes mistakes, and everyone can make things better again."

If Geraldo knows the answer to your question "What do we do next?"—that is, getting a sponge and cleaning up the mess—he will probably be happy to do that, relieved he's not getting criticized or punished. And if he doesn't yet know how to clean up a milk spill, this is a good time to teach him. You might also set up a spot where he can safely pour liquids between containers without wasting anything or making a big mess. You may be encouraging his scientific curiosity, as well as getting a kitchen helper.

There are, of course, bigger problems than the ones depicted in these scenarios. If your child is being aggressive or destructive, you have to stop it. With kindness as well as firmness, do what's necessary to stop what's happening. If your child is hitting someone, take their hands in your hands, so they can't continue doing that. If they're kicking someone, sit them down on the floor and hold their feet. If your child had a dangerous weapon in their hand—a knife, say, or a gun—you wouldn't hesitate to take the weapon away. Hitting, scratching, kicking, and biting are no different. Hands, nails, teeth, and feet are the weapons available to your toddler. It's your job to ensure they learn they cannot use their weapons on others.

Next, take your child to a private place, even if it means picking them up and carrying them, kicking and screaming. That can be a quiet corner of a store or parking lot or a separate room in a home. This gives your child a chance to calm down away from the situation where they were hitting (or scratching, etc.), and it gives you a chance to deal with it away from the eyes of others. That allows your child to maintain their dignity. Even for a toddler, it's embarrassing to have a problem addressed in front of others.

When you've found a quiet spot and are still restraining your child, or they're no longer hitting, and so forth, look them in the eye, and tell them firmly and calmly something such as, "In our family, we do not hit." No matter how you are feeling—angry, worried, embarrassed—do your best to stay calm, kind, and strong, as well as clear about the message.

As soon as possible and once your child's rage has passed, explain what is wrong about what happened, and tell them what you want from them going forward. For example, "Hitting is never okay. When you notice you're about to hit [or scratch, etc.], please let me know how you feel. Instead of hitting, maybe you can say, 'I'm tired, Mommy' or 'My tummy is rumbling' or 'I really need you to listen to me, right now.' And if you can't find your words to tell me about it, let me know some other way. Maybe you can look at me and clap your hands together."

It may seem funny to expect a young child to pause and think before going through with the hitting action or to clap instead of hitting. But by suggesting one or more of these options, you are teaching them that you are there to help them get their needs met. You are also teaching them to be aware of their needs. More than that, you are teaching them that their human needs—whether it's hunger, needing to use the toilet, or needing to express a big emotion—are acceptable, not something to be ashamed of. We never grow out of these needs; we just learn better ways to deal with them.

Childhood: 6 to 10

At the beginning of the chapter, I presented a scenario involving 9-year-old Molly, who had created a big mess in the living room—books, games, and other things strewn everywhere. I offered three response options: Yell at Molly and tell her she must clean it up immediately, with no screens, dinner, or other activities until she's done; calmly give her a time-out before cleaning up the mess yourself and putting her things into boxes that she won't get access to for 24 hours; or say, "You have a big job ahead of you. You know what's next, right?"

As with younger children, in the interest of things going well for Molly, yourself, and the rest of the family, you don't want to yell at her, give her a time-out, or punish her in any other way. Instead, once again, your best response is to welcome this as an opportunity to figure out what's going on with her. There's some kind of message in this mess, and it's important you figure out what it is. Offer to help her clean it up; that will give you a chance to spend some time with her, and she may give you some clues about what's going on. If she grumbles and keeps playing, you might suggest a starting place: "How about we do the books first? If you collect them, I can put them back in the bookcase."

If Molly continues to play or leaves the room, remind yourself that her state of mind is more important than a tidy home—even if you will be working from there as your office—or bending her will to your demands. You might say something such as, "Is something bothering you? Can we talk about it?"

If she refuses to talk or start the cleanup, tell her you want to know what's going on with her, but in the meantime, you're starting the cleanup yourself. Let her know you're available to talk when she's ready, but for now, you're packing her stuff into a box, and she will lose access to it for a specified time, maybe a day. Stay alert to subtle messages she may send that will help you understand what's troubling her.

When people feel threatened—no matter their age—they can sometimes get angry and act with defiance. That's true whether it's a real and external threat, such as a person with a weapon, or it's a perceived and internal threat resulting from feeling sad, lonely, disappointed, or embarrassed. Behaving badly can relieve the powerless feelings and make a person feel stronger in the moment.

A child under 10 has neither the physical strength to deal with a big scary monster (e.g., an angry adult) nor the cognitive maturity to deal well with disappointment or embarrassment (e.g., being yelled at). They don't have what it takes to soothe themself or modulate their reactions, so it's not only unfair to punish them for making mistakes, breaking the rules, or getting defiant, but it will also make things worse. They'll feel worse about themselves, not better, which will only escalate their bad behavior.

It will help if you realize that your child's defiance or misbehavior is an indication of suffering of some kind, something not okay in their life. Try to welcome it as a chance to learn what's going on with them, quite possibly something they haven't put into words for themselves. Before responding to their problematic actions, think about possible threats from their perspective. It's normal, but not useful, for a parent to react with annoyance or even anger to a child's misbehavior. If you speak harshly to your child or punish them, though, you'll be making their world scarier and increasing the likelihood of further explosions. Instead, try to keep yourself calm. Model the skills your child needs to calm themself down.

It will also help if you reassure your child that you understand. When your child knows you understand why they're upset (whether or not it seems reasonable to you), they feel safer and are better able to feel the vulnerable emotions driving the behavior. That's true whether they're feeling grief over a broken toy, hurt over a harsh word, or fear of a bully.

Let your child know it's okay to be angry or upset. Welcome your child's feelings and express gratitude if they trust you enough to show you their feelings, even if it's through unacceptable behavior. Your acceptance of their feelings will allow your child to accept those troubling feelings instead of trying to repress them, which never goes well. If your child is showing defiance, it means they're afraid. They need reassurance that they're safe before they can calm down and carry on. Don't give your child a time-out, which will make them feel more alone and afraid. Instead, hold them close. Give them a "time-in."

You might want to dramatize some anger management techniques. You can do some role-playing with your child, where each of you enacts, in turn, the angry child and the villain who made the child angry. Feel free to exaggerate. Use props and costumes if you like. A witch's hat might be useful or a hero's cape. Watch tears turn to laughter and creative solutions arise as your child feels listened to and understood and also sees a glimmer of possibility that they might be able to control their behavior.

One of your important jobs as a parent is to help your child develop the coping mechanisms they need to navigate life's challenges successfully. Once the storm has passed, find a quiet moment to discuss what happened and different ways they might handle things in the future. Help your child feel more powerful as they learn to prevent problems and gain control of their reactions. It takes a long time and many setbacks before a child learns how to regulate their emotions and behave with maturity, so be patient, both with yourself and your child, as they learn to recognize and manage their emotions and behavior.

Family therapist Jane Nelsen recommended taking four factors into consideration when responding to a child's misbehavior.[12] Ideally, your reaction is (a) related to your child's misbehavior; (b) respectfully communicated, without blaming your child, shaming them, or causing them pain; (c) reasonable relative to the severity of the misbehavior; and (d) helpful in getting your child to do better in future.

Finally, some behavior problems can't be easily solved without professional help. If you're seeing a lot of aggression or defiance to the point that it's explosive or oppositional and you're not able to handle it alone, look for help.

Adolescence: 11 to 18

The teenage problem scenario I posed at the beginning of the chapter involved learning that your son, Deon, had been truant for half of the days during the preceding 6 weeks. When you ask him about it, he admits he's been skipping school and spending time with friends at a downtown mall. The response options were to shout at him and impose an escort to take him to and from school each day and also confiscate his phone and any other electronic devices he has, with no screen privileges for the foreseeable future; ground him for 2 weeks, with strict orders to spend all time outside of school hours with one of his parents; or ask him about what's going on in his life, trying to understand what's happening with him.

You probably know that the third option is the one I'd recommend. It is imperative for Deon's future well-being—and your relationship with him—that you put your emphasis squarely on understanding his needs and doing everything you can to help him make good decisions now and as he gets older. Try to welcome your knowledge about the truancy: It gives you a chance to understand what's happening in your child's world and answer his call for help.

Most responsible parents take school attendance seriously and would be upset to hear about this kind of truancy, worrying perhaps that Deon was throwing away any chances of a successful high school career and diminishing his postsecondary opportunities and, therefore, future career options. As children get older, there can be real-world consequences for infractions like this, but yelling at Deon and punishing him for staying away from school (or not doing his homework or failing subjects) won't help. At this stage, you can't punish or control him into good behavior; if you do, it will have a high cost in self-esteem and/or repressed anger.

Your best path forward is to work to understand if Deon is having problems with school—maybe he has a learning problem not yet diagnosed; maybe he's experiencing bullying, racism, or fear of gun violence. Or if the problem isn't school per se, then you want to know the reasons he's seeking the company of other kids who are skipping school. And maybe there's something else entirely. Perhaps he's dealing with depression, anxiety, loneliness, social isolation, drug use, or something else.

Sometimes a teen's annoying behavior signifies nothing, but sometimes there's something deeper going on, and the young person needs something from you. In either case, just like when they were a toddler, they feel safe only when they know they can trust you to remain calm and strong, no matter how many of your buttons they push. If you know you're about to explode, back off until you've regained your equilibrium and you're strong enough to stay calm.

Whether you're dealing with a problem such as truancy or not, you and your child will both benefit from scheduling a regular time together, maybe a few minutes daily, when you talk about anything they want to talk about. Or make a weekly date to do something together. Go for ice cream, take a walk in the neighborhood, take an exercise class together. Your teenager might try to get out of your together time, but you should proceed regardless, solo if necessary. Your teenager probably won't let you know it—at least, not until they're a bit older—but this time together could be a lifesaver.

I'm not saying you should abandon your beliefs. You should tell your child as firmly as necessary (with respect and without hostility) why you think it's important they attend school regularly, why you need them to behave respectfully, or why you want them to turn off all electronics by 10 p.m. It probably doesn't feel like this at the time, but it's actually good to argue with your teenager, as long as you're respectful and affectionate. Kids do best in the long run when they grow up in a home that's characterized by lots of heated discussions, as well as lots of love and warmth.[13,14]

If your teenager is making you crazy, you might try completing this sentence in your mind: "It must be hard . . ."—for example, "It must be hard to crave independence while living with your parents," or "It must be hard trying to be a man but finding your schoolwork challenging."

When you encounter problems with your teenager, try to remember, "Yes, they'll make mistakes—they're new at life and decision making—but that's the only way they learn." Before puberty, most children are blissfully unaware of the perceptions of others, but teens believe that everyone is looking at them with critical mocking eyes. So, work hard to avoid nagging and criticism. Make sure your teen feels your positive gaze. That can make the difference between them losing their way in harmful directions and finding and living their strength.

Let your teen know you're always available to listen or do some problem solving with them if they want that, but don't try to solve their problems for them. When they want to talk, be fully present (no distractions, no devices) and be fully positive (no criticism, no judgment). Offer no solutions, just patient attention and acceptance. If your child asks what you think they should do, do your best to avoid giving an answer. Instead, try to ask questions that lead them to identify the solutions. Any solution they feel they've invented will be worth a hundred solutions you give them.

A final recommendation for parents of teens is to strengthen your family's network of social support. Many teens feel dramatically misunderstood by their parents and, therefore, lonely in their own homes. Connecting with grandparents, aunts and uncles, friends of the family, and others can help your child see you and themselves through different eyes and provide a safety valve for talking about what's bothering them. Feeling like a member of a closely connected network of social support can help your young person find more confidence and a healing sense of connection.

It might comfort you to know that challenging one's parents is a healthy part of growing up, so at least some of the trouble your kid might be causing you is helping them develop into a successful and resilient adult who knows how to manage their life. There's a limit to how much challenge is healthy challenge, however. If your teenager is defiant, oppositional, and consistently surly, you may need help. If your teenager is seriously troubled (by drugs, violence, etc.), it's time to look for professional help. Take advantage of the small parenting window you still have before your teenager is an adult. Get the help you need to provide them with a more solid foundation for moving into independent adulthood.

Young Adulthood: 19 to 24

The problem scenario I posed for young adults was 21-year-old Amanda's being fired from another job for having a bad attitude. She doesn't want to go to college and just wants to continue living at home with you, taking a few months off. The options were exploding and telling her she couldn't continue living at home if she wasn't going to school or working; telling her she'd have to pull her weight as family shopper, cook, laundress, and cleaner; and collaborating with her to design a daily schedule, including some household maintenance, part-time learning or training, community service, and career counseling.

This may be the most controversial of my recommendations. Once again, I choose the third option. I understand a parent choosing either of the first two options, but the research is pretty solid in showing late adolescence or early adulthood to be another potentially vulnerable time in a person's life.[15,16,17] It's a time when a person's identity is volatile, when they're working (consciously or unconsciously) to figure out who they are in the world. Many young adults have a hard time at this stage; parental guidance and support can make all the difference in the outcome.

As with each of these scenarios, this is a simplified version of a real-life situation, but real life is immeasurably more complex and nuanced than this. Your situation is unique. Knowing the research can help you make an informed decision, but only you can know the personalities, history, and context that will allow you to figure the next steps. What I know for sure is that it's always wise to find a perspective that welcomes as a learning opportunity what life presents as a problem and that early adulthood is a tough passage and best navigated with ongoing support.

As with the other stages, there are some problems that require professional help. If you have concerns about substance abuse, violence, psychological or psychiatric problems, or some other serious or life-threatening behavior, you need help. You can't do this on your own, and there are professionals available to help you find the services your young adult needs and the support you need, too.

Adulthood: Responding to Mistakes Made by You and Others

The adult scenario I provided at the top of the chapter was that you'd missed an important deadline at work because your kids had been sick, and you'd been doing more than your share at home. Your boss had warned you you'd be replaced if it happened again. The response options were to blame your partner; say nothing to anyone, vowing to do better next time; and acknowledge to yourself that something had to change and work together with your boss and/or partner to take care of both family and work.

I expect you realize by now that my recommendation is that you welcome this problem as an opportunity to consider your options for a more sustainable work and home situation. Every circumstance is different. Some jobs allow for more flexibility—maybe you can work from home at least part of the time when you have a sick child, maybe your partner can do that, maybe you or your partner can bank sick days to use for situations like this, or maybe you can train someone else to take over your work if necessary, perhaps with you on call as needed—and some jobs don't. Some employers are reasonable, understanding that this is a normal and predictable issue they should find a good way to manage; some employers aren't. Some partners are more flexible; some are not. Regardless, if this problem has happened once, there's a good chance it will happen again, so it's worth looking at as a learning opportunity and making whatever changes you can make. It won't help you in the long run if you blame your partner or ignore this problem and hope it never happens again.

We all make mistakes. We all have problems and failures and disappointments. The more I can find it in myself to look at setbacks as learning opportunities, the happier I am and the more successfully I navigate my responses to the problems.

As adults navigating imperfectly through our own complicated lives, we know that we need a variety of tools to help us feel successful and cope when things are hard. Maybe you are great at putting dates in your calendar. You can be relied on to take the family vehicle in for an oil change or arrange with your mom to go to her dialysis appointments. But when emotions are high, you'd rather flee to your room until your pulse slows down a bit and afterward pretend nothing is wrong. It's easier to leave the problem underneath those difficult emotions well alone and just hope it works itself out in time.

You have likely developed many excellent tools to smooth over imperfections in some areas of your life, but you still need work in other areas. Remember that your child is going through the same thing while their body, brain, and hormones are constantly changing! As you review the "right" or "best" scenario responses given earlier, my greatest hope is not that you learn them by heart. My hope is that as you practice them, you adopt a compassionate view of your imperfections or limitations, both as a human and as a parent and that you begin to see yourself as someone with great potential to grow and change—just like your child.

TAKING IT INTO THE COMMUNITY: MAKING LEMONADE WHEN LIFE GIVES YOU LEMONS

Angela was beside herself with worry. She'd always been flexible with demands on her 15-year-old daughter, Jesse, but for the past 3 weeks Jesse was staying out most evenings, sometimes not returning home after school until 10 o'clock. She'd call home around 5 to give some good reason for the absence—she was grabbing a sandwich and studying at the library, she was having dinner at a friend's house and then doing homework together, or there was a band practice after school, and they were having a pizza party afterward.

Jesse had been an easy child and had always had lots of friends. She was usually cheerful and cooperative at home and good with her little brother. She wasn't an academic star, but she enjoyed school and mostly did her homework. Angela hadn't had any problems with her before now, but she felt uneasy about the situation. Whenever she pressed for more details, Jesse was ready to provide them. Angela trusted Jesse to tell her the truth but felt that these stories about her after-school activities just didn't ring true.

Angela talked to a couple of friends who had daughters in Jesse's grade at the same school. They both advised her to come down hard on Jesse. "You need to ground her!" said one. "Kids this age can get into all kinds of stupid and dangerous things. She can't do this night after night without some kind of repercussions." "I'd take away her phone and other screen privileges until she's arranging these things ahead of time," said the other mother. "I let my daughter have one late night like this a week and that's only when I have lots of notice."

Feeling a bit desperate and seriously worried, Angela talked to her mother about the situation. Her mother raised her eyebrows and asked why she was being so gullible: "There's something going on here, Angie. It's not like Jesse to lie, and I doubt she's doing anything terrible, but she could be in trouble and need you to get involved. I really think it's time you challenged her on these stories she's telling you."

That evening when Jesse returned home a little after 9, Angela was waiting for her in the kitchen. She asked Jesse to sit down at the kitchen table. "I need to talk to you, Jesse," she said. "You're not in trouble, but we need to talk. We had chicken stew for dinner, and I saved some. Can I warm it up for you? Or make you some hot chocolate?"

Jesse seemed apprehensive and said, "Sorry, Mom, I don't have time. I'm really beat, and I still have 2 hours of homework."

"No, sweetie. We have to talk now."

Jesse grumbled and sat down on the edge of her seat. "What?"

It took a while, but eventually, that evening, Angela learned that Jesse had been lying to her because she was honoring a friend's request for secrecy. Her friend Marisol was being abused by her stepfather.

Marisol had tried to talk to her mother, Jesse told Angela, but her mother denied the possibility and told Marisol she had to rein in her evil imagination. Jesse had been sitting in a local coffee shop or the library with Marisol or walking endlessly with her until 9 most nights when Marisol's mother came home from work. After that, Marisol said, she was safe.

Angela was relieved she hadn't punished Jesse as her friends had suggested and glad she'd taken her mother's advice to check into the situation, taking into account both Jesse's history of being honest with her and her worries that something was wrong. Angela said, "I love it that you're a loyal friend to someone in trouble—and we need to talk about how to help Marisol—but I am not happy that you have told me so many lies about what you've been doing."

"Marisol made me promise I wouldn't tell a soul. Now I feel terrible about breaking my promise," Jesse said, beginning to cry. "I don't know how I'm going to face her tomorrow."

"I'm worried about Marisol. Let's start by talking about how we might be able to help and then get back to what you'll say to her tomorrow and my issues with your lying."

"There's nothing we can do. That's what Marisol and I talk about every day. If she talks to a teacher or guidance counselor at school, they'll have to call Children's Services, and then maybe they'll put her in foster care. She can't go to the police for the same reason."

Angela nodded. That was a real possibility.

Jesse continued, "Marisol has tried to talk to her mom, and she won't listen. She just accuses Marisol of flirting with her stepfather and making things up."

"So, Marisol feels safe after her mother comes home from work?"

"Yes. Luc looks all innocent and disinterested then. Marisol and her mom have a great relationship other than this."

"What about weekends?"

"Not a problem. Her mom just works during the week."

"How about you bring Marisol home with you every day after school? You can do your homework together here, and she can go to her place once she feels safe."

"But then she'd know I told you!"

"You can tell her that I pushed you on all your excuses and forced you to tell me what was going on, and then I made this suggestion."

"She'll feel betrayed. I promised. And she won't want to be a burden."

"She won't be a burden. You girls can help with the cooking and some of the other chores. Once she's had some time to think about it, I think she'll see it's best for her to have an adult to talk to and a safe home where she's welcome."

Jesse nodded. "Maybe. I'll talk to her tomorrow, and we'll see. She might just turn away from me and lose her only true friend in the world."

Angela agreed. "That's a risk, but I think it's a risk worth taking."

"I'll never lie to you again, Mom. I should have come to you with this immediately."

"You were in an impossible situation, Jesse, and I am proud of what a good friend you've been to Marisol. But yes, please trust that no matter what you think you need to lie about, I'll listen to you, and maybe together we can find a better pathway through the situation. And if I don't listen very well sometime, please remind me of this conversation."

The next day, Marisol came home with Jesse after school. Angela—who worked from home—greeted them and brought them to the kitchen, where she'd set out some snacks. Angela reassured Marisol that her secret was safe with her and took responsibility for Jesse having shared it with her. They talked about what had been happening, and Angela told Marisol she had a place to stay whenever she needed it, day or night.

After 2 weeks of Marisol coming home every day with Jesse, Angela learned of a house in her community that provided shelter for families in unsafe situations. She spoke to the leader of the non-profit group that ran the house and learned that she and Jesse and Marisol could do some volunteer work there. The girls could work with young children who were being helped, providing them with friendly warmth, as well as tutoring in reading, and Angela could do some counseling with the mothers.

Jesse and Marisol loved doing the tutoring. They both felt good about helping the children through a tough time, and it made Marisol realize that she wasn't the only one living in bad circumstances. After they'd been volunteering at the house for a few weeks, Angela talked to the leader of the organization that ran the home. She asked what else they could do to support families in need. She learned that funding was always a problem and that the local city council was trying to close them down. She talked to Jesse and Marisol about this, and together the girls organized a social media campaign, providing awareness about the need for this resource in the community.

Their efforts led to local and regional media interviews with the girls and to pressure being put on the city council not only to increase funding but also to set up more homes in different parts of the city. And not only did their efforts lead to more reliable and generous funding for this service, but there were also repercussions on the personal level. Marisol's mother was surprised one day when she turned on the TV and saw Marisol being interviewed. She was proud that Marisol was doing good work in the community, but it made her rethink what might be happening in her own home. After some heartfelt conversations with Marisol, her mother realized she had to leave her husband. Marisol's problem was resolved, but she and Jesse carried on with their volunteer work.

Human beings do make mistakes—and there are a lot of them in this story—but with a growth mindset, they can be fixed and become turning points for important learning, growth, and change. Jesse lied to her mother. Angela waited 3 weeks before addressing her worries. Marisol wanted to keep her situation a secret. Marisol's mother didn't listen to her daughter. The city council tried to shut down an important service. All these problems would have ended differently if some of the participants hadn't looked squarely at the problems as learning opportunities and engaged in problem solving instead of blaming someone or something.

KEY TAKEAWAYS: USING A GROWTH MINDSET TO RESPOND TO MISTAKES AND FIX THEM

The best news emerging from the mindset research is that mindsets are habits. They aren't hardwired, and they can be changed. Like any ingrained habit, it isn't easy to change a mindset, but it is relatively simple.

- **It starts with you.** Learn to welcome the obstacles you encounter as opportunities to learn what you don't know yet or need to adjust somehow.
- **Think about intelligence and other skills and abilities as dynamic.** Remember that your skills and abilities, like your child's, develop over time with motivation, effort, and opportunities to learn. Try adding the word *yet* after failures: "I can't cook," "I can't master this new software," "I can't do math" becomes "I can't cook yet," "I can't master this new software yet," "I can't do math yet." Do the same with your child's perceptions of failure. Show them how they can't run fast YET, they can't make friends YET, they can't write an essay YET.

- **Welcome your child's misbehavior and other setbacks as learning opportunities.** Do your best to treat a disappointing behavior or result as a positive and welcome chance to learn something about what needs attention or more work. Be sensitive to your child's feelings, but help them reframe the setback as a chance to figure out what they need to do to do better next time.
- **Avoid blaming anyone or anything.** When your child experiences an obstacle, setback, or failure, don't look for who or what is at fault. Your child didn't do well on a math test. Maybe the teacher isn't as friendly as you or your child would like, maybe the test included items that hadn't been taught, or maybe your child wasn't feeling well the day of the test—none of that really matters. Instead, ask your child what they can learn from how they did on that test and how they can do better next time. You want your child to take ownership and learn what can be learned from this, so don't blame your child, either.
- **Don't set limits on what's possible.** Recognize that your child's potential is invisible and unmeasurable. And so is yours.

What to do about mistakes and misbehavior is an important question for most parents, and it doesn't get easier as kids get older. If your child is still young, invest the time and energy now in establishing a good strong relationship, so your child feels secure enough to venture into the world with confidence and come back to you for guidance and support as they encounter obstacles. No matter your child's age, it is never too late to see their problems as opportunities to figure out how to fix them and do better going forward.

CHAPTER 3

ACCEPT AND BE MINDFUL: TAKE A BREATH, YOU ARE ENOUGH

Be the silence that listens.
—Tara Brach, *Radical Compassion*

Mindfulness is the term used for bringing one's attention to what's happening in the present moment without judgment. It means consciously attending to being here, in this moment now. Doing that is much harder than it sounds because our active brains are constantly taking us back into pleasant, confusing, and disturbing memories; forward into plans, hopes, and worries for the future; and sideways into our email messages, to-do lists, dinner plans, and all the other distractions that surround us. When we can learn to "be the silence that listens" (in the words of psychologist and meditation teacher Tara Brach[1]), we find the stillness in our centers, helping us be present to what's happening in our bodies and minds and in the lives of those who we encounter.

Mindfulness Quiz

"Mindfulness" has become a bit of a buzzword. Most people have encountered the word and have a general sense of its meaning, but there are a lot of misconceptions about it, too. Before getting into what it is and how it might be useful in your life, you might find it interesting to take

---

(continues)

Mindfulness Quiz (*Continued*)

this true/false quiz that targets some of the prevailing misconceptions. I address each of these topics in this chapter, but in the meantime, you can see the answers in the endnotes.[2]

1. There is no solid scientific research on mindfulness. (T/F)
2. People who practice mindfulness are calmer and wiser than others. (T/F)
3. To become mindful, a person has to study meditation. (T/F)
4. Mindfulness practices improve cognitive functioning, attention, and memory. (T/F)
5. If you take one or two yoga classes a week, in a year or so, you will become mindful. (T/F)
6. Mindfulness is a Buddhist religious teaching and not practiced by devout Christians, Muslims, or Jews. (T/F)
7. There is brain research showing that mindfulness reduces anxiety and stress. (T/F)
8. The range of emotional expression is muted in those who practice mindfulness; their serenity means they experience less sadness and less happiness than others. (T/F)
9. Mindfulness has been proven effective in pain management. (T/F)
10. Before age 12, children are too young to learn mindfulness techniques. (T/F)

HOW DOES MINDFULNESS WORK?

Mindfulness practices offer a dramatic illustration of *neural plasticity*, also called brain plasticity or neuroplasticity. Neural plasticity is the brain's ability to form and reorganize connections between brain cells in response to a person's experience. The nature of the experience, coupled with the brain's maturity at the time, determines whether the brain change is beneficial, as happens when a child spends time making things with building blocks and develops an appreciation for spatial relations, engineering, or architecture. Neural plasticity can also be detrimental, however, as happens when a person experiences chronic stress, repeated abuse, or severe maternal depression.

Findings from Harvard neuroscientist Sara Lazar show that mindfulness reduces the neural indicators of stress and anxiety, improves attention and memory, and promotes self-regulation and empathy.[3,4] By using mindfulness practices, you can not only improve your brain's functioning, but you can also gain some big advantages that will help you in many important dimensions of parenting.

We have to be careful not to overinterpret the neurological research on mindfulness because it is still in the early stages and often contentious. At the same time, many experts have observed mindfulness-related brain changes that lead to reduced anxiety and depression, increased coping and wellness, and more effective responses to problems with learning, emotions, health, and behavior. Harvard University offers courses on the "Cognitive Neuroscience of Meditation" and "Mindfulness for Educators." The University of Oxford has a Mindfulness Research Centre, where mindfulness practices are taught and studied. Oxford also offers a graduate program in mindfulness-based cognitive therapy, as well as mindfulness courses for staff, faculty, and students. At Stanford University, mindfulness and mindfulness meditation are taught and studied at The Center for Compassion and Altruism Research and Education.

Mindfulness is sometimes associated with the religious practices of Buddhism, but there is no religious aspect to the practice of attending to here and now without judgment. There are many ways to become mindful, including meditation, yoga, focusing on gratitude, spending time in nature, and paying conscious attention to one's breathing. Prayer can also be a form of mindful meditation.

SOME EXAMPLES OF MINDFULNESS IN PRACTICE

Mindy has a high-stress job as an emergency room doctor. She has found mindfulness training invaluable when dealing with frightened, intoxicated, and demanding patients. Before responding to their fear, confusion, or anger, she takes a deep breath, focusing on being present to the patient's experience. She no longer takes so much of her stress home with her after work, and she's become known by her colleagues as the right person to call when dealing with a particularly difficult patient.

Shakir teaches science in an inner-city high school. He enjoys working with challenging young people, and he loves sharing the mysteries of science with them, but because of the stress he experiences daily, he had been thinking about leaving the profession before he learned about mindfulness. He started practicing simple breathing exercises for 10 minutes a day during his lunch hour and has become better at managing the disruptions in the classroom. Instead of feeling overwhelmed, Shakir feels better able to prioritize his responses, and he has even developed new systems for preventing or minimizing the most common disruptions. Not only does he enjoy his work again, but he's also less tired when he gets home and much better able to enjoy his young family.

Rollo is a stay-at-home father, and he is also running a web design business from home. His partner has to travel frequently in his work, so Rollo is often home alone for a week at a time, trying to make work deadlines and parenting their energetic young children, one of whom is highly spirited and one of whom is on the autism spectrum. Rollo talked to a friend about his fears that he couldn't manage much longer. His friend recommended an online mindfulness course that she'd completed. After about 6 weeks, Rollo noticed he was coping better. When he felt pushed beyond his limit, he would stop and take a few mindful breaths before responding to the situation at hand. His life remains enormously demanding, but he's no longer desperate and is finding himself able to enjoy the children, his partner, and his work a lot more than before.

Every person's life has its unique blend of stressors, but I don't know anyone—least of all a parent—who lives without some kind of pressure and strain. Think about where you might not be coping as well as you want to be or what's stressing you more than is comfortable. That's a place where mindfulness can help.

MINDFULNESS MEDITATION: GETTING STARTED

There's a widespread misconception that it's hard to do mindfulness meditation, but it's actually profoundly simple, in that there are only a few steps to follow and no special equipment is needed. It can be done, start to finish, in just a few minutes. However, some people do find it hard or even a bit scary to quiet their minds. The important thing to remember is that even if your mind tries to keep chatting, it doesn't mean you are bad at meditating. Meditation is a practice—it's both a good habit and something that you can get better at with repetition over time.

You can take a course—there are courses offered in every community and online—or you can start on your own by following these steps:

1. **Settle in.** Find a quiet space at a time you probably won't be disturbed. Sit on the floor, a cushion, or a chair, or lie down. Get comfortable.
2. **Soften your gaze or close your eyes**—whatever feels most comfortable to you.
3. **Breathe.** Take a deep breath. Feel the rise and fall of your chest. Notice your body relaxing. Attend to the expansion and contraction of your belly.

4. **Take another breath.** Notice how the air feels as it fills your lungs. Don't try to control your breathing; just feel it as it enters and fills your body.
5. **Take another breath,** and come back to being here, now.
6. **Take another breath, and slowly, another.** Thoughts will come to your mind. Notice them, and don't judge yourself for being distracted. Instead, gently shelve your thoughts to attend to later.
7. **Return to focusing on your breath.**
8. **Do this for 10 minutes.**
9. **Do it again tomorrow.** After a few days, you'll probably begin feeling the benefits. You might also notice it gets easier to find 10 minutes daily. Some researchers have observed that maximum benefits are achieved with 20 minutes twice a day, but my experience, and that of others with whom I've worked, suggests that doing this for 5 or 10 minutes a few days a week means a noticeable change in a surprisingly short time.
10. **Integrate your practice into your life.** When you're feeling stressed, irritable, or anxious, observe your breathing. Just paying attention to it works to regulate it and slow it down. It won't be long before you're feeling calmer and more in control of your emotions and reactions. Soon others will start noticing too.

There are many other ways to meditate other than "sitting meditation." Some people do "walking meditations," listen mindfully to music, cook mindfully, or use affirmations, all of which I discuss next.

WHY IT'S GOOD TO BE A MINDFUL PARENT

There are many reasons to be a mindful human being: You'll be calmer, healthier, more reasonable, and nicer to spend time with. But the reasons to be a mindful parent may be even more urgent.

One of the pressing learning challenges of childhood is self-regulation—coping with setbacks and managing emotions. You'll be infinitely more effective at teaching your child about self-regulation if you're good at managing your own reactions. By becoming mindful, you become a better listener. When you're more patient, less irritable, and more present to your child's feelings, you're better able to respond thoughtfully and well. Mindfulness gives you the capacity to choose how you react in the moment instead of being overwhelmed by your feelings.

Children have an uncanny ability to identify their parents' emotional buttons and push them, which can lead to parents behaving badly. A mindful parent learns to recognize when this is happening. If you're practicing mindfulness, you'll still feel the emotional reactions, but instead of getting upset, shouting at your child, or punishing them without thinking about it, you can take a few deep breaths, analyze what's happening, and respond more appropriately. In that moment, you are modeling emotion regulation and increasing the likelihood your child will eventually regulate their childish responses to stressors.

Being mindful doesn't mean you won't feel anger, disappointment, irritation, exhaustion, and all the other negative emotions that are part of everyday life, especially with children. It does mean you'll be more aware of what you're feeling, less likely to act on those feelings without thinking, and more likely to act in your child's best long-term interest.

RELAX AND BE HAPPY, ESPECIALLY IF YOU'RE A MOTHER

Mindfulness practices help people relax and be happy, and that's a good thing. It's good for all humans, but—contrary to so many cultural expectations—it's especially important for mothers.

One of the most persistent and damaging cultural myths is that mothers should be martyrs to their children. The research shows that it's quite the reverse: Too much self-sacrifice and too little self-care on the part of a parent (especially a mother), combined as it so often is with a heavy sense of having two full-time jobs (one at work and one at home), does not lead to happy or healthy children. For your child to thrive, you need to do what you need to do so you can thrive, too.

Michael Ungar is the principal investigator of the Resilience Research Centre at Dalhousie University in Halifax. He and his colleagues have done pioneering work considering why some children thrive in the most problematic circumstances, and others don't, even in highly privileged circumstances.[5]

One of the variables Ungar identified as important for healthy and happy children, regardless of their family and community situations, is parental happiness. He observed that things go better for children when their parents—and mothers, in particular—are relaxed and happy than when they are stressed. If you're a parent, he said, you should do your best to take good care of yourself, even if that means letting household chores and other obligations slide a bit. He wrote, "A little benign neglect could give our kids the edge we want them to have by placing in their life a role model for work-life balance and reasonable expectations."[6] By "benign neglect," Ungar is referring to neglecting some of the duties you might feel obligated to do if you were a "perfect parent" (e.g., laundry always up-to-date, every night a homemade nutritious and delicious dinner, the house always spotless). He is NOT talking here about genuine (and harmful) neglect, such as ignoring your child's unhappiness, forgetting to pick them up after school most days, or regularly leaving them alone to forage for their meals.

The most damaging home environments—those where children have high anxiety, poor emotional adjustment, and low self-confidence—are those where parents argue a lot or don't share problems with each other and where parents are short tempered and demanding. What matters to children is love and kindness, not where they live, how tidy their house is, or how much money their family has.

It's also important for your child that you find satisfaction in your role as a parent and that you feel you have a strong network of social support. Your source of support can include a spouse, but it can also consist of friends, extended family, neighbors, religious or other community members, or colleagues at work. When you feel you're getting the support you need, you're able to be a happier and calmer parent and are more available to your child, both emotionally and physically. In *Happy Parents Happy Kids*,[7] Ann Douglas makes this point, describing parents who are struggling with the challenges of becoming happier and calmer, as well as all the reasons that's worth doing.

HOW TO BE A MINDFUL PARENT

Your objective with mindfulness is not to stay calm and centered— in my experience, nobody who has children can do that all the time— but rather to notice when you are not calm and centered and then bring yourself back to center before doing any real damage.

Most parents are too busy to add anything to their schedule, but you might find that 10 minutes of mindfulness meditation a few times a week is a good investment. You can use walking in a natural setting, quietly listening to music, or even cooking mindfully as your mindfulness practice instead of the breathing practice I outlined earlier.

Mindful walking means paying attention to each foot taking each step, noticing how your body feels, attending to your breathing and the sounds and sights around you as you walk a familiar path, preferably in a natural setting. Mindful music listening is stilling your mind, letting other thoughts and stimuli go as you listen—truly, deeply listen—to the notes and the sounds of the music. Mindful cooking was my entry point to mindfulness meditation. I read the *Tassajara Cookbook*[8] shortly after it was first published in 1985 and initially found it odd to thank each ingredient, each utensil, each bowl, each saucepan, as I got it out, used it, and cleaned it. But after doing that a few times, I found it oddly soothing—meditative even—to be so appreciative and focused on each step through the cooking and cleaning process.

Pretty much any activity can be done mindfully. All you have to do is attempt to be present in the activity, being here and now while you are doing it. Interruptions are part of life for most of us and also part of the practice. Mindfulness means being present to the interruptions, dealing with them mindfully if that's the right (or necessary) thing to do, and ignoring them if they don't need attention in the moment.

In addition to enhanced health, happiness, and well-being, mindfulness practice saves time repairing problems you might otherwise cause with your impatience or annoyance. You can look at mindfulness practice as preventive self-maintenance, keeping your emotional equilibrium fine-tuned so you're ready to respond to the challenges that come along.

AFFIRMATIONS AND MANTRAS

One technique many mindfulness teachers recommend is the use of affirmations or mantras. An *affirmation* is a saying that helps you connect with your center so that you can act from a place of calm. Ideally, you repeat one or two affirmations every day, perhaps as part of a mindfulness practice, perhaps while you're washing the dishes or having a shower or any other time it works for you. A *mantra* is similar to an affirmation—a word or set of words that help you stay calm and focused—but mantras are more frequently associated with meditation.

There are dozens of books available, as well as hundreds (maybe thousands) of lists of affirmations and mantras on the internet, some for children, some for dealing with problems with self-esteem, anxiety, financial worries, or anything you can think of. Here are a few that I like:

- "Thank you for another day of loving."[9]
- "Let this be a quantum day. Let me be open to the infinite possibilities that this day brings."[10]
- "My task is not to seek for love but merely to seek and find all the barriers within myself that I have built."[11]

Carole Matthews[12] is a yoga and meditation teacher who sometimes uses this poem as an opening to a meditation class:

> Breathing in, I calm my body. Breathing out, I smile.
> Dwelling in the present moment. I know this is a wonderful
>   moment.
> Breathing in, calm. Breathing out, smile.
> Present moment. Wonderful moment.[13]

Matthews told me that the mantra for her meditation class became "Breathing in, calm; breathing out, smile." Then it became "In, calm. Out, smile" and sometimes "Present moment, wonderful moment." "It's a short mantra," she told me, "But it works because it's related to the poem. It's not complete in and of itself, but it reminds us to breathe mindfully."

She starts the meditation practice by having the participants sit comfortably and focus on their breath, noticing the inhale and exhale. She then reads the poem a few times slowly, gradually shortening it, allowing participants to focus on their breath and the present moment. She said, "It's a great way of helping people find calm in the present moment, even in the midst of stressful situations." She smiled and added, "This would have been a GREAT mantra for me when my kids were little!"

At a time when my life was beyond turbulent, I found the following affirmation helpful: "I have everything I need to enjoy my here and now, unless I am letting my consciousness be dominated by the dead past or the imaginary future."[14] I memorized it, and when I felt that I was on the edge of my coping capacity, I would repeat it slowly and intentionally in my head or (if I was alone) aloud. Over time and use, I discovered that it's always true. Even in the midst of highly stressful situations, I have learned that I always have everything I need to enjoy my here and now. Remembering that usually gives me the presence of mind to stay calm, make better decisions, and not make things worse than they already are.

And of course, what works for one person in one situation doesn't always work for another person in a different situation, so Carole's mantra and my affirmation may not work for you at all. I provide them as illustrations of the usefulness of having one or two of these sayings in your repertoire to pull out as you need them. You will find thousands of possibilities online, or you can craft your own, something that reflects your personality, circumstances, and needs.

The beginning stage of mindfulness is noticing when you're off center. If you consciously pay attention to your moods and inner state, you'll learn to recognize when you're tired, anxious, sad, or irritable. When you notice you're distractible, impatient, or otherwise not centered, try to stop what you're doing. Repeat a favorite affirmation or mantra, and take a slow, deep breath through your nose to the count of five. Release the breath just as slowly. Repeat.

You may be justified in being tired, anxious, disappointed, or irritable, but being mindful means noticing it and then doing your best to let it go. Even when you deserve your tantrum, it's always within your power to be a grown-up. When your child makes you crazy, maybe it helps to think back to a time they gave you joy. Maybe that was last night when they were sleeping. Maybe they did or said something wonderful last week or last year. Try to respond with love to the challenging situation.

It takes time before mindfulness practice works reliably. Keep practicing, though, and it will happen. Someone will surprise you one day and describe you as calm and reasonable. You'll realize your child is calmer and happier, too.

HOW TO NURTURE YOUR CHILD'S MINDFULNESS

Over the long run, the best way to teach your child to be mindful is to be mindful yourself, but it might be years before your child notices what you're doing and tries it themself. In the meantime, you can teach your child one or more of the following techniques. All of the techniques work, in one form or another, across all ages, so if you like one of these ideas but your child is not in the designated age range, you can always adapt it to make it more suitable.

The Early Years: Birth to 5

You may think your child is too young for mindful breathing, but I've seen it work with children as young as 2½. A young child who learns one or more mindful breathing techniques is better able to focus their attention on cognitive, emotional, and physical activities, and they're less likely to behave badly because they're frustrated or angry.

When your young child is veering out of control, ask them to stop and breathe out the bad feelings with you. Say, "Breathe in to the count of five. Now hold your breath while we count to five. Now, breathe out loudly, like a dragon, while we count to five one more time."

Once your child has settled down enough to hear you—maybe an hour or two later—give some examples of when you were angry or upset and used your breathing to get through it without doing any damage. Next time you need to decompress when your child is present, talk them through what you're doing and why.

Once you and your child have been through this a few times, you can use a code to signal it's a good time for this kind of breathing. Maybe hold your hand up in a stop signal and demonstrate a dragon breath or say, "Want to breathe out your fire?"

Mindfulness is great for dealing with everyday concerns, but it's also helpful when dealing with bigger problems. For example, a while back, I received a message from a woman named Shandra saying, "My 3-year-old was diagnosed with social anxiety by a developmental specialist. When I told his preschool teacher, she told me that my son Kyrone is 'just shy.' Should we worry that the teacher is not taking the diagnosis seriously? What can we do to help Kyrone?"

To begin with, I told Shandra, young children vary greatly in their sociability. Some have an easy confidence when they encounter strangers and enjoy meeting new people. These kids can be thought of as socially confident. Others are openly skeptical and resist interacting with people until they're familiar with them. These children might be described as shy. The third group of children—those who can be described as socially anxious—have an intense fear reaction to situations where there are people they don't know well.

I told Shandra it was impossible for me to confirm or contest the diagnosis she'd been given without having a much deeper knowledge of Kyrone, the family, and the context but that the teacher questioning the diagnosis was a good sign. The teacher sees Kyrone in a social context every day and also has a wide experience of what's normal. Her opinion that he is shy and not socially anxious means that he is probably managing the social classroom environment sufficiently well. I told Shandra it was also worth thinking about the developmental specialist's observations and keeping her eyes open to Kyrone's social development.

In the meantime, I suggested to Shandra that she think about how she might be able to ramp down any possible stress Kyrone might be experiencing in social situations. As always, I told her that means becoming mindful about her own stress and coping, particularly in social circumstances. A good place to start doing that is to learn some of the basic mindfulness strategies I describe in this chapter.

I suggested that Shandra pay attention to whether and how she greets people on the street and whether she enjoys being sociable herself. Or does she try to avoid people and see social events as painful obligations? She may be unconsciously teaching Kyrone to avoid social encounters.

Another area where mindfulness could be helpful for Shandra is paying attention to how she's reacting to Kyrone's interactions with others, both children and adults. It's important that she avoid being judgmental or critical because that can make any anxiety he might be experiencing worse. From a position of mindful self-attention, Shandra can work on being only positive and supportive with Kyrone in social circumstances.

Shandra can also teach Kyrone to become mindful and to start to pay attention to his feelings. If he notices he's feeling worried or anxious, she can help him learn to take a few deep breaths to calm himself down as needed. There are other things Shandra can do with Kyrone to help him become more socially confident—role-playing about social situations, reading stories about shy kids becoming confident, and looking for social activities Kyrone enjoys—but mindfulness (hers and his) will make all the difference.

Childhood: 6 to 10

Bedtime is a great time for mindfulness practices with your child. It can help them get to sleep and improve the quality of their sleep, which has all kinds of benefits that I describe in the next chapter. One simple technique is to help your child use their breath to calm themself at the end of the day. If they're still wide awake after you've completed a slow and loving bedtime routine—teeth brushing, lullabies, stories, and the rest—talk them through a breathwork body scan.

Lie down beside your child. Start at the toes and work up the body to the top of their head, saying, "My toes are asleep," accompanied by a long, slow breath, "My feet are asleep," accompanied by another long, slow breath and all the way through their body up to the top.

You can get up now and go to the door of their room. If they are still wide awake, ask them to do it two more times, once with you standing there and the next with you out of the room. It usually works. In fact, I'm feeling sleepy as I write this.

Some kids worry more than others, and sometimes this body scan won't be enough. If your child tends to focus on how sad, lonely, or hurt they feel, you can help them turn that around by reinforcing an attitude of gratitude just before they go to sleep.

As part of your bedtime routine, maybe before you do the body scan, ask your child to tell you about one good thing that happened that day. Maybe a child they like invited them to join in a game. Maybe they enjoyed the lunch you packed for them. Maybe they did well on a test. Then ask, "What role did you play in making those good things happen?" When good things happen, we've almost always participated in one way or another, even if only by being in the right frame of mind to notice.

In doing the bedtime gratitude exercise, you're helping your child focus on the positive rather than the negative aspects of their experiences. You're also encouraging them to consider their role in the good events of their life. If you persist with this, you'll probably notice over time that your child is sleeping better and has a deeper sense of well-being.

Another situation where you can use mindfulness with your child is dealing with a fear. For example, some children think about death a lot at some point. Triggers for these worries vary from a story that's been told to the child, a cemetery they've walked past and wondered about, or a death in the family. Sometimes worries about death stem from something metaphoric, such as the feeling of losing a parent through divorce, and sometimes it's the loss of one's position in the family, as can happen when a sibling is born.

There are books available that can help a sensitive child come to terms with most fears, including death. *And So It Goes*[15] by Paloma Valdivia is a beautifully meditative story showing how change is inevitable. Through subtle mindfulness messages, it illustrates that the best comfort in a time of loss is to appreciate the love and beauty in our lives in this moment: "Those of us who are here are just here. And so we'd best enjoy ourselves."[16] Some parents steer away from everything to do with death, worrying that it might upset their child, but children actually feel safer when they understand what's happening. One of the things I like about *And So It Goes* is the easy balance between sadness and celebration, honoring the pain of loss while reassuring young children that life goes on: "And so it goes, just as spring follows winter. Some arrive while others take their leave."[17]

Regardless of the specific fears or circumstances, you can use mindfulness techniques to help your child handle their worries so they don't become overwhelming. As with pretty much everything when it comes to parenting, it starts with you. If you can use one or two basic mindfulness techniques, you'll be better positioned to support your child through a challenging time, whether it's you who is suffering, or your child, or both of you.

Pay attention to your child's comments about their worries and fears. Reassure them that it's your job to keep them safe. If their fears concern someone's death, talk to them about the nature of all life—the way plants grow, form seeds, and die, and then the next year, a new plant grows. Seeing the truth of biology can reassure your child that you are being honest with them. In that case, what your child is most worried about is probably their own death or yours. Tell them you're planning to live long enough not only to see them grow up but that you also intend to know their kids and maybe even their kids' kids. Be as honest and positive as possible if they want to talk about what happens after death. If a family member has died, you can talk about how the one who is lost lives on in people's memories: "Grandma will always be with us, in our hearts. She doesn't come to our house anymore, but she's still here with us."

One of the basic mindfulness principles that works particularly well with children concerns focusing on the beauty in this moment, now, in this place, here. So, celebrate being alive. Discuss with your child how you can affirm the beauty of life. Take a walk, and pay special attention to all the forms of life your neighborhood contains. Say thank you to those who make you happy in one way or another. Be grateful. Show your child how much you appreciate their presence in your life and how much you appreciate your home, work, friends, and whatever else you feel grateful for. Help your child express gratitude, too. When people focus on the sources of gratitude in their lives, their world feels brighter.

There's a lot more (other than mindfulness techniques) you can do to help your child weather a worrisome storm. You can keep to the usual routines, trying to maintain the usual schedule of bedtimes, mealtimes, and so forth. Kids experiencing loss or worrying about something like death are reassured by predictability. You can also ensure a healthy balance, making sure your child is getting what they need to maintain their equilibrium: cuddles, time outdoors, visits with friends, exercise, playtime. I should add that there are times when the fear of death is not abstract and needs a different kind of attention. If you or someone else close to your child has a life-threatening illness, or if you can't soothe your child's fears, it's time to seek help.

Adolescence: 11 to 18

When you take the time mindfully to openly appreciate life's small gifts—a sunny day, a good meal, a deep sleep—you're helping your child or teenager notice what's good in their life. A person who focuses on what they have to be thankful for is practicing mindfulness. The research shows they're happier than others, more optimistic, empathic, enthusiastic, and well-liked. Lisa Feldman Barrett is a neuroscientist at Northeastern University who wrote a book called *7½ Lessons About the Brain*,[18] in which she described the powerful effect of gratitude on the brain. She wrote that feeling awe can increase our sense of meaning and satisfaction: "This practice has had a huge effect on my life. On my daily walk, I stop to notice the little weed pushing up from the crack in the sidewalk—to marvel at the unconstrained exuberance of nature."[19]

Negativity corrodes family life, but it isn't a problem only at home. Not surprisingly, negative people don't do as well at work or in relationships as those who are more optimistic, positive, and pleasant. Nobody enjoys spending time with someone who whines, sulks, complains, or criticizes. Thankfully, there is a bright side to this. Negativity is a habit of mind, and like all habits, it can be changed. With help, even the grumpiest teenager can become someone with attitudes that others—including their families—can enjoy. One of the approaches that has received research support in recent years focuses on helping kids move from a sense of entitlement to one of gratitude.

In "The Science of Gratitude," a white paper for the Greater Good Science Center at the University of California, Berkeley, Summer Allen reviewed the research illustrating the neurological, physiological, and psychological advantages of gratitude.[20] Cardiac patients who are more grateful report better sleep, less fatigue, and lower inflammation. Grateful people experience less depression and more resilience following traumatic events. Grateful adolescents are more interested in and satisfied with their school lives, are kinder and more helpful, and are more popular with their peers.

One of the corollary benefits of this approach is that using a mindfulness approach to changing your teenager's habits of mind from negativity to positivity is bound to affect everyone else in the family, including yourself. Your teenager is not the only family member who will benefit from acquiring more positive habits of mind.

Young Adulthood: 19 to 24

Across the lifespan, there's no age when mindfulness practices aren't useful. Diana Brecher is a clinical psychologist and professor at Ryerson University in Toronto, who has worked with Deena Kara Shaffer to develop "Thriving in Action,"[21] a series of courses and materials for students, faculty, and staff, with resources now being made available more broadly. Inspired by the positive psychology movement, Brecher and Shaffer have developed some practical strategies for putting mindfulness principles into action, strategies that have proven highly effective with the young adults they work with, as well as with the professors and other staff members at their university and others.

One of these strategies—the 20-second rule—was an adaptation of an approach recommended by Shawn Achor.[22] It helps young people tackle the bad habits that fuel anxiety and procrastination. Applying the 20-second rule means identifying the first 20 seconds of obstacles to achieving better habits and then eradicating those obstacles.

If the young adult in your life takes ages getting dressed in the morning and then worries about being late or is chronically late, help them make sure they have their clothes and everything else they'll need in the morning organized the night before. When they wake up the next day, they won't have to think about what they're going to wear or scramble to get their things together so they can leave the house on time. They've eliminated the first 20 seconds of their morning routine, facilitating their being on time and reducing their anxiety.

Maybe your young adult wants to have more friends or wants to find a romantic partner, but they tend to be too enthusiastic in approaching people they're interested in. Talk about what happens in the first 20 seconds after sighting someone they'd like to get to know better. Instead of rushing over, they might take a couple of deep mindful breaths while pretending to look for something in their pocket or purse or putting on and taking off a jacket or scarf—anything to slow themself down and greet the other person calmly.

Help your almost-grown child to identify the times they most need destressing—entering a new course where they don't know anyone, getting an assignment done on time, applying for a job—and then identify how the 20-second rule might help them manage it.

TAKING IT INTO THE COMMUNITY: BEING MINDFUL ABOUT RACISM AND EQUITY

As I write this, we're in the throes of a global pandemic that has not only shattered lives and disrupted almost everything we do but has also shed light on problems that undermine some people's chances to create meaningful lives for themselves. We're seeing an upsurge in attention to problems experienced by certain groups in our society, including the systemic racism that undermines people from Indigenous, Black, and other non-White cultures. In the United States, for example, professional organizations, as well as municipalities, counties, and states, have issued declarations or resolutions on racism as a public health crisis. At the time of this writing, over 200 jurisdictions have done so in response to racial disparities related not only to COVID-19 rates and vaccine access but also to a host of other health-related areas, such as infant mortality, violence, elevated levels of lead in drinking water, and chronic disease.

June Callwood was a Canadian journalist, author, and social activist, who observed, "Once you witness an injustice, you are no longer an observer but a participant." Similarly, John Lewis, an American statesman and civil rights leader, said, "When you see something that is not right, not fair, not just, you have to speak up. You have to say something; you have to do something." These leaders were advocating social mindfulness, attention to the circumstances of each member of your community and the world, and also observing that as we learn more about these inequities, we're responsible for doing something about them.

One thing you can do as a parent is to encourage your child to be aware and be part of the solution instead of part of the problem. Children feel injustice deeply and worry a lot about fairness. You can show your child how to use those feelings and worries productively and enable them to find their own contribution to making the world a better place.

As early as 3 months of age, an infant notices differences in people's skin color. Racial bias can show up by 2½. Children of 4 and 5 can show an obvious prejudice or feel the impact of racial discrimination. By the age of 12, a child can have an ingrained racial bias unless they're growing up with antiracism values at home or school.[23]

In a race-conscious society, it's easy for a child to adopt subtly racist views. When I was growing up in London, Ontario, "Newfie" jokes were popular. In these jokes, people from Newfoundland were ridiculed as stupid and unsophisticated. Whenever my mother heard one of her children telling a Newfie joke, she would stop us and insist we say "WASP" (White Anglo-Saxon Protestant) in the place of "Newfie." When we did that, the joke was no longer funny, of course, and that was her point. She had grown up White in Brantford,

Ontario, which is close to a First Nations (Indigenous) reserve. She had seen firsthand the terrible damage and indignities that otherwise decent White citizens were inflicting on Indigenous people. She bristled openly at any tinge of racism or bullying and was proud as our family diversified through marriage. I believe it was at her insistence that we recognized the humanity of each person we encountered that led to the rainbow of races, religions, and points of view among her children-in-law, grandchildren, and great-grandchildren.

As a socially mindful parent, you can have an important role in moving the needle on racism and equity. As with so much else, your attitude and behavior will probably be the most powerful factor in whether or not your child will grow up with racist attitudes. Pay mindful attention to your reaction to racial differences. Are you less comfortable or respectful with those from one race or another? Your child is acutely sensitive to what you're doing and saying, so do what it takes to be actively antiracist in your mind and heart, as well as your words and actions.

Kirsten Ivey-Colson and Lynn Turner are the founders of AntiRacist Table.[24] They wrote an article for Berkeley's *Greater Good Magazine* in which they outlined 10 steps toward antiracism, describing the connection between mindfulness and antiracism. They wrote, "Setting the intention to have an open heart and open mind in order to be anti-racist affects how one shows up. Present-moment awareness links with our intention to pull us out of autopilot and into conscious pursuit of our goals."[25]

You can expose your child to positive experiences of different religions, races, socioeconomic status, political points of view, languages, and sexual orientation. On a personal-gain level, the more diversity your child experiences, the bigger their world of possibilities will be going forward. On a larger societal level, the more comfortable each child is with diversity, the fewer problems we will collectively experience with systemic racism.

When your child points out differences, acknowledge that, and remind them of the similarities, too: "Yes, that boy's skin is a different color from yours, but he's about the same height as you. Just like everybody else, he's different in some ways, and in many ways, he's also just the same as you." Find videos, movies, books, and other media that illustrate human diversity in action. You might want to start by watching a video or reading a book together that introduces racism topics (e.g., *The Undefeated* by Kwame Alexander and Kadir Nelson[26] or *The Proudest Blue* by Ibtihaj Muhammad and Hatem Aly[27]).

If your child has been hearing about antiracism protests, ask them what they think about that. Make no judgment—as with all misconceptions, children can pick up racist attitudes very young. Instead, use their observations to teach them that every human has the same range of feelings and desires as they do. Help them understand the profound truth that we are all the same under the skin, and that means we all deserve to be treated with respect.

Older children can be taught about White privilege, how race or other identities can combine with life circumstances to give some people a boost in society, while others experience disadvantages. For example, when school graduation rates or lung disease rates are wildly unequal for people of different racial backgrounds, this means something is wrong at a system level. Special attention is needed so that all high schoolers get the support and resources they need to graduate and so that more people across all races can be healthy. And while this special attention may sometimes look like unequal treatment, its purpose is to reduce the systemic inequities, empowering and equipping those who didn't have power before.

Remember that, as with teaching any other kind of mindful attitude, it's best to take things slowly. Expose your child to media and situations where they'll experience diverse people. Answer their questions as they arise, at the level your child is ready for. Discuss issues in the world around you, but don't push the topic too hard or at too high a level for their understanding. Of course, when there's a threat within your immediate circle—for example, if your child is the target of racism—you may not have the option to take things slowly. In these cases, mindfulness may look like you serving as a buffer for your child to protect them from the worst that is happening, or it may look like you reaching out for supports that you need to keep your family safe.

As your child becomes aware, discuss what the two of you can do to combat racism and other social inequities at a level that makes sense to your child. Be honest about the enormity of the situation, and also help them realize how change happens with the small steps each person takes. Even the youngest and least powerful person—a child—can contribute to the change that needs to happen. Help your child learn to challenge racism and inequity wherever they see it happening. As my mother knew, even apparently harmless language can support racism and exclusion. Just as early feminists challenged media stereotypes of women, it's important for antiracist parents to be mindful of the stereotypes all around us.

When your child is ready, you can talk about what it means to be an ally or ask for support from allies. There is increasing attention being paid to the importance of allies in fighting racism. An ally is someone not from an underrepresented group who takes action to support people from a group that is being discriminated against. There are some good kids' books on allies, such as *IntersectionAllies: We Make Room for All*, by Chelsea Johnson, LaToya Council, and Carolyn Choi.[28] Discuss what that means in your child's life, both now and in the future.

You can also talk with your child about possibilities for school-based antiracism advocacy. Schools are increasingly implementing antibullying, LGBTQ-friendly, and mental health programs. Talk to your child's teacher or principal about possibilities for including antiracism programs as part of an equity and diversity agenda. If that doesn't go very far, you might think about getting involved with other parents in advocacy efforts, something I address in Chapter 10.

KEY TAKEAWAYS: LEARNING TO BE HERE NOW

Mindfulness practices have proven remarkably effective not only at changing people's attitudes and behaviors but also their brains. They help reduce a person's stress, improve coping, enhance mental and physical health, and increase their enjoyment of life. Mindfulness also helps you be a better parent—not perfect, of course, because you don't want that, but better: more present to your child and a better model of healthy self-regulation. In short, there's no area of life, whether personal or professional, that isn't enhanced by mindfulness. Here are some of the main takeaways from this chapter:

- Whether you choose breathing techniques, meditation, affirmations, mindfulness walks, or something else, find your best way to connect to your here and now, so you can respond with calm strength when it's needed.
- You're not too old to change your brain's programming. No matter your circumstances, you can learn some mindfulness techniques to help you enjoy your life more, become happier, and respond more positively to your child.
- Learn some mindfulness techniques, and make time, even 5 minutes a day, to practice them.
- Your child will also benefit from mindfulness techniques, whether you practice them, teach them to your child, or (the best option) both.
- Accept and be mindful. Smile. Take a breath. You really are enough.

CHAPTER 4

CARE FOR YOURSELF, AND YOU'LL HELP YOUR CHILD CARE FOR THEMSELF

In nature, nothing is perfect and everything is perfect. Trees can be contorted, bent in weird ways, and they're still beautiful.
—Alice Walker (attributed)

In Chapter 3, I talked about mindfulness as one way to care for yourself. In this chapter, I talk about other ways to care for yourself, ways that (like mindfulness) help you both enjoy your life and respond more vibrantly to your child. Although I'll be discussing nutrition, exercise, sleep, and more, this chapter is not about nagging anyone or encouraging them to regain or retain their youthful energy and body—quite the reverse. It's about doing what needs doing to share Alice Walker's perspective on the beauty of our natural imperfections, appreciating oneself fully, contortions and all. By taking care of our needs for play or leisure, good nutrition, exercise, time in nature, and enough sleep, we improve our capacity to accept our imperfections and our children's. We enhance our ability to enjoy our lives and be present to others in our lives, very much including the children.

I don't know a parent who hasn't gone through at least one period of sleep deprivation. For many parents, reducing their hours of sleep feels like the only way to have enough time to do everything that needs doing, let alone have any "me-time." For many reasons, it can be impossible to follow good nutritional rules or participate in the kind of exercise regime you might have engaged in before becoming a parent.

Karen recently started her own business. She has three young children and is finding herself in the middle of a cyclone. Her business is doing better than she'd anticipated, which is great, but she's finding she has to get up at 4 in the morning to get her work done and have time for her home and family. Mona, a single mom and the sole support for her two kids, has gone back to school and is juggling her studies, kids, and job. Edward has taken a part-time sales job in addition to his full-time job and is also doing most of the family's child care and other household duties. His wife is having health problems and isn't able to work or do much around the house.

In all these cases, these people are doing what needs to be done and having to make some sacrifices in the moment. But they can't sacrifice their leisure, exercise, and sleep indefinitely. I've learned this the hard way, by getting run down and then sick, operating for too long at less-than-full capacity, getting more frazzled and irritable and less capable of enjoying anything or anyone as time goes by.

No matter your circumstance, caring for yourself is not a luxury option. It's a basic physical and psychological necessity over the long run. If you want to keep or get your body functioning well, get much joy from being alive, or be a good-enough parent over the long haul, you need to find ways to care for yourself.

A Self-Care Quiz

1. Which one or more of these statements best reflects your current situation?
   (a) I prioritize my health. I get 8 hours of sleep most nights, I get enough outdoor exercise, and I make sure to work some leisure activities into my schedule.
   (b) There aren't enough hours in the day if I don't work late into the night or get up early. I'm doing okay on 6 hours sleep a night, occasionally a bit less.

A Self-Care Quiz (Continued)

(c) I can't afford fresh fruit and vegetables and all those other good expensive healthy things, so I just stay away from those aisles in the grocery store. To be honest, I've never learned what to do with most of them.

(d) Exercise? I'm working all the time at home and work; I haven't had time for exercise since my child was born.

(e) I don't see the point of spending time outdoors. I just don't have time for it. I open the windows in the car or the house when I can, and occasionally, I walk my child to school, and that has to be good enough.

(f) I gave up having time for my own interests when my first child was born. I'd love to get back to regular nights out with my friends, but I just don't see how I can make that happen.

(g) I'm like everyone else. Sometimes I get enough sleep but mostly not. Sometimes I get exercise but mostly not. Sometimes I spend time in nature but mostly not. Once in a while, I see my friends, but it's hard and expensive for me to arrange a babysitter.

2. "We are all just one small adjustment away from making our lives work."[1] In that spirit, if you answered something other than (a) in Question 1, what's the first step you'd like to take toward better self-care?

(a) I'm going to do my best to go to bed 15 minutes earlier than I do now. It's not a lot, but it's a start.

(b) I'm going to find one inexpensive fruit or vegetable at the supermarket every week and learn how to prepare it.

(c) I'm going to find a 15-minute online stretch class and do it in the morning before I go to work.

(d) Maybe I can organize a playdate on the weekend with friends and kids and kill a few birds with one stone—go to the park with the kids, get some outdoor time, and see my friends.

(e) I'm going to make a point of taking my lunch outdoors when the weather's good. There's a park two blocks away from work, and I can walk over and eat there.

(continues)

107

A Self-Care Quiz (*Continued*)

(f) Maybe I'll try a little of everything—do a smorgasbord of self-care: get to bed a bit earlier, do some stretching before bed, and take a walk outside after dinner. Maybe I'll take the family with me or arrange to meet a friend.

For the first question—asking which statement best reflects your situation—I'm guessing few parents can truthfully answer (a)—that is, that they're taking excellent care of themselves in all regards, unless they have a part-time or not-too-demanding job or are a stay-at-home parent and also have a housekeeper.

The vast majority of parents are juggling a lot of demanding responsibilities. That's just the way it is, but they're forfeiting their own care in the process. Unless it really can't be helped (as in the cases I mentioned earlier of Karen, Mona, and Edward), that's not smart. In a blog for new mothers for the American Academy of Pediatrics (AAP), pediatrician Whitney Casares wrote,

> The reality is, the only way to take the best care of your family is to make sure you're taking time to take care of yourself. Can you push through and be a mommy martyr for the next 18 years? Sure. Will it leave you resentful and angry? Most definitely.[2]

As for the second question, it doesn't really matter how you answered it. There aren't any right or wrong answers, but I hope it got you thinking about whether there's a small step you might take toward a more satisfying and healthier life. If you want your child to be healthy and happy, why not show them what that looks like? As your child gets older, you can also teach them more directly about the choices you make every day—both for yourself and on their behalf—that lead to good health and happiness. All of us need enough playtime, good nutrition, physical exercise, time outdoors, and sleep on a regular basis.

THE EARLY YEARS: BIRTH TO 5

When your baby is born, you can see they have important physical tasks to master, including the gross motor skills that will allow them eventually to walk, run, and play and the fine motor skills that will allow them to dress themselves, put puzzles together, and nourish themselves without too much mess. Many factors have to come together to allow them to master those tasks.

Playtime: Good for the Mind, Body, and Spirit

There are a variety of definitions, but there's a general consensus that play is an activity that is voluntary, fun, and spontaneous and engages the person's active interest or enthusiasm. It can include experimentation, risk taking, and boundary testing and is buffered from serious real-world consequences.

Jean Piaget, a pioneering child development expert, said, "Play is the work of childhood,"[3] an idea that the children's TV personality Mister Rogers echoed when he said, "Play is often talked about as if it were a relief from serious learning. But for children, play is serious learning."[4] Play matters not only for your child's physical development and as a way to enliven their spirit, but it's also important for building their brain and giving them the tools they need in a rapidly changing world.

Recognizing that play is essential to all aspects of children's development, the AAP is now recommending that doctors write prescriptions for play. Explaining this recommendation in *Pediatrics*, the official journal of the AAP, Michael Yogman and colleagues wrote, "Research demonstrates that developmentally appropriate play with parents and peers is a singular opportunity to promote the social-emotional, cognitive, language, and self-regulation skills that build executive function and a prosocial brain."[5] They went on to describe how play stimulates brain development, social development, creativity, academic skills, and resilience and to specify ways parents can best support their children's play experiences.

THE BENEFITS OF PLAY

Spend a few minutes watching your young child at play, alone or with others. Although it might seem that they're just fooling around, wasting time, if you look a bit deeper, you'll see some important things happening. Play motivates babies and young children to master and refine their language skills, the foundation of further learning. This is most obvious when your child is playing with others, but it's also true when they're playing independently. You might hear your little one talking to themself as they pour water or sand from one cup into another or as they build a tower. Playtime also increases your child's strength, flexibility, dexterity, coordination, and confidence.[6]

Playing with your baby or young child is good for you both. When you play with them, you experience an attunement that feels good for you both and also enhances bonding, affection, and trust. This builds your child's confidence and motivates further learning.

WHAT'S YOUR ROLE IN YOUR YOUNG CHILD'S PLAY?

Most parents see their job as ensuring their child is loved, fed, clothed, healthy, and able to succeed at school. Those are all important, but if you also help your child get the most out of playtime, you increase the chances they'll thrive over the long run. At heart, early learning is motivated by the desire for social connection, and you'll enhance your young child's playtime just by being present and engaged, sharing with them your delight in their discoveries and achievements.

One way to encourage creative play is to make simple objects available for them to manipulate: blocks, balls, paper, crayons, pots and pans, pillows, and cardboard boxes. Help your child make a costume box for old scarves, hats, shoes, clothes, and fabric. And keep technology use to a bare minimum in the early years (more on that in Chapter 9).

Be available if you're needed when your child is playing, but try not to comment too often or give too many suggestions, other than when it's necessary for safety or by way of encouragement. Even with encouragement, though, be careful that you don't rob your child of a sense of owning their activities during playtime.[7]

Play has more to do with attitude than with activity. When you or your child is frayed and grumpy, maybe it's time for a dance break. Take on character roles while you're making dinner together—be a troll, a princess, or whoever you feel like right now. And if you're just too tired to make that happen, ask your child for help. By age 2½ or 3, you'll be surprised at the creative ideas they have for fun in everyday situations.

Finally, support play-based learning at your child's day care and school. Up to about 7, play-based learning leads to the best long-term learning outcomes.

Nutrition: Let Your Child Win the Food War

Good nutrition is essential to healthy bodies and brains. Knowing this, many parents worry about their children's eating habits, starting with breastfeeding. Although there are solid health and bonding benefits to breastfeeding, babies can grow healthy and strong even if they're not breastfed. What's most important is that they're surrounded by love, affection, and care and given enough nourishment to grow and thrive. The best recommendation for parents worried about the breastfeeding versus formula question is to relax and enjoy your child. Yes, breastfeeding has lots of benefits, but it's more important that you keep yourself calm so you can be warm and nurturing than that you feed your baby in any particular way.

That same principle applies to the food challenges you face as your baby gets older. In some families, the arguments about food begin as soon as the child begins to eat independently. Your toddler might refuse food altogether or eat only one or two things meal after meal. They might play with their food or throw it. As they get older, they might want to eat all the time but only candy and crackers.

There is so little that young children can control it's no wonder some of them use food to assert their autonomy. If you're bribing, threatening, rewarding, or punishing your child for food behavior, you're showing them how important their eating is to you. You're losing the food war if your child knows you care more about what they eat than they do. The same principle applies here as to the breastfeeding question: It's more important to your child's long-term development that you keep yourself calm, patient, and loving than that you ensure your child eats certain amounts of certain foods. You can control the available food choices, but you can't control what they actually put into their mouth, chew, and swallow.[8]

The crafty secret of good nutrition in the long term is to let your child win the food war while doing your best to make sure most of their available options are healthy. Here are some ideas for making that happen.

Maybe grocery shopping feels like just one more chore in your life, but it can be a great multisensory brain-building experience for your child and support good eating habits. If you take your child with you and treat it as an excursion, you can have an unrushed learning and bonding experience. Answer your child's questions, and let them make as many choices as possible. Talk about which fruits look good today, which vegetables they might like to try, and let them choose a reasonably healthy treat or two. Talk about the smells, colors, textures, and appearance of the various options.

Another way to entice your child to eat healthy food is to let them help in the kitchen, especially if that involves getting their hands dirty and learning real-life skills. It's much harder for them to resist food they've helped make. Be patient, though. Cooking will be slower and messier until your child masters the necessary skills. As early as 2½ or 3, you can let them choose their cutlery and tableware and (with some foods) decide whether they want to cut their own food or have you cut it and in what shapes.

When there is nothing your child wants on the menu for a given meal, let them choose among a few additional healthy options. Some items you might keep available: whole grain bread or crackers, fruit, cheese, peanut butter, unsweetened yogurt, vegetables in bite-size pieces, hummus, nuts.

Serve a variety of foods to your family, but don't force your child to try something new. Instead, you might ask them to sniff the new food. If they want to taste it, fine. If not, that's fine too. You can do the same thing next time the family has that food. Eventually, the child will try it. Or not.

One great way to create eating problems is to pay too much attention to what your child eats and doesn't, so do your best to avoid being the food police. Put away your badge and gun, and enjoy your own meal. Family mealtime is about more than just food. Eventually, your child will see they can't make you crazy by not eating and will quietly pick up a spoon.

For some delightful hints on how to do this, see *Bread and Jam for Frances* by Russell and Lillian Hoban.[9] In that story, Frances decides the only thing she wants to eat is bread and jam. Her parents start off trying to entice her to eat other things, extolling the tasty virtues of what they're having and pointing out how the baby in the family is trying it and enjoying it. Frances doesn't budge, and her parents capitulate. For a few days, Frances has bread and jam for breakfast, lunch, and dinner. Nobody tries to convince or entice her to have anything else. After a few days, Frances gets bored of bread and jam. She starts looking longingly at what her family is having at mealtimes and what her friends have in their lunch boxes. One night she asks if she could maybe have some of the spaghetti the family is having for dinner. The next day, she requests a variety of foods for her lunch box and enjoys each bite, having lunch with her friend, who also enjoys his selection of tasty, healthy foods.

Sometimes children (like adults) use food for solace, stimulation, boredom relief, or revenge on a controlling parent. If you're worried your child is overeating or undereating for emotional reasons, consider how you can better meet those needs. Get professional help if you need it.

The bottom line here is that you can't control what your child eats. Give them healthy food options. Be kind and relaxed at mealtimes, and let them decide how much to eat. If it's mealtime and your child says they're not hungry, that's okay. Tell them you want them to join the family for mealtime—and do your best to make it a pleasant time for them as well as yourself—but if you want them to be a healthy eater long term, don't pressure them to eat what you want them to eat.

Physical Exercise: Your Young Child Needs 3 Hours Spaced Throughout the Day

Babies, toddlers, and young children should be active several times a day, accumulating 3 hours of varying kinds and levels of physical activity spread throughout the day.[10] Your child shouldn't be inactive for long periods, except when they're asleep. The 3 hours—180 minutes—can include light activity, such as standing up, moving around, rolling, and gentle roughhousing with a parent, sibling, or friend, or more energetic activity such as skipping, throwing a ball, playing in the water, hopping, running, chasing, or jumping.

It's through frequent energetic movement that your child's muscles and gross motor skills develop. And as with their muscles, physical stress supports their bone health, strength, and growth, helping your child become stronger and more flexible and have better stamina. When your child is active, their heart's functioning also improves.

An additional benefit of exercise that isn't as obvious is that when your child exercises, they're cleansing their system of toxins and thereby increasing their body's ability to combat illness. A fit child is less likely to get a cold, develop allergies, or suffer from many diseases, including cancer. And not least among benefits is that beta-endorphins and serotonin, associated with feelings of well-being, are stimulated by exercise, so your child will sleep better and feel better if they get enough exercise each day. In addition to being stronger and healthier, your child will feel calmer and happier when they're getting enough exercise.

Outdoor Time: Your Child Needs Outside Time Every Day

There is a growing body of research showing the benefits of spending time outside for every human, across the lifespan, starting at birth. Natural settings are best—places where you can see different forms of nature as they change through weather and seasons. The benefits of time outdoors can be significant, even for babies, including a greater sense of well-being, enhanced immunity, enhanced attention, greater attunement to nature and the environment, and an enhanced capacity for inspiration and wonder.[11,12,13]

In spite of the benefits that come from spending time outside, many parents find it easier to keep their children indoors, and in fact, most kids today aren't getting as much outdoor time as they need for their optimal health and well-being.[14] Parents can feel they have more control over what the child is doing when they're inside, as well as finding it easier to do what they want to do themselves, whether it's housework, their own work, or leisure activities.

One way to increase outdoor time is to limit your child's use of electronic devices, which can easily gobble up a lot of time indoors. Another way is to look for opportunities to walk or bicycle where you're going and reduce your child's time in the car.

Look for outdoor activities your child wants to do. If you have a backyard, maybe you can install a sandbox or swing set or get a water table or some simple outdoor toys. If you live in an apartment building, see if you can find a nearby green space you can use as your backyard and take your toys there once a day when the weather allows, or get together with neighbors and advocate for a children's playground on the property or nearby.

Another way to entice your child and yourself outdoors is to grow some food. Invite your child to help plant, weed, water, and harvest some food for your family. In one family I know, each member of the family gets to choose at the local garden store one or two things to plant and take care of in a tiny backyard patch. Later, they harvest it and share it. In the meantime, everyone is thinking and talking about how they will serve their produce to the family—maybe tomatoes will be sliced on hamburgers, carrots might be made into a cake, or blueberries will be eaten with a dollop of whipped cream. This can happen on your own outdoor patch, whether a balcony or a backyard, a windowsill, or a community garden.

Try to choose a day care, preschool, or kindergarten that values and provides ample outdoor time. If there's not enough outdoor time during the usual course of your child's day, you might suggest that your child's day care or school extend outdoor periods. If your child still isn't getting enough outdoor time and you don't have time to supervise it yourself, maybe you can coordinate with other families who live close by to watch your kids during outdoor playtime on your workdays, with you taking their kids for some outdoor play on the days you're not working.

Don't push it, though. Try for at least an hour a day of outdoor time, but when your child isn't feeling well, or your family system is under duress, loosen the pressure on yourself and your child and amend the schedule.

Sleep: Essential to Intelligence, Health, and Well-Being

For many families, sleep becomes overwhelmingly important when a baby is born. Some babies "sleep like a baby," but many don't, and for a lot of parents, getting enough sleep for themselves and their infants seems like an impossible dream.

Chris Winter is a neurologist and sleep specialist who has written a book to help parents understand their children's sleep needs.[15] He opens the book with a chapter called "Sleep 101: How Sleep Works in Your Kid's Brain," in which he reviews current sleep science findings, starting with the prenatal stage. I found it a delightfully well-written book, knowledgeable, good-humored, and reassuring, filled with practical suggestions. If you have any issues with your baby or child and sleep, take a look at this book.

On the basis of an extensive review of the research findings, the American Academy of Sleep Medicine (AASM) made some recommendations for young children's daily sleep needs.[16] In each case, the recommended number of sleep hours includes naps as well as other sleep in a 24-hour period:

- 4 to 12 months: 12 to 16 hours
- 1 to 2 years: 11 to 14 hours
- 3 to 5 years: 10 to 13 hours

(Between birth and 4 months of age, the AASM found there was too much variability across infants and insufficient evidence to make recommendations.)

WHY SLEEP MATTERS

Sleep is important for your child for a number of interconnected reasons. Best known perhaps is sleep's contribution to growth and physical health. The hormone that your child's body needs for growing, breaking down fats, and daily repair is released by the pituitary gland while your child is sleeping. Their immune system, needed for disease prevention and an effective response to infections and disease, only functions well when they're getting enough sleep.

You may be surprised to hear that there's also a learning and memory function to sleep time: While your child is sleeping, their brain is filing what they've experienced and learned that day, sorting and storing it for later retrieval. While your child is asleep, their brain is connecting the day's new learning to what they've learned in the past. This establishes associations across topics and enables deeper level learning they can make use of the next time those ideas are relevant.

There's also an important brain health function: As a result of cognitive activity, toxins build up in your child's brain during their waking hours; sleep is when those toxins are flushed out.

Finally, sleep is necessary for emotion regulation. When a baby or young child doesn't get enough sleep, they get irritable, moody, and anxious, undermining their ability to soothe themself. When your child is well rested, they're more likely to have a sense of energetic well-being and to be positive in their moods.

HOW CAN YOU ENCOURAGE YOUR CHILD TO GET THE SLEEP THEY NEED?

You know that sleep is important for your child, essential for regenerating their body and brain and making the best of tomorrow, but it's not always easy for them to shut down their active brain at bedtime. They might be thinking about what they've learned during the day, about monsters and other scary creatures, or about everything they'd rather be doing than sleeping.

If your child resists going to sleep, consider the sleeping environment. Is your child's sleeping space clean, comfortable, quiet, and safe? Have you established a reliable and consistent wind-down routine, with snuggles and a story and a lullaby or two? If you can stay calm and take your time with this, it will go faster than if you try to rush through the routine.

Many children have worries about separations, including the daily separation of bedtime. At least for the last hour before bed, do your best to avoid criticism and arguments. As bedtime approaches, make sure your child feels secure in your love.

If your child is fearful at bedtime, don't dismiss those fears or tell them not to worry. Instead, show them how they're safe. A night light might help. Perhaps a stuffed animal can become the "guard bear." Help the bear look in the closet and anywhere else your child thinks danger might lurk. When the inspection is done, the guard bear can report, "All safe here," before going to his guard spot on the bed or by the door.

On a physical note, avoid sugary food in the hour before bedtime. When your child has sugar at bedtime, their blood sugar spikes and then later drops, leading to hunger during the night. If they want a bedtime snack, try something with protein, such as an unsweetened dairy product (milk, yogurt, cheese) or whole-grain crackers with peanut butter or hummus.

Finally, your child will have a better sleep if they've had enough exercise and play, preferably outdoors.

When your child's bedtime is calm, reassuring, and dependable, they have a better chance of getting the healing regenerative sleep that will help them have a happier day tomorrow.

CHILDHOOD: 6 TO 10

As your child gains some autonomy and masters the basics of self-care, and as they move more into the world beyond your home and family, you will probably feel freer than you did in their infancy and early childhood. This assumes that things are going well and that they're growing and learning as expected. By the age of 6, you already know or are beginning to suspect if they have problems that require special attention. Whether the issues are physical, cognitive, psychological, or behavioral, this is a good time to get help if you need it and haven't done that yet. Your family doctor can be a good source for a recommendation or referral, as can your child's school.

Play in Childhood

Through the years from 6 to 10, play continues to be important for your child's development in every dimension of their lives—physical, intellectual, social, and psychological. It is essential to brain building and giving them the skills they'll need as they get older. The AAP was thinking of school-age kids as well as young children when they made their recommendation that doctors write prescriptions for play, describing how play stimulates brain development, social development, creativity, academic skills, and resilience.[17]

THE BENEFITS OF PLAY

As your child grows into and through the years from 6 to 10, play contains more of the risk-taking, experimentation, and boundary-testing dimensions than it did when they were younger, but it retains its voluntary, fun, spontaneous qualities, free of serious real consequences.

Play continues to be important in enhancing your child's communication skills. It also hones their attention, self-control, intellectual flexibility, and working memory. Too little playtime—because of too much time spent on screens, academics, extracurricular activities, commuting, or something else—has been linked to rising numbers of children with attention problems.

Play has important psychological benefits, too. Unstructured play—when adults refrain from giving instructions—helps your child discover what they like doing, who they are, and what they want to learn more about. It also has an important function in buffering toxic stress. Play reduces your child's anxiety and helps them cope with stressful circumstances, such as a new school, a family move, or a change in family structure.

Play stimulates your child's creativity. When they're actively engaged in following their interests, they're developing their curiosity, imagination, love of exploration, and creativity.

Play also builds a healthy body, increasing your child's strength, flexibility, dexterity, coordination, and confidence. Playful physical activity reduces the risk that your child will experience unhealthy levels of stress, fatigue, injury, depression, and obesity.

Finally, play builds your child's social and emotional intelligence. Playing with other kids is one of the best ways for your child to learn how to share, negotiate, solve problems, resolve conflicts, and advocate for themself.

Play is essential to your child building 21st-century skills. The rapidly evolving information economy demands more innovation than ever before—more agency and creativity and less conformity. To thrive in tomorrow's fast-changing world, your child needs ample time now to play.

WHAT'S YOUR ROLE IN YOUR CHILD'S PLAY?

As in early childhood, you can make sure your child has the tools they need to invent their own fun. Through the years from 6 to 10, that might include supplies for arts and crafts, puzzles, balls, and games. Even more than when they were younger, be available, but don't interfere or try to direct their play. Many of the benefits of play—autonomy, creativity, problem-solving skills, and more—come from deciding what to do and how to do it.

Another important role for you in maximizing the benefits of your child's play is to keep their schedules sufficiently open that they have ample unstructured time to invent their own activities. If they're attending an after-school day care, talk to the care providers about options for the kids to invent their own activities.

Take a look at the amount of time your child is spending on screens. Technology can be great when used for specific purposes such as winding down at the end of the day, providing a change of pace when needed, or teaching certain information or skills. Most kids today, however, are spending so much time online that they don't have enough room in their schedule for healthy amounts of play.

Commuting time is another potential time gobbler that eats into playtime for a lot of kids. Do what you can to keep your child's commutes as brief as possible. Put "within walking distance" on your priority list for choosing schools and activities.

Encourage your child to play with other kids. When they play with others without intrusive supervision, they learn to communicate effectively, think about fairness, listen to others, negotiate rules, solve problems collaboratively, and be inclusive.

Nutrition: Once Again, Let Your Child Win the Food War

Most parents are well aware of the connection between long-term health outcomes and a child's eating habits. At the same time, however, there are many reasons to worry about eating disorders in children and teens.[18]

As with younger kids, children between 6 and 10 can use food as a means—usually unconscious—of asserting their autonomy, rebelling against controlling parents, or managing frustration, sadness, or anxiety. At this stage, it's even more important to allow your child as much decision-making power as possible when it comes to food. The one rule I recommend is that they be expected to attend family mealtime but, otherwise, not be bribed, coerced, coddled, or persuaded when it comes to what they put into their mouths.

In a position statement on nurturing children's healthy eating, a team of scientists defined a healthy diet as occurring "when one's usual eating patterns include adequate nutrient intake and sufficient, but not excessive, energy intake to meet the energy needs of the individual."[19] After reviewing the epidemiologic and intervention research, they concluded that an authoritative parenting style leads to the healthiest long-term eating habits in kids.

The scientists came to the authoritative parenting conclusion by analyzing the four key themes they identified that encourage and support healthy eating practices among children. The first theme was a positive parental attitude to food. They recommended that parents avoid food restrictions, allow children to make their own food choices, and encourage their children to decide on their portion sizes. The second theme focused on eating together, emphasizing the important role of socializing and regular family meals in children having a healthy diet. The third key theme was a healthy food environment at home. What they meant by that and recommended was having healthy food choices available and accessible to kids and parental modeling of healthy choices. The fourth theme was all about the pleasures associated with eating. Kids develop the best habits when they associate healthy eating with pleasure through repeated exposure to good nutritious foods, enjoyable social meals, and discussions of the qualities and value of healthful foods.

This means as much as possible choosing natural whole foods with no additives and being stingy with fast, processed, and junk food. Try to save those for occasional use, and do your best to avoid soft drinks, added sugar, and chemicals. Include your child in grocery shopping, meal planning, cooking, and cleanup, shaping them toward healthier options. Let them make as many choices as reasonable.

Regular, pleasant family mealtimes are important for children for many reasons, including nutritional. This means holding off during mealtime on any criticisms you feel you need to make or suggestions for doing things differently. Share those with your child after the meal, offered kindly in private. Try to make mealtime a sociable time for discussion and sharing both food and news of the day. Keep the focus on acceptance and appreciation. If your child whines or complains about the food or having to sit while you're eating after they've finished, ask if they have anything they're happy about. If they can't think of anything, ask the other family members for ideas. If that doesn't get things started, you might point out your gratitude for good food to keep you healthy, a loving family, a safe place to live, and so much more.

It's also important that you model a healthy attitude toward eating. If you're not happy with your own weight or food habits, you can be honest about that with your child, but do your best to prevent your child from experiencing the body-shaming and food guilt so prevalent in our culture. If you hear yourself talking about your body in a negative way or comparing your body with someone else's, try to get out of the habit. You can start talking about what your body can do instead and encourage your child to do the same— for example, "I sure am glad I can touch my knees, because it really feels good to stretch my back out like that! I guess if I keep working at it, maybe I'll be able to touch my toes, too, like you can."

If you have concerns about your child's eating and all the other factors are good (good family atmosphere, especially around food; good parental eating habits; regular family mealtimes; no coercion about what they're eating, when, or how much), consider whether your child has other needs that aren't being met. As noted earlier, sometimes, children (like adults) use food for solace, stimulation, anger management, or boredom relief.

Good nutrition matters. Somewhat counterintuitively, the best way to ensure your child eats well and continues to eat well across their lifespan is to let them decide when, what, and how much they'll eat. Do have sociable family mealtimes and provide healthy and delicious food options, but otherwise back off. Let it be theirs.

Physical Exercise Builds Your Child's Brain as It Builds Their Body

As in early childhood, getting enough exercise leads to a variety of physical benefits, including improved heart and bone health, better fine and gross motor skills, lower body fat, and more. More surprising perhaps is that children who get enough exercise do better on measures of psychological, social, and cognitive development. Children from 6 to 10 years old should get at least an hour a day of moderate to vigorous physical activity, mostly aerobic. More is better, but an hour is a minimum for building a strong and healthy body, as well as for your child's psychological and cognitive health. Included in your child's exercise should be muscle- and bone-strengthening (weight-bearing) activities at least 3 days a week.[20]

For one example of the power of frequent, regular exercise, students in Finland do exceptionally well in comparisons of educational outcomes around the world. This is surprising because Finnish children don't start their formal education, including learning to read and write, until the age of 7, and they attend school less than 6 hours a day. There are many other factors involved in Finland's high standings in international academic rankings (great support for parents starting at birth, excellent training, support, and remuneration for teachers, and more), but analyses of the Finns' high academic global standing suggest that one of their most potent success factors is that children get 15 minutes out of every hour for recess or outdoor play.[21] In Chapter 10, I discuss the ways you might get involved in advocacy at your child's school or after-school program for more recess time and physical exercise being built into their daily routines.

THE BENEFITS OF EXERCISE FOR CHILDREN

There are many compelling reasons to ensure that your child gets enough exercise. The first group of reasons—perhaps the most obvious—concerns physical health. Energetic movement strengthens your child's bones and muscles—including their heart muscle—as well as their gross motor skills. When your child exercises regularly, they develop strength, flexibility, and stamina, as well as resilience to many kinds of illnesses. Kids who get enough exercise sleep better and burn more calories, resulting in a much lower likelihood of obesity and diabetes.

There are a whole lot of neurological and cognitive reasons, too, for getting enough exercise. It's one of the best ways to increase blood flow to your child's brain. That delivers the oxygen and glucose they need to concentrate on tasks that require focused attention. Physical activity improves reaction time, short-term memory, and accuracy. When your child is physically fit, they are faster and more accurate on challenging cognitive tasks. With all these advantages—better concentration, attention, reaction time, and short-term memory—it's no wonder that physical fitness is associated with better academic grades. Finally, a more active body means a more active mind, bringing with it more creativity and originality.

And if the physical and cognitive reasons weren't enough, there are several psychological benefits, too. Your child feels more energetic when they exercise. If they're hyperactive, exercise helps them regulate their energy better. Exercise increases norepinephrine and endorphins, reducing your child's feelings of stress and enhancing their mood. At the same time, it improves their sense of well-being, as well as their appearance and self-confidence. Beta-endorphins and serotonin, chemicals our brains make that are associated with feelings of well-being, are also stimulated by exercise. Your child feels calmer and happier when they're getting enough exercise.

If your child is not fit today, that's not ideal, but it's not terrible, either. Research on sedentary children who increased their physical activity showed they achieved all the benefits enumerated here.[22] If your child gets 15 minutes of active playtime an hour, starting now, they will not only tone their body but will also reboot their brain, so they're able to return to their studies or other activities more ready, willing, and able to concentrate.

How Can You Encourage Your Child to Get Enough Exercise?

If you make fitness a personal priority, it will be good for you, but it will be great for your child. As with everything else, they're more likely to do what you do than what you tell them to do. You might look for physically active things you can do together. Go to a playground, take a hike in the neighborhood, play ball together, go for a bike ride. One family I know tries to take an after-dinner walk each evening. Even if it's just a 15-minute walk around the block, it helps with digestion and leads to better sleep for everyone. It's also a great time to notice changes in the seasons and the neighborhood and to chat about what each of them has done all day. Taking a walk can be conducive to loosening your child's worries about telling you something that's troubling them.

Maybe you can build physical activity time into the weekend. Go for a hike or a bike ride, build a fort in a local park, or play a game of soccer or baseball. Or you can make fitness time social, getting together with friends, neighbors, or family to do something active together.

If your child isn't getting enough exercise, consider screen time limits. Too much time watching television, playing video games, or surfing the web can easily consume all of your child's free time, reducing time for physical activities. Look for ways to commute on foot or bicycle with your child instead of driving places.

You might also give your child active chores, including making beds, scrubbing floors, raking leaves, or washing the car. Include physical activity as school decision-making criteria. Choose a school where your child will spend time outside and be physically active throughout the day, or perhaps you can become an activity advocate. Talk to your child's teacher and other parents about daily activity opportunities. This is especially important for children under 8, boys, and kids with attention issues, but it's healthy for everyone.

Physical activity is hugely beneficial for your child, but it should be woven into their daily life as seamlessly as possible. When your child isn't feeling well or is experiencing unusual stress, loosen your expectations regarding exercise. Maybe you can find longer activity periods later when they can be worked more easily into their life.

Outdoor Time

Time outdoors has most of the physical, cognitive, and psychological benefits of physical activity, with the added advantage of a closer connection to nature and an enhanced sense of social connection.[23] Time outdoors—particularly in nature, whether it's a pocket park or the wilderness—has been shown to increase a child's happiness and optimism, their feelings of well-being, their balance, coordination, and strength and lead to lower stress, better coping skills, and increased resilience. Outdoor time improves your child's attention, focus, critical thinking, academic achievement, and social skills and leads to a greater attunement to the environment.

If you realize the value of outdoor time but are wondering how to make it happen, take a look at how your child is spending their indoor time.

You might want to establish technology limits for your child or look for ways to minimize their commuting time to sports, school, and other activities. Maybe there are ways to make outdoor time part of your daily routine, whether it's walking to school, riding a bike to a friend's house, or walking to local shops. Talk to your child about creating or finding an outdoor happy place—a fort, certain playground, sandbox or dirt pile, water feature, or swing they like to swing on.

It's good to have a reason to go outside, other than it being good for you. If you have a dog, that will take you out a few times every day; make sure your child is participating in that activity. Maybe you can grow something in a garden patch, windowsill, or community garden. Invite your child to help choose plants, weed, water, and harvest some of your family's food or flowers. Perhaps you and your child would enjoy being part of a local citizen science project. Search "citizen science" or "participatory science" + "[your state or city]", or go to Canada's citizen science portal, *National Geographic*'s citizen science page, or *Scientific American*'s citizen science page.

As with everything else, don't try to be perfect on this one. Yes, the benefits are enormous, but your frame of mind and your child's are far more important. Do your best to ensure an hour a day outdoors, but if things are unusually hectic or otherwise stressful, loosen the schedule until things are easier.

Sleep

Every parent knows that sleep is important, but not everyone knows why it's important or how to encourage their child to get the amount of sleep they need. According to the AASM, your child needs between

9 and 12 hours of sleep every night between the ages of 6 and 12. The AASM stated, "Regularly sleeping fewer than the number of recommended hours is associated with attention, behavior, and learning problems. Insufficient sleep also increases the risk of accidents, injuries, hypertension, obesity, diabetes, and depression."[24]

According to neurologist and sleep expert Chris Winter, "We are losing battles against ADHD, diabetes, depression, and obesity, but all the while these diseases are quietly being caused by or fueled by unrecognized and untreated sleep disorders."[25] He underlines how important it is for parents to pay attention to the role of sleep in their children's problems, citing the National Sleep Foundation's estimate that two out of every three children in the United States experience a sleep problem before reaching adulthood.

WHY YOUR CHILD'S SLEEP IS SO IMPORTANT

Getting enough sleep is essential to brain health. While your child is sleeping, their brain is making orderly sense of what they've experienced that day, connecting the day's new learning to what they've learned in the past. This allows them to make use of the new, more complex understandings next time those ideas are relevant. Sleep is also when the toxins that are by-products of brain activity are flushed out, allowing your child to wake up refreshed and ready for more experiences and learning.

Sleep also has significant physical implications. As happens in early childhood, your child's immune system only functions well when they're getting enough sleep, and the hormone your child's body needs for growing is released while your child is sleeping. Children who don't get enough sleep are also more likely to have problems with obesity and diabetes.

Learning and academic ability are also affected by sleep. When your child doesn't get enough sleep, they're more distractible and impulsive and less able to concentrate. When they do get enough sleep, they learn better and are more likely to do well at school.

You've probably noticed the emotional and psychological implications of insufficient sleep. It impairs your child's judgment, so they react to small problems and frustrations as intensely as to bigger concerns, with more irritability, moodiness, and anxiety. Somewhat predictably, then, your child is more likely to behave badly if they're not getting enough sleep. When your child is well-rested, they're more likely to have a sense of energetic well-being and to be positive in their moods.

How Can You Help Your Child Get Enough Sleep?

You know how important sleep is to your child's development, but getting enough sleep is harder for some kids than others. Kids who are intensely curious, imaginative, or active can find their brains racing as they try to fall asleep. Children who are experiencing change, stress, or disruption often find their sleep troubled.

If your child isn't sleeping as well or as much as you'd like them to, take a look at their sleeping environment. To the best of your ability, make sure it feels calm, safe, and soothing, that it's clean, quiet, and comfortable. Ideally, there aren't any electronic devices in the room where your child sleeps, and they've had at least 1 hour without technology before they've gone to bed. Try to avoid sugar for at least an hour before bedtime. If they want a snack, look for something with protein and without sugar.

Some other things to think about if your child isn't getting the sleep they need include, Have they had enough exercise and play, preferably outdoors? Are you following a dependable bedtime schedule 7 days a week? Have you followed a sleep-conducive wind-down routine (maybe teeth, toilet, goodnights, a snuggle, a story, and a chat)? (Hint: If you can stay calm and take your time, this will go faster than if you try to rush through the routine.) Have you kept the last hour or two before bedtime calm and conflict free? Many children have worries about separations, including the daily separation of bedtime. As bedtime approaches, ensure your child feels secure in your love and affection.

A child who has trouble getting to sleep can sometimes do better when the emphasis is on relaxation instead of sleep. Give your child some strategies for relaxing their body and mind. Visualizations can help: Suggest they imagine they're in a quiet place they love, doing something peaceful and calming. Or you can ask your child to tell you about one good thing that happened today. Maybe someone said something kind or funny to them. Maybe they helped someone else. Maybe they did or made something they're proud of.

Something else that works for some kids is to ask them to set an intention for the next day—for example, "I will sleep soundly and wake up in the morning feeling refreshed," or "Tomorrow I'm going to spend some time painting." Mindfulness practices like this are a good way to help a restless child get more sleep. You might suggest to your child that they breathe in through their nose as they count slowly to five. Then breathe out through the mouth, counting slowly to five. Repeat five times and then again if necessary.

Sleep is important on so many levels. As you follow these routines with your child, you may also be learning what you need to get the calm, regenerative sleep that will allow you to face tomorrow refreshed and ready for whatever storms it brings.

ADOLESCENCE: 11 TO 18

By the time your child is 11, it's great if they've established healthy habits regarding play and leisure, nutrition, exercise, outdoor time, and sleep. There's always time to establish good habits—even into old age—but it gets harder over time because the longer we have a bad habit, the harder it is to override in favor of something healthier. Nonetheless, anytime you or your child decide it's time to do better in one of these dimensions, it's completely worth the effort in terms of the lifetime benefits.

Playtime and Leisure

Teenagers need play as much as younger children do, but it takes a different form. Much of adolescent development involves social interactions, learning about emotions and relationships, which tends to be the focus of a teen's leisure time. They like to get together with friends just to hang out together, playing music, sports, or video games or going to concerts or movies. Sometimes a teenager's play takes the form of "doing homework" together—homework that sounds to a listening parent like it's heavy on conversation about what happened at school today, who they or their friends are interested in romantically, how impossible their families are, or what they're doing on the weekend and light on academic assignments.

Sometimes adolescents' leisure time is spent watching videos or television or on social media, something that parents can find worrying. As long as it doesn't start interfering with other interests, including time for exercise, sleep, or academic or household responsibilities, it's usually good to see these activities as a form of leisure. Remind yourself that what looks to you like wasting time may be necessary for your child's mental health, as well as providing opportunities for social learning. Pay attention to the balance in their life, and intervene only as you think necessary if you see your teenager losing perspective on what's important.

There are early adolescents and teenagers who get in trouble with substance use, sex, truancy, and other risky behaviors. I address these concerns in Chapter 10, where I emphasize the importance of getting help when things get serious. Some problems are too big to solve on your own, and it's a sign of wisdom to know you don't have to do it alone.

Nutrition

By the age of 11, your child's food habits are pretty well set. As with all habits, they can be changed, but by this age, it's up to your child to figure that out and make any changes they decide to make. And as with younger children, it won't help if you nag or criticize. The best you can do is accept your child just the way they are, try to model good eating behaviors yourself, make sure there are healthy and tasty food options for them, and offer to be available if they want help making any changes.

Family dinner can be an important touchstone for a teenager who is having trouble at school or with friends, and one of the best resiliency factors for a healthy adolescence is regular family mealtimes. Unless there's an urgent reason to have a phone on(e.g., you're an on-call doctor or someone you know may require immediate assistance), all electronic devices should be off during mealtime, yours as well as your child's. Eat together as often as possible, on as regular a schedule as possible. Don't try to avoid your teen's anger, irritability, or silence—in fact, welcome negative emotions as opportunities to see that there's something that might need your attention—but try to keep your focus on being positive and supportive, especially at mealtime.

Physical Exercise and Outdoor Time

Exercise and time in nature continue to be important across the lifespan and can be particularly important during adolescence. As I discussed in the section on childhood, these activities offer many important health benefits across physical, psychological, social, cognitive, and academic dimensions and can be essential to a teenager retaining a positive perspective through a potentially challenging period.

Laurence Steinberg wrote a book called *Age of Opportunity: Lessons From the New Science of Adolescence*,[26] in which he discussed teenagers as exquisitely vulnerable but also filled with enormous possibilities. The years from 11 to 14 are particularly important in defining a life pathway, second only to the early years in terms of the brain's plasticity. Neural pathways and connections are being reorganized during adolescence, so it's a great time for your child to form new habits and follow interests that strengthen their skills, resilience, and emotion regulation.

All of this has implications for parenting, of course. Whether your child appears to be pushing you away or asking more from you than ever, they need you to become "the guide on the side" of their life, not "the sage on the stage." They need you to move away from being proactive in making decisions for them to being patiently attentive and reactive, allowing them to make their own decisions as much as safely possible. Be ready, willing, and able to provide support when necessary or when they invite that from you, but for most aspects of their lives—including diet, exercise, and sleep—it's time for them to figure it out.

Sleep

Sleep during adolescence has all the benefits I mentioned in connection with sleep needs during the childhood years, and—because their body and brain are still growing—your adolescent continues to need more sleep than an adult. The AASM recommends 8 to 10 hours until the age of 18, observing that "Insufficient sleep in teenagers is associated with increased risk of self-harm, suicidal thoughts, and suicide attempts."[27] Too much sleep can also be problematic, although that's less common. According to the AASM, "Regularly sleeping more than the recommended hours may be associated with adverse health outcomes such as hypertension, diabetes, obesity, and mental health problems."[28]

Frances Jensen is a neuroscientist and parent who wrote a wonderful book called *The Teenage Brain: A Neuroscientist's Survival Guide to Raising Adolescents and Young Adults*.[29] She wrote,

> Sleep isn't a luxury. Memory and learning are thought to be consolidated during sleep, so it's a requirement for adolescents and as vital to their health as the air they breathe and the food they eat. In fact, sleep helps teens eat better. It also allows them to manage stress.[30]

Many of the same strategies apply to helping teenagers get the sleep they need as apply to younger children. The one difference is that your teen will have to take responsibility for it themself. You can offer to help them with sleep strategies, but there's little you can do to make it happen except modeling good habits yourself and doing your best to be positive and loving with them, especially in the evening.

There may be something else you can do. Sleep specialist Chris Winter thinks school shouldn't start before 8:30 and that many school start times are too early for kids' optimal sleep. He stated,

> In my opinion, school is the clearest and most present threat to your child getting a healthy amount of sleep. If the COVID crisis has taught us anything, it is the fact that the removal of a rigid, in-person school schedule has resulted in a dramatic increase in sleep time for many children.[31]

He cited research showing that kids' school performance and health improve when school starts later. If you think school start time may be affecting your teen's hours of sleep, you might consider advocating for a later school start time. There aren't a lot of issues more important than their health and well-being, and you'll probably find other parents, as well as teachers and kids, support your cause.

YOUNG ADULTHOOD: 19 TO 24

By 19, your child is (or ought to be) making all their own decisions about leisure time, nutrition, exercise, and sleep, unless their decisions have an impact on the rest of the family's lives somehow.

Young adults—and older adults, too—need playtime, just as children and teens do. Playtime looks different in adults than in kids, but many of the benefits are the same as I discussed in connection with children, most important perhaps being refreshing our spirits. We need time for leisure activities that we choose simply because we enjoy them. Our play can come in the form of getting together with a friend, taking a bike ride, taking up a hobby, going on a trip, joining a choir, participating in a local drama group, going bowling, playing video games, reading a book, or anything that feels like it nurtures your spirit.

According to the American Heart Association, young adults (and other adults, too) need at least 150 minutes a week of moderate-intensity activity, preferably spread throughout the week.[32] The benefits include a lower risk of heart disease, stroke, Type 2 diabetes, high blood pressure, dementia, several types of cancer, and some complications of pregnancy. Getting enough physical activity also leads to better sleep; improved cognition, including memory, attention, and processing speed; less weight gain and obesity and fewer related chronic health conditions; fewer symptoms of depression and anxiety; and a better quality of life and sense of overall well-being.

To get the neurological, emotional, psychological, and health benefits of sleep that I described in connection with children's sleep, adults need 7 or more hours each night, according to a joint consensus statement of the AASM and Sleep Research Society.[33] In that statement, they observed,

> Sleeping less than seven hours per night on a regular basis is associated with adverse health outcomes, including weight gain and obesity, diabetes, hypertension, heart disease and stroke, depression, and increased risk of death. Sleeping less than seven hours per night is also associated with impaired immune function, increased pain, impaired performance, increased errors, and greater risk of accidents.[34]

The AASM and Sleep Research Society went on to say that some people may need more than 9 hours a night, including young adults, people recovering from sleep debt, and those who are sick. Sleep is when the toxins that are by-products of brain activity are flushed out, allowing you to wake up refreshed. This does not get less important as we get older; there are research indications that insufficient sleep in middle age may increase the risk of dementia.[35]

It's good to know these things, but when it comes to nutrition, exercise, and sleep, there's not much you can do for your young adult child anymore. If your young adult has established good habits through the years of childhood and adolescence, they'll probably retain them or come back to them in a few years when they've fully settled into their lives. If not, that will be up to them to figure out as time goes by. It's no longer your problem or your concern, so don't nag, criticize, or lecture.

If you have serious concerns about the way your young adult is spending their time—you think it may be dangerous or destructive—the best you can do is be positive about what you think they are doing well and offer to provide whatever other supports they might need if they want that. If they're misusing their time and living at home still and not contributing to household income or chores, you can think about how you want to respond, something I discuss in

Chapter 5. Otherwise, do your best to respect their choices and love them for who they are. This book is about building a relationship with your child that can weather any storm. That means, in essence, focusing on your connection with them while also taking care of yourself.

TAKING IT INTO THE COMMUNITY: SUNNYDALE ELEMENTARY SCHOOL'S GARDEN

Good nutrition is important for so many reasons, and having access to fresh produce has important physical, psychological, and cognitive benefits. In many communities, however, there's neither much by way of available nutrition information for parents nor easy, reasonably priced access to fresh produce.

In one such community, where many families are struggling financially, the parent–teacher association decided to create a community garden. They allocated a section of their schoolyard to growing food they'd make available to the community as they harvested it. In September of the first year, each class in Sunnydale Elementary School had a task to complete in the planning process. The sixth graders (the oldest students) were asked to consult local gardening experts and draw up a schedule of what needed to be done and when it should be done to create a bountiful garden with good soil that could grow herbs, fruit, and vegetables, and a planting, tending, and harvesting schedule.

Sunnydale's fifth-graders were asked to do some research and figure out the best crops to grow, thinking about what they would have the best luck with, given the local climate and soil conditions; what would be most nutritious; and what people would most enjoy.

The fourth graders were asked to take care of the finances, including calculating the costs of preparing the soil, buying the seeds, and anything else. They were also asked to think about how they could generate the money they needed for the garden project.

The third graders were asked to find good recipes using fruits, vegetables, or herbs that they might be growing, and as the decisions about what to grow were firmed up, they were to make sure there were good recipes for that produce in their recipe collection. At the end of the year, their assignment was a recipe book to give out with the produce.

The second graders were asked to design and execute a huge to-scale map of the school and the schoolyard, showing the playground, parking lot, and garden. They were asked to consult with the fifth graders in figuring out how much room to allocate to each crop.

The kindergarten and first graders were in charge of illustrating the recipe book and decorating walls throughout the school with art and poetry celebrating healthy food and gardens.

In the assembly in the first week of school the first year, the principal announced the project and asked that each of the students talk to their parents and neighbors about whether they'd be able to help out anytime or take over from the teachers in the summer when there was no school. They had monthly assemblies where each grade gave a garden project progress report, identifying equipment or services needed that the students couldn't provide themselves. As necessary items were identified, the principal asked everyone to see if they could find someone who could provide it—items such as a rototiller, for example, or some garden shovels or watering hoses. As time went by and the project gained momentum, the students' excitement grew. As often happens with innovative, hands-on, real-world projects, some of the kids who'd never enjoyed school much were the most enthusiastic participants.

The Sunnydale staff, students, and parents learned a lot in the first year. The second year began with each class analyzing what had happened the year before, what had gone well, and how they could do it better. At the first assembly the second year, the principal gave the floor to the garden project coordinators for each grade, who reported on their grade's analysis. The coordinators agreed they'd been a bit ambitious in trying to grow things that didn't do well in their soil and sunshine conditions. They wouldn't try cauliflower again—their cauliflower plants had been overrun with bugs—and corn was probably a mistake—it needed too much room. They were surprised by how well the herbs had done. They'd had a bumper crop of sage, parsley, basil, mint, and rosemary. It didn't take a lot of space to grow a lot of herbs, and their families and neighbors had loved having the fresh herbs, which are normally pretty expensive.

Over the course of the second year of the garden project, they assigned the tasks in a similar way, but the different grades did more coordinating with each other. They instituted monthly meetings of representatives of all grade levels, which cut down on a lot of duplication of labor, and the experience ran more smoothly once they got into planting season. That spring and summer, a local newspaper ran a feature on the Sunnydale garden project, with weekly photos of different kids and the garden as it grew. They had more community volunteers helping out, and the students and staff at the school all had a sense they were doing something good.

By the spring of the third year, there was even more media attention, and it felt like the whole community was involved. That summer, they had more volunteers than they knew what to do with, so they decided to expand the garden the following year, making an annex in a neighboring park. Community members would organize the annex, consulting Sunnydale students and staff as needed.

The benefits of this garden project went way beyond the nutritional benefits to the community, of course, in ways I discuss in Chapter 10, in connection with Eric Klinenberg's book *Palaces for the People*.[36]

KEY TAKEAWAYS: SELF-CARE IS THE FOUNDATION OF EVERYTHING
ELSE IN LIFE

- From infancy through into adulthood, play and leisure are essential to every aspect of your child's development: physical, psychological, cognitive, social, and emotional.
- Children develop good eating habits when their parents have a positive attitude toward food and allow their kids to make choices; when families share pleasant mealtimes together; when kids have access to healthy, delicious food, and parents model good food choices; and when kids are encouraged to associate pleasure with food.
- Physical exercise builds muscles, bones, strength, flexibility, and stamina. A fit child, teen, or adult is healthier in every way and sleeps better.
- Outdoor time increases optimism, well-being, and balance. It lowers stress and improves coping skills and resilience. By improving attention, focus, and critical thinking, academic achievement is also improved. People who spend time outdoors have better social skills and greater attunement to the environment.
- Getting enough sleep is essential to a healthy brain and body. It's necessary for focus and self-regulation and contributes to academic success. It's also essential for good judgment and behavior, a positive mood, and a sense of energetic well-being.
- When you care for your own needs for leisure, nutrition, exercise, time in nature, and sleep, you enhance your ability to enjoy your life and be present to others in your life, very much including your child.

CHAPTER 5

EACH OF US IS UNIQUE: BRAIN BUILDING TOGETHER

*Reading to children at night, responding to their smiles with
a smile, returning their vocalizations with one of your own,
touching them, holding them—all of these further a child's brain
development and future potential, even in the earliest months.*
—T. Berry Brazelton (attributed)

T. Berry Brazelton was a pediatrician and Harvard professor of
pediatrics who was fascinated by how babies' and children's brains
develop.[1] Current findings in the neurosciences are proving him
right: Reading to children at night, holding them, responding to
their smiles with a smile, and echoing their vocalizations is building
their brains and nurturing their abilities. How that happens—and
leads to the wonderfully unique person each of us is—is the subject
of this chapter.

The human brain is one of the most exciting frontiers of scientific research, and you have a front-row seat on the miracle that is
your child's brain as it develops, one neuron and one synapse at a time.
Over the past several decades, knowledge about the brain's workings
has been changing dramatically. Translating research into practice is
always painfully slow, encountering the usual human resistance to
changes in the status quo, but over time, evolving knowledge about
the way the brain works is transforming our approaches to supporting human development across the lifespan because that affects early
child development, education, mental health, brain damage, neurological differences, and so much more.

Here are some questions to get you thinking about how the brain-building process works.

Questions to Consider About How the Brain-Building Process Works
• Do you think you have a role to play in how your child's brain develops?   • Do you think your child has a role to play in their own brain building?   • What can you do (if anything) to support your child's brain-building process going well?   • Is there anything you might do—habitually or occasionally—that could undermine that process?

NEURAL PLASTICITY

In Chapter 3, I talked about neural plasticity when I discussed how mindfulness changes the brain. Neural plasticity (also called neuroplasticity or brain plasticity) is an essential idea for understanding how each person's brain is constructed and how it is that each of us has a unique personality, essence, and life experience. The term *neural plasticity* refers to how your genetically designed brain forms connections between brain cells (also called neurons) as you interact with the world. Through this process of genetic possibility being influenced by and making sense of the people and experiences you encounter, your brain is constantly changing, even into old age. What this means is that the social, sensory, and physical environments you inhabit and travel through—and your responses to them—are constantly affecting your brain, changing it, and building it.

Some changes are beneficial, as happens when you study the piano or learn a new language; you're creating new pathways in the brain, stimulating learning and growth, so next time you attempt to play a musical piece or speak that new language, you'll have a richer recall and find yourself a bit more fluent. Your brain has retained something from the earlier experience, so you approach it with a slightly different brain next time you attempt it.

Other brain changes are harmful, as happens when you experience something traumatic or sustain high anxiety levels over time. In these cases, you may find yourself less fluent emotionally, unable to remember certain events or processes, or less able to find pleasure in activities you used to enjoy. You probably know that neural plasticity can be detrimental for children when they experience chronic stress, repeated abuse, or severe maternal depression. Damaging ongoing experiences like these can be toxic to a child's developing brain.[2]

Tabitha and Marni were delighted when their son Terry was born. For the first few months, they took him to work with them. They owned and operated a high-end crafts and clothing shop in a small town that was a popular summer theater destination. From April through October, they were run ragged taking care of customers and restocking shelves as they sold out, and during the rest of the year, they visited their suppliers' workshops—often necessitating travel—and got ready for the next busy season. The business was doing well, but they had a lot of debts to pay off, and rents were going up. They knew that if they didn't continue investing their energy in it, they'd lose the business they'd been dreaming about for years.

By the time Terry was 3 months old, Tabitha and Marni realized it wasn't working to take him to work with them—they had to sacrifice attention either to their shop or their child. Their extended family lived too far away to help out, and they decided to put Terry in day care. Initially, they'd planned that Terry would spend a maximum of 4 hours a day in day care, but as time went by, that grew bit by bit, until Terry was spending 10 hours there most days and 12 hours some days. During the shop's off-season, they were able to spend more time with their son, but he was still in day care at least 8 hours a day.

Mornings with Terry were terrible. After his first week in day care, he started refusing to allow them to put him into his car seat, and once they'd buckled him in, he wailed all the way, fighting with every ounce of his strength not to leave the car or their arms. The day care providers told Tabitha and Marni that he settled shortly after they left and was fine after that, but drop-offs continued to be painfully heart wrenching for both moms and also for Terry.

This pattern continued—painful drop-offs and long days for Terry in day care—until he was 4 and started preschool plus after-care. He was there the maximum amount of time the preschool allowed—from 8 a.m. to 6 p.m. By the time he was 4, drop-offs were no longer filled with tears and resistance. Instead, Terry walked slowly, dragging his feet, into the preschool. He didn't greet the other kids or his teacher but just proceeded into the early-care classroom to wait until preschool started. He wasn't a behavior problem, but the preschool teacher described him to Marni as "sullen and disinterested" one day when she picked him up at the end of the day.

Tabitha and Marni did their best to provide Terry with stimulating toys and books and happy activities when they spent time together. They wished he could be more cheerful but decided that his usually sorrowful face and lethargic behavior reflected his personality. They couldn't see anything more they might do for him. The business was doing well, and they were able to provide him with things and experiences they'd never had.

Terry had trouble learning to read and couldn't seem to master writing at all well, but his parents hired a tutor, and his literacy skills seemed to be progressing.

Terry was in Grade 3 before they realized there was something wrong. By then, he'd started hurting himself. They'd find cuts and bruises on him that he couldn't explain, but then one day, Tabitha saw him repeatedly bashing his elbow against the wall, with tears streaming down his face. They found a family therapist—

Dr. Robinson—and started seeing her. She had play therapy sessions with Terry and saw Tabitha and Marni separately, together, and with Terry at different times.

After a few months of therapy, Dr. Robinson arranged for a case review with Marni and Tabitha. She said that Terry was carrying a lot of repressed anger that was showing up as lethargy and sadness. It was affecting his cognitive processing, which was why he was having trouble with school. He'd developed a habit of tuning out and wasn't learning and growing as he should be. She suggested that one or both of the parents take some time off work and begin the process of reestablishing a strong bond with their son. She recommended they continue with school but not enroll him in early care or aftercare.

Marni and Tabitha were filled with guilt. They looked back on the previous 8 years and wished they could take them back and spend more time and attention on their son. It felt like a desperate situation.

Dr. Robinson explained that as toxic as some experiences can be—and Terry had experienced his long hours in day care and away from his parents as toxic—the great advantage that our brain's plasticity gives us is that rewiring the brain is pretty well always possible. Even in cases of posttraumatic stress disorder (PTSD), she said, the fact that the brain is still malleable means that new habits and reactions can be learned.[3] That doesn't mean it's quick or easy or that a person can recover from PTSD without a lot of help, but the fact that it's possible to grow past toxic situations offers enormous hope to us all.

"Terry doesn't have PTSD," she said, "but if you think you've damaged your child or that he's had experiences that damaged him past repair, there are ways to help him recover and strengthen."

The family continued to work with Dr. Robinson for the next 2 years. Marni and Tabitha hired a store manager and started working fewer hours in the shop and spending more time with Terry. As time went by, he became a fluent reader and a surprisingly good artist. He opened up and began to enjoy outings with his mothers and friends.

Maya Angelou said, "Do the best you can until you know better. And then when you know better, do better." These words gave me a lot of comfort and strength at a few points when I realized I should have handled things differently with my own kids. It can help you move forward from those moments of realization if you remember that your child's brain is plastic and that each of us has our own unique pathway to parenting, our own challenges and limitations. None of us is perfect, and that is okay.

There is a growing consensus among brain researchers that the brain continues to develop across the lifespan.[4] Neurons can be produced in some parts of the brain even in later adulthood, and although neural plasticity is greatest in infancy and childhood, some capacity for learning is evident into old age. Knowing something about neural plasticity can inspire you to keep learning and transcending self-imposed limits and also help you better understand what's happening with your child, so I'm going to take a bit of time now to review the basics of how the brain develops, connecting that back to practical ideas and suggestions.

THE EARLY YEARS: CONCEPTION TO 5

When a young child has a huge reaction to a small frustration—say a temper tantrum because you won't let them have one more cookie—you might feel justified in being annoyed. You could be forgiven for asking, "Really?!? You're having a fit over this?" What you might not know is that your young child's brain isn't able to manage disappointments yet. It isn't sufficiently mature to make sense of the frustration so your child can cope better with it.

Your little one is not being bad. Their brain just isn't sufficiently sophisticated to put things into perspective, soothe themself, or respond more appropriately. That means that punishment is not only useless in teaching them to do better, but it's also unfair and, perhaps more important, it's counterproductive. As I discussed in Chapter 2, punishment for a crime the child can't help committing only makes your young child feel confused, powerless, unhappy, and sometimes angry.

A parent's steady, loving gaze is a powerful brain builder. When you sit patiently with your baby or young child, mirroring the baby's sounds and actions, smiling with affection, as Berry Brazelton described in this chapter's opening quote, you are communicating warmth, safety, and responsiveness, the most important conditions for optimal brain development in the early days, weeks, months, and years.

Developmental cognitive neuroscientist Charles Nelson is a Harvard professor of pediatrics and widely respected as an expert on neural plasticity and brain development in childhood.[5] He studies both typically developing children and children at risk of neurodevelopmental disorders. Nelson and his colleagues have described how a healthy brain develops and also what can go wrong along the way.

Conception to Birth: In Utero

The first brain cells, or neurons, start to form about 16 days after conception. Over the next few weeks, the brain and spinal cord start coming together. Once the neural tube has been established, brain cells (also called neurons or nerve cells) begin to multiply. Once a neuron is formed, it migrates to its final destination. This begins about 8 weeks into gestation and ends 2 or 3 months later.

As neurons migrate to their final destinations in the brain, they establish synapses, or connections with other neurons. The developing nervous system becomes more densely packed, and the surface of the brain acquires the convoluted form we're familiar with. The central nervous system, consisting of the brain and spinal cord, is formed through an intricate sequence of processes and is vulnerable to many internal and external factors. This vulnerability, or plasticity, has enormous benefits after birth in terms of growing, learning, and adapting to challenges, but it also carries heavy risk factors in this earliest stage of development. Even the smallest disturbance during any of the fetal brain-building processes can severely alter a child's developing brain.

Infancy and Early Childhood: 0 to 3

By birth, your baby has about 100 billion brain cells. As the neurons make connections with one another, they create pathways of connected neurons throughout the brain. The early years of life are characterized by a rapid and explosive proliferation of connections between the brain cells: More than a million new connections (synapses) are formed every second. Shortly after birth, the brain cells produce far too many axons, preparing your infant's brain to respond to the environment. To stay viable, these axons must make connections with other neurons.

Some synapses form in utero, but most develop after birth. This process is particularly dynamic during the first year of life, although the schedule of synapse formation varies across different areas of the brain. The sensory pathways for vision and hearing develop first, followed by language and, a bit later, higher level cognitive functions such as reasoning. In the proliferation and pruning processes, simpler neural connections form first, followed by more complex circuits. The timing is genetic, but your child's early experiences determine whether the circuits will be strong or weak. The most important take-home message for a parent is that a secure and loving environment and a wide variety of rich experiences lead to better brain building for your child.

Myelin is a fatty sheath that insulates axons and speeds up impulse conduction, which is how information travels from one neuron to another within the brain. As one might expect, the areas of the brain that become functional first are the first to myelinate. For example, the axons that connect the neurons that control body posture are fully myelinated before birth, so your baby already has some physical abilities at birth—such as sucking or turning their head in response to someone touching their cheek. In contrast, frontal areas of the brain responsible for higher level reasoning and other complex processes continue to myelinate through adolescence and early adulthood, not reaching mature levels until age 30 or later. Disruptions in myelination in the frontal areas of the brain can lead to distractibility or impulsivity and can occur for a variety of reasons, including hypothyroidism or poor nutrition.

The brain's early development is shaped by your child's genetic makeup in interaction with their experiences and the environment. One of the most important early brain-building experiences is the "serve-and-return" process, which is what happens as you affectionately mirror your baby's sounds and gestures, returning to them the sounds of their early babbling and their facial expressions. When that serve-and-return process doesn't happen—or is unreliable, inconsistent, or inappropriate—it can lead to problems in many areas, including learning and behavior, in another example of the downside of neural plasticity.

The brain is most plastic early in life and, at that time, can accommodate a reasonably wide range of environments and interactions, but as your child matures and their brain becomes better able to handle more complex functions, their brain also becomes less plastic, less able to adapt to new challenges. For example, by the age of 1 year, the parts of the brain that differentiate sound are attuned to the languages the baby has been exposed to, and the child is already starting to lose the ability to reproduce sounds found in other languages. Although the window for foreign language learning remains open, these brain circuits become increasingly difficult to alter over time, as you'll know if you've tried to learn a new language in adulthood. It's doable (and highly beneficial in keeping your brain active and growing) but not as easy as it once was.

For optimal brain development in the early years of life, in addition to receiving the basics of good nutrition, sleep, and physical exercise, your infant or young child needs to feel securely loved, safe in the world, and encouraged to explore. They also need a wide range of sensory stimulation.

Stimulating the Senses

Your child's brain is developing from conception through adulthood. There are many approaches to thinking about how that happens and what you can do to ensure it happens as well as possible. One helpful perspective is to break the process down into the five senses.

A young child's environment affects both the structure of the child's brain and its functional pathways. Each of the five senses— sight, smell, touch, hearing, and taste—is constantly processing information and sending it to the brain. That information is critical in forming synapses, neural pathways, and neural networks, all of which enable your child to make sense of subsequent experiences. For optimal brain building, stimulate each of your child's senses starting early in infancy. As time goes by, help your child enjoy the complex possibilities in multisensory experiences.[6]

Some children are especially sensitive to one or more of the senses and are easily overwhelmed by certain experiences. They can find a particular stimulus too intense to process and need your help in coping with it. I recently overheard a father say to his little boy,

"You left the table suddenly when Mom brought the pickles to the table, right? You have a very sensitive nose. Do you think maybe the smell was too much for you?" The 3-year-old nodded solemnly, grateful that his experience had been validated instead of causing him to be chastised for running off in the middle of dinner.

Once your child is old enough, you can explain how it's through their five senses that their brain is growing. When they've had a particularly good or bad sensory experience, help them figure out which of the senses were most active and how. Open yourself to the range of sensory experiences in your child's world, and help them explore and consider those smells, sounds, sights, textures, and tastes when you're out for a walk or doing something together.[7]

VISION

At birth, your baby can't see far—about 8 to 12 inches—and their vision is blurry. They see in black and white, mostly shapes and shadows. By the second week, they can discriminate their caregivers' faces but only when they are close. By 4 months, your infant can see farther and in color and can track moving objects. By 5 months, they're beginning to develop depth perception. As they learn to crawl and then walk, they can use depth perception to judge distances as they explore.

To stimulate your child's visual development, try to provide a colorful environment, including bright colors and distinct shapes. Place your face in your baby's line of sight, talking, singing, and smiling, allowing them to focus on your face and watch its movements. At 3 or 4 months, start playing games such as pat-a-cake and peekaboo to stimulate your baby's hand–eye coordination.

Starting when your baby is born, take them on outdoor walks, protecting them appropriately from the elements, of course. Take different routes, and go different places. You'll be further enriching the brain-building experience if you're also talking to them as you walk, naming features of the environments you are walking through. When something catches their eye, stop and let them look at it. Comment on it, naming what you think they might be looking at.

Give your young child a wide range of visual stimuli, including moving objects such as tree branches, shadows, and bouncing balls. As they get a little older, give them tools for coloring and painting. Play matching games with cards. Play "I Spy" when you're going somewhere together. That encourages your child to pay closer attention to their visual environment and learn the names of what they're seeing.

HEARING

Hearing begins to develop during pregnancy, so your voice is already familiar to your baby when they're born. For the first while, they respond best to high-pitched, exaggerated sounds and voices. Newborns startle at loud noises—one of the signs of a hearing problem is that they don't startle—and some infants are soothed by the steady hum of a vacuum cleaner or clothes dryer.

With this, as with everything else, every child is different, but somewhere around 2 months, a baby begins to mimic basic sounds such as coos, and at about 4 months, they begin to babble. If you haven't already been talking to your baby, at 4 months, it's time to start. Speak slowly and carefully, repeating sounds and words so your baby can watch your lips and tongue, making sounds such as "bay-bay-bay-bay-baby!" By about 6 months, your baby should be trying to imitate sounds, and by 8 months, they should be babbling freely and responding to changes in your tone of voice. Language development is an enormous contributor to brain building, and it happens best via conversations you have with your child in the first years of their life.

Listen carefully to your baby or young child, mirroring their sounds and utterances. Play rhyming games and share books with them right from birth. Spend time both inside and outside, paying attention with your child to the sounds of the environment. Play different kinds of music, starting at conception and continuing right through childhood. As they get a little older, play clapping games, clapping out different rhythms and asking them to clap them back, then giving them a chance to be the clap leader. Use household instruments to play the same game—spoons, bells, a fork and a cup, maracas, whatever you have that can be used to create a rhythm. Ask your child which sounds and rhythm patterns they like best.

As with the other senses, some children have exceptionally sensitive hearing. Your child may be overwhelmed by a noisy environment or find certain sounds unbearable. Do your best to protect your young child from experiencing a sensory overload of any kind, including auditory. As time goes by, you will discover workarounds and compromises, such as time limits at parties, malls, and other noisy places or quiet-place hideouts for a bit of respite, as needed.

TOUCH

Touch is one of the best-developed senses at birth: Your newborn is already able to distinguish temperatures, textures, and shapes. They need to feel skin-to-skin contact to bond with you, and that bonding is the foundation of much that is happening in their brain in the early months and years. Close, warm cuddles help your baby feel secure enough to reach out and explore the world around them.

Some experts recommend gentle baby massages, or you can rub baby lotion over your infant's body after a bath. You can also use different textures to rub gently over your baby's body: a stuffed animal, a towel, a sweater, a bumpy ball.

As they get a bit older, one of a baby's best vehicles of exploration is their mouth; they like nothing better than to suck or chew anything they can find. Babyproofing a home starts with putting out of harm's way anything small enough to go into a child's mouth and become a choking hazard.

To stimulate your child's sense of touch, provide a variety of shapes and textures they can manipulate and help them feel the differences. There are tactile books designed for young children, such as *Pat the Bunny* and *Peter Rabbit Touch and Feel*. Give them toys they can play with in the water and opportunities to spend time at sand and water tables. Let them squish their toes in the mud and play in the sand. You can play touch-based guessing games, allowing your blindfolded young child to feel something with their fingers or feet and guess what it is. You might include grass, wood, playdough, sand, and more. Ask them whether it's rough or smooth, cold or hot and if they like it. You can do a guessing game with a pillowcase or soft bag into which you put a familiar object. Ask the child to feel the object through the bag and tell you how it feels, guessing what it is.

As your child gets a little older, touch continues to be an important way to explore the world. Give them opportunities to make a mess with clay, finger paints, water, and playdough. Tactile letter and number boards are good ways to stimulate touch and also encourage literacy and numeracy skills.

SMELL

Babies are born with a good sense of smell. They recognize their mother's scent shortly after birth and recognize the scents of other people within the first several days. Within a short period, they identify some smells as comforting and others as alarming.

At least in the first several months, it's best to avoid artificial smells, including perfumes, room deodorizers, and scented laundry detergent because these mask the important smells in the baby's environment, such as your natural pheromones. Familiarity is comforting to your infant, so regularly use the same low-scent or scent-free personal and household cleaning products—soap, shampoo, laundry detergent.

Almost immediately, you can start naming for your infant the smells in the environment, just as you do with people, objects, and sounds. That way, you're exposing your baby to language and also helping them attend to their olfactory sense. As your child gets older, point out the smells of foods, flowers, and nature. You can play a blindfolded guessing game with smell, providing sniff opportunities with chocolate, cinnamon, and other foods and objects around the house that have a distinctive smell. When you go somewhere new, notice the smells, and discuss them with your child.

As with the other senses, some children have an exceptionally well-developed sense of smell and are easily overwhelmed by certain scents, even to the point of allergic reactions. I'm one of those people who choke in response to mildew and many perfumes, as well as room deodorizers and scented candles. I feel like I can't breathe and have to get away. I'm just as extreme on the other end of the spectrum; some smells fill me with delight, such as summer rain or the ocean. If your child has a problem with particular smells, respect that as legitimate, even if you can't smell it or aren't bothered by it.

TASTE

A baby is born with fully functioning taste buds. They can detect flavors from their mother's diet in their breastmilk, and otherwise, they prefer sweetness. Eat a variety of healthy foods while breastfeeding because that familiarizes your baby with a range of flavors.

Once your baby is eating independently, the same rules apply as with the other senses: Give them a wide range of tastes, textures, and colors. Your baby's taste preferences will develop based on what you ate if you were breastfeeding and/or what you feed them in their early years. As they get older, help them name the different tastes and textures—for example, "Applesauce tastes sweet, but it also tastes a little tart, doesn't it?" Ask them what tastes they prefer.

As your child gets a bit older, you can make tasting plates together, creating multicolored, multitextured patterns of different foods on a plate. You might have three or four carrot sticks, two or three cheese cubes, some apple slices, a few grapes, a small pile of nuts, a couple of broccoli florets, a little mound of hummus in the center, and a few crackers. Even young children enjoy creating their own food art, participating in the selection, design, and demolition (by eating) of their plate.

As with smells and touch and sound, you can play a blind-folded guessing game with tastes. With the child's eyes covered (or yours—you'll be taking turns with this), put into their mouth (or yours) a small bite of something you know they like (or at least don't hate). Ask them to describe it, using words such as salty, sweet, tart, sour, bitter, fruity. Then ask them to identify what it is. You might include honey, raisins, apple slices, nuts, juice, breakfast cereal, or anything else that isn't too spicy or strong for their taste buds.

Just like the other senses, some children have exceptionally sensitive taste buds, and it's just as important as with the other senses to respect your child's sensitivity. You don't want to create an eating problem, so keep calm and positive during mealtimes and avoid making an issue about what your child eats. You want your child to enjoy the sense of taste as much as the other senses.

CHILDHOOD: 6 TO 10

One of the most harmful misconceptions about brain development is that the brain is built in the first 3 years of life and that, after that, parents and others don't have an impact on a child's intelligence. Yes, the first 3 years are critical, but the brain continues to develop and change during childhood.

The peak number of neural synapses (connections between brain cells) is reached at about age 11[8] and then reduced by approximately

40% over the next several years until achieving adult values later in adolescence. The periods of overproduction and pruning vary by area of the brain and are influenced greatly by your child's experience. Synapses in the visual cortex (affecting sight and visual perception) reach adult numbers by the time your child is 5 or 6, whereas synapses in the frontal cortex (which is responsible for complex functions such as planning, judgment, and attention regulation) don't reach adult numbers until early adulthood.

During childhood, the brain is not changing as quickly or dramatically as during early childhood or the early teen years. It is an extremely important time in your child's brain development, nonetheless. This is a time for exploring diverse interests, acquiring solid foundations of knowledge, and consolidating learning. It's optimally a time when your child is not only gaining competence in many areas but also learning about assessing their priorities, managing their time, and establishing other habits that will be valuable as they go forward at school and, later, at work.

During childhood, sleep, exercise, and nutrition continue to be important, both for physical and neurological health, including affecting the volume of gray matter being formed in your child's brain. Gray matter is rich with neurons and affects muscle control (including speech), sensory perception (e.g., seeing, hearing, tasting), memory, emotions, decision making, and self-regulation. It's developing through the childhood years and into adolescence, so you're right to tell your child they need to get more sleep (or better nutrition or more exercise) if they want to protect and strengthen their intelligence and other cognitive functions.

Between the ages of 6 and 10, in addition to encouraging healthy habits, support your child in discovering their interests and exploring them. Look for opportunities that allow them to gain skills and knowledge in domains of life that they find meaningful, whether that's academics, social and emotional intelligence, athletics, the arts, or something else entirely—carpentry, video game design, or bees and other pollinators. This is not only important for their brain's development but it's also an important resiliency factor as they take on the challenges they'll encounter when they enter puberty.

ADOLESCENCE: 11 TO 18

It's sort of unfair to expect teens to have adult levels of organizational skills or decision making before their brains are finished being built.[9]

—Jay Giedd

The teen brain can be perplexing to a parent. One day, your teenager seems like a perfectly reasonable human being: kind, thoughtful, funny, and intelligent, a person you enjoy being with, who surprises you sometimes with the extent of their knowledge or the depth of their wisdom. But then, perhaps later the same day, they've transformed into a dangerously angry risk-taker with no insight or self-restraint. The challenging times may look to you like stubbornly intentional defiance, but as with your toddler, your teen's brain is undergoing massive changes that are out of their control. One of the most important changes is happening in the prefrontal cortex, the brain's center of self-awareness, decision making, and conflict management, which is not fully mature until a person reaches their mid- to late-20s.

What can you do about this? Start by realizing that your child or teen can't behave like an adult—they don't have the neural equipment—but that you can make a difference in what happens going forward. You can learn to relax and be patient while you nurture your child's growth and your own. Neuroscientist Frances Jensen wrote, "It's important to remember that even though their brains are learning at peak efficiency, much else is inefficient, including attention, self-discipline, task completion, and emotions."[10]

Emerging brain research findings are offering new explanations for why teens can be so unpredictable, moody, and disorganized; why they sometimes make such tragically short-sighted decisions; and why many of the most serious mental illnesses emerge in adolescence. In *The Teenage Brain: A Neuroscientist's Survival Guide to Raising Adolescents and Young Adults,* Jensen stated that the teen years are critical to an individual's brain development, as volatile and crucial as early childhood: "That seven years in their life [the teen years] is . . . as important as their first seven years of life."[11]

Adolescence is a time for massive experience-based pruning of brain cells and developing new synapses, creating a heightened "use it or lose it" situation during the teen years. Neural systems and pathways that were developed in childhood that are then used in adolescence form new connections and strengthen, while those that are not used die or diminish. So, if your child is hanging out with buddies and lazing around the house, those are the brain connections that will be strengthened; if your teen is investing energy in athletics, mathematics, or art, those are the neurons and synapses that will survive.

Because their brains are still developing, teenagers can be vulnerable to stress and stress-related disorders, such as anxiety and depression. Mindfulness practices can be especially important at this stage to help your adolescent calm themselves and regain a healthy perspective.[12]

The neural volatility of this period makes teens susceptible to addiction, potentially fatal risk taking, and problems with impulse control, conflict resolution, and decision making. When chronic stress is added to the mix, whether resulting from family violence, a dangerous neighborhood, poverty, abuse, bullying, or something else, the teen is at risk of serious mood disorders and learning problems, as well as risky behaviors.[13]

For healthy brain development during adolescence, your teen continues to need your active involvement in their life. They need support, latitude, and stimulation to continue to explore, learn, and master areas of interest. They also need your love, guidance, and boundaries so they don't go too perilously off the rails.

YOUNG ADULTHOOD: 19 TO 24

Many parents don't realize that their child's brain is still developing well into their 20s. As a result of this ongoing development, most experts now define adolescence as lasting until the age of 25.[14] One important aspect of decision making in late adolescence is the powerful influence of the social context in which a young adult finds themself: "As compared with adults, adolescents are particularly sensitive to external social stimuli, easily aroused emotionally, and less able to regulate strong emotions."[15]

"Failure to launch" or "Peter Pan syndrome" are names given to describe young adults who aren't supporting themselves and living independently by their mid-20s. The reasons for failing to commit to a career and/or a relationship are many and complex and vary from person to person, but one of the more common reasons is a problem with *pathological perfectionism*,[16] where no job is good enough or just right, nobody understands your capabilities, no boss gives you a chance, or there's no training or graduate program that interests you. This can result from many things, including being told during childhood that you're capable of anything but never learning to overcome obstacles or cope well with failure—in short, having a fixed mindset (which I discuss in Chapter 2). A different but allied reason for failing to launch is choosing security and safety over the decisions and risks of adulthood. Some Peter Pans retreat to their parents' basement to play video games because they perceive the real world to be annoyingly difficult, even dangerous, for them.

Regardless of the reasons for a failure to launch, it's worrying when it happens and underlines both the vulnerability of early adulthood and the ongoing role that parents can play in their young adult's life. It emphasizes the importance of giving your child opportunities to make decisions (even bad ones) and learn how to handle setbacks when they're younger, but early adulthood isn't too late to acquire new habits. In fact, while the brain is still developing, late adolescence is a good time to provide the social support your adult child needs to develop a growth mindset. They're susceptible during this window of opportunity to social influences. If you think you might have a Peter Pan situation, you may need professional help, but it's not time to give up.

Just as it's unfair to expect younger children to behave like adults, recent findings on the brain's continuing development well into a person's 20s suggest that parents should continue to be available for support and guidance for their young adult kids. As is true when they're younger, it can make the difference between a positive outcome and a harmful change in the course of your child's life. They still need you, whether they're hanging out at home or have left home and are trying to go it alone. Whether or not your adult child appears to be completely self-sufficient, they can benefit from your loving care, attention, and availability.

HOW TO SUPPORT YOUR CHILD'S OPTIMAL BRAIN DEVELOPMENT

Neuroscientist Jay Giedd told PBS's *Frontline*

> The more technical and more advanced the science becomes, often the more it leads us back to some very basic tenets. . . . With all the science and with all the advances, the best advice we can give is what our grandmother could have told us generations ago: to spend loving, quality time with our children.[17]

Similarly, Ellen Galinsky, a renowned social scientist, observed, "Even though the public perception is about building bigger and better brains, what the research shows is that it's the relationships, it's the connections, it's the people in children's lives who make the biggest difference."[18]

In *Beyond Behaviors: Using Brain Science and Compassion to Understand and Solve Children's Problem Behaviors*,[19] Mona Delahooke wrote about the relationships that Jay Giedd and Ellen Galinsky emphasized, drawing connections between those relationships, children's developing brains, and their behavior. Sharing case histories from her work with children considered challenging, Delahooke described how misbehavior is a child's unconscious way of adapting to the environment they're experiencing and provides a window of understanding into their internal realities. Many adults are blind to the opportunities that misbehavior provides, often because of the adult's own anxiety.

Delahooke observed that all behavior, whether bad or good, is an attempt to adapt to our environment or to get the environment to change in our favor. A parent can respond most effectively to a child only when they consider what might be motivating the child's misbehavior. With the caveat that each of us is unique and that what works well for many children won't work at all with other children, she identified some basic principles to think about when you're trying to understand what's going on with your child. Knowing what underlies your child's behavior can help you turn things around if you find yourself parenting a challenging child and can also help you stay on course if things are going well.

To illustrate Delahooke's recommendations, I'm going to go back to two families I introduced in Chapter 1. The mothers in those families were Elizabeth and Sara. They were friends who had children at about the same time, and in each case, their child was quite spirited, a challenging baby who was hard to soothe, who grew into a demanding child with strong reactions to pretty well everything. I'm using these cases because they provide dramatic illustrations of the principles under discussion, but that doesn't mean these ideas apply only to parents dealing with spirited kids. They work for every parent and every child.

Make Sure Your Child Feels Safe

A child who is confident they're valued and that someone is looking out for them is more likely to feel calm and to be engaged in learning and growing. All children need to feel loved and connected to thrive, but some kids feel threatened even when they're objectively safe. If you have a child who frequently misbehaves, provide as much reassurance as you can, showing them they're safe and secure in your love. If you observe your child being more challenging than usual, think about what might be going on with them, but also think about yourself. Are you feeling less energetic, more irritable, less loving than usual? That's enough to make a child feel less secure and use bad behavior to get your reassurance that you still love them.

Right from conception, chronic stress damages a child's brain functioning. Ongoing stress can lead to lifelong problems in learning, behavior, and physical and mental health. This is true whether the stress is caused by poverty, abuse, maternal depression, or other environmental factors. Positive stress (moderate, short-lived physiological responses to uncomfortable experiences) is an essential component of healthy development and resilience, but chronic stress is toxic to your child's developing brain.

Mona Delahooke integrated findings from neuroscience into her clinical experience and concluded that misbehavior is often an unconscious response to stress: "When we see behavior that is problematic or confusing, the first question we should ask is NOT 'How do we get rid of this behavior?' but rather 'What is this telling us about the child?'"[20]

In the early years, this was one of the biggest differences between Sara's and Elizabeth's parenting styles. Elizabeth saw little Ezra's crying fits and refusals to sleep, try new foods, or be strapped into his car seat as a challenge to her parenting skills and worked hard to impose her will and change his behavior. She went into parenting thinking—as so many new parents do—that it was her job to shape her child's behavior in a certain direction. Sara, however, read little Suzy's crying spells and refusals to comply as indications that Suzy was worried about something and needed comforting and soothing. She responded with reassurance to Suzy's insecurities, anger, and noncompliance and, over time, established a solid connection that helped Suzy settle down into more compliant behavior.

So, when your child misbehaves, don't move directly to correct the behavior. Instead, ask yourself why your child doesn't feel safe. When you learn to welcome your child's misbehavior as a window into their inner world—instead of resisting that behavior and trying to change it—change becomes possible.

Your Child Is Unique, and So Are You

Each of us is unique, both in our genetic makeup and our environmental experiences. Over time—minute by minute, day by day—the countless interactions between our genes and environment create a complex and particular brain. That's as true for you as it is for your child. A book like this can help you think about what's happening, based on research on the brain and child development, but when you're trying to solve a problem, you have to find what works for you and your child, understanding that that will be different than what works for other families in other situations.

From the vantage point of objectivity and knowledge, it's easy to look at Elizabeth's response to Ezra's behavior and judge it as damaging to her child or, at least, as unsuccessful. But that would be unfair. Elizabeth came to parenting from her unique combination of personality, temperament, and life experience. Happily, she recognized before too long that she needed help, and she got it, which allowed her to find a better way forward with Ezra, but it's important to respect that each person—whether it's you or someone else— has to find their own unique way with parenting, as with everything else. Not only is it okay to get it wrong, but also being comfortable with getting it wrong can help you figure out the best way to move forward and do things a bit better. I don't know any parents—myself included—who didn't get parenting wrong in one way or another.

Look at Misbehavior as a Clue, Not as a Disorder

Rather than looking for a label—attention disordered, behaviorally disturbed, or something else—try to identify the problems underlying your child's troubling behavior. Ask what your child's inner experience might be that leads to the misbehavior, not what label best applies. I'm not saying you should avoid diagnostic labels altogether—they can sometimes be useful in getting a child the services they need—but it's good to know that labels can also carry complications that erode a child's self-concept and confidence. (I address labels more fully in Chapter 6.)

Elizabeth saw Ezra's misbehavior as his problem. She thought it was his behavior that was getting in the way of family harmony. Sara, however, worked hard to understand and address what was motivating Suzy's misbehavior. It may sound like a subtle difference, but focusing on misbehavior as a clue and not as a problem makes all the difference in what happens next.

Is Your Child's Misbehavior Top Down or Bottom Up?

Mona Delahooke distinguished between behavior that is rooted in the senses and in unmet needs (which she called "bottom-up" behavior) and behavior that has a conscious component ("top-down" behavior). Rational approaches such as logical consequences can help if you're dealing with top-down behavior, but bottom-up behavior needs a different response entirely. Logical consequences assume a level of self-awareness and self-regulation that a young or difficult child doesn't have, and logical consequences don't touch bottom-up causes of misbehavior. Because stress derails your child's capacity to reason, always start by ensuring your child feels safe.

With young children, misbehavior is always a bottom-up problem—maybe the child needs soothing, perhaps they need food or sleep, or they might need to be protected from stimuli they find threatening (e.g., too noisy, too bright, too smelly). Sara responded to Suzy's problems by considering these bottom-up causes, whereas Elizabeth tried too early to use top-down instructions and explanations with Ezra ("Stop doing that! You'll break it!" "No snacks now; it's almost lunchtime" "You need to get into your car seat. It's not safe otherwise").

Take Good Care of Yourself

Your child is exquisitely attuned to your feelings and moods. The more sensitive they are, the less safe they feel when you are anxious, impatient, or irritable. To be effective in helping your child manage their emotions better, start by paying close attention to your own moods. It may be that your calming, kind, and attentive presence is enough to make the difference.

This was another difference in the early parenting experiences of Elizabeth and Sara. Both moms are intelligent women with many interests and not a lot of natural patience. Elizabeth didn't notice how Ezra was picking up on and echoing back her impatience and irritability, whereas Sara realized she had to find ways to take sufficient care of her own needs that she didn't impose her moods on Suzy.

It's not always easy—and in some situations, it feels impossible—but if you want things to go as well as possible for your child, it's extremely important to take good care of yourself.

TAKING IT INTO THE COMMUNITY: PARENTING CENTERS

Most parents don't have the benefit of much of the information in a book like this. They don't know how to handle tricky situations with their kids and don't realize that help is available as they try to muddle through. Having easy access to knowledge and support can be a game changer for a parent and, multiplied many times over, for a community.

One of the best investments a community can make is in a parenting center (also known sometimes as a family resource center), where parents can connect with other parents and are given the information and support they need to enjoy parenting and feel they're succeeding at it. When a parent realizes they're not alone and understands the important role their relationship with their child plays in their child's development, including in their child's brain development, as well as their body, mind, and social and emotional strengths, and they're helped to put those understandings into practice, everyone benefits: the parent, the child, and the whole community.

Sometimes parenting centers are located in hospitals, such as the Mount Sinai Kravis Children's Hospital in New York City. This center "aims to transform the way pediatric healthcare is delivered by maximizing opportunities to promote strong parent-child relationships and early child development within everyday healthcare interactions."[21]

Sometimes parenting centers are located in community centers, such as the EarlyON centers in rural Simcoe County, Ontario.[22] These centers attempt to create an environment for children, families, and caregivers to grow and learn. Google reviews of these centers include: "Highly recommended for any new parent or family newly located to the area. Helpful staff and a warm, friendly, and caring atmosphere"; "Lots of toys and activities for the kids. They encourage parents to spend active time with their kids, rather than the kids playing alone"; "I honestly love this place and she fosters the most friendly environment"; and "These guys are the BEST! Great support for new moms, and those who've been at it for a while. Love the registered programs, holiday parties, information, lending library for toys and books, and drop-in play time."

Other times, parenting centers are located in schools, colleges, and universities. They vary, of course, and each parenting center is unique, reflecting the community and the people who established it and are running it. Some of the common themes across most centers are an emphasis on parents connecting with their children and other parents; resources to help parents navigate daily life, as well as troubling situations; books and toys available in a drop-in center or lending library; and referrals for professional support, as necessary. Ideally, a parenting center provides a place where parents feel welcome; where they can get together and offer and receive peer support, as well as getting professional support and referrals as needed; where they can take their children for activities such as reading circles and play experiences.

There's an extensive body of research showing the importance of society taking seriously the needs of all children and the benefits to communities that do that. One of the oldest and still best examples comes from the Abecedarian Project of the 1970s. Craig Ramey and his colleagues demonstrated long-term cognitive gains for disadvantaged children who were provided with good nutrition and welcoming preschools, as well as parenting support, such as that provided in parenting centers.[23] The parents were helped to implement the evidence-based recommendations discussed in this book: the importance of listening and talking to your baby, the need for patience and loving attunement to your growing child, the value of reading and other forms of intellectual stimulation, and more.

The Abecedarian Project and other similar investigations have shown that for every dollar spent on parenting centers and high-quality early childhood education for high-needs kids, the community saves at least five dollars over the next 20 years. Over time, the children are less likely to experience behavioral and psychological problems, less likely to get involved with the criminal justice system, less likely to get pregnant as teenagers, more likely to complete high school, more likely to go on to postsecondary education, and more likely to become taxpayers. These are all good reasons to support parenting centers in your community.

There are many ways you can support a family resource or parenting center. If you have one locally, you can make use of the center, taking your own children or grandchildren there or other kids in your life. You can spend time there as a volunteer or a parenting mentor. You can donate money or items they're looking for. Toys, books, and children's clothing are always welcome, whether new or used, in good condition. You might want to host a diaper drive through the National Diaper Bank Network[24] or get involved in advocating for better funding or establishing a new center in a community that could benefit from that. Depending on your skills and interests and the available facilities, you might get involved in other ways, tutoring kids who need or want it, conducting after-school reading circles, leading sing-alongs, providing cooking classes for parents or kids, or teaching gymnastics.

KEY TAKEAWAYS FOR HEALTHY BRAIN BUILDING

- **Talk to your child and listen.** The more you mirror the sounds your baby makes, talk to your child from birth on, and listen to them, the better their language development, which is the foundation for so much more exploration and brain building.

- **Support healthy habits of sleep, nutrition, and exercise.** It is as important to your child's developing brain as it is to their developing body that they eat nutritious food and get enough outdoor exercise and sleep.
- **Remember that everything develops.** The biggest gift of neural plasticity is the possibility of learning in every domain and across the lifespan. If your child has learning or behavioral problems, they can be helped—over time, with motivation and the right kinds of support (including professional help, as needed)—to overcome those problems. Provide meaningful learning experiences in a context of warm support, and look for other resources that might be helpful.
- **Stimulate your own brain, too.** Neural plasticity applies across the lifespan. Unless there's serious brain disease or degeneration, even seniors can learn to play a musical instrument, speak another language, or write a book. You're a better role model for your child's healthiest brain development when you're learning and fulfilled in your own life.

CHAPTER 6

DON'T STOP LEARNING: YOU CAN KEEP GETTING SMARTER

It is not that I'm so smart. But I stay with the questions much longer.

—Albert Einstein

A child doesn't achieve adulthood (other than perhaps in the legal sense) the minute they turn 18 or even when they hit 25. As we discussed in Chapter 5, the brain is still maturing during that period from 18 to 25. Even after 25, your child's brain and cognitive abilities are still developing. Wisdom will take longer if they ever get there, developing with experience over time.

By the same token, no one would say that becoming a parent completes our journey to adulthood. In fact, many of us still struggle with what our friends on social media might call "adulting." Putting off making appointments, forgetting to do the laundry, shunning the evening cleanup to binge-watch a favorite show—we all do it sometimes because being an adult is hard. Adulthood does not mean that we know everything or that we've reached the pinnacle of our intelligence. So why do we feel uncomfortable or less than when we don't know the answers to the questions our children ask? And why do we sometimes feel impatient with our children when they struggle in school? Why do we worry when their intelligence seems well developed in one area and woefully lacking in another?

People used to believe that babies were born gifted, average, or intellectually slow, just like they were born to have blue eyes or brown. This perspective has changed dramatically over the past

30 years. Research in psychology, education, and the neurosciences has informed a growing awareness that intelligence develops, just like wisdom and other skills and abilities. It turns out that intelligence is not a gift of genetics but rather the result of complex and interacting developmental processes in which a baby, child, or adult actively engages with ideas, environments, people, and circumstances. Albert Einstein was prescient in his understanding of intelligence, as he was about so many other things, when he insisted that his knowledge and discoveries were the result of hard work and persistence rather than innate ability.

People vary in their genetic predispositions—some are more readily drawn to mathematics and some to the natural world, for example—but nobody is born with a higher level of developed intelligence than others. As with strength and fitness, babies, children, teens, and adults are active participants in learning processes that are more complicated than but not as mysterious as often imagined.

Sometimes when a parent learns about the role of stimulation in intelligence building, they go overboard in providing their child with all the stimulation the child can handle. One of the messages I hope you come away with here is that—whether or not you think a high IQ score matters—the loving, listening, playful time you spend together is by far the most important encouragement you can give your child. For most parents, the message they need to be their imperfect good-enough best is to relax and enjoy your child. Focus on building your relationship with them, and the rest will follow.

That intelligence develops over time—under the right circumstances and given sufficient motivation—and that it is not stable over time are among the many emerging facts that counter prevailing misconceptions about intelligence. Here's a true/false quiz that addresses some of the other misconceptions. The answers are in the endnotes.[1]

> ## Quiz: How Does Intelligence Work?
>
> 1. There's nothing you can do to raise your intelligence, and the same is true for your child. T/F
> 2. A person's physical health has nothing to do with their intelligence. T/F
> 3. If you're socially engaged and active, that increases your intelligence. T/F
> 4. A child with a high IQ is exceptionally capable in all academic subject areas. T/F
> 5. White and Asian people are naturally smarter than those from other races. T/F
> 6. Most highly intelligent people don't have good common sense. T/F
> 7. Exceptionally high intelligence usually goes along with social and emotional problems. T/F
> 8. Kids who are unusually smart do fine on their own; they don't need special educational accommodations. T/F
> 9. High intelligence means you learn things quickly. T/F
> 10. If a child learns to read before the age of 5, they're gifted. T/F

CONTROVERSIES AND MISCONCEPTIONS

Intelligence is a highly controversial topic. In 1995, the American Psychological Association (APA) convened a task force to consider the nature of intelligence.[2] This was in the wake of a controversy that resulted from the publication of *The Bell Curve: Intelligence and Class Structure in American Life*,[3] in which the authors made much of differences by race and social class on certain intelligence tests.

The APA task force experts could not agree on a definition of intelligence and, in fact, were not even close to a consensus. They did agree, however, on three important dimensions of intelligence: There are individual differences in how people interact with the environment, IQ test scores are not stable (i.e., they change over time), and assessment results and test scores vary depending on the criteria used.

My clinical work with children has provided many illustrations of each of these principles. To begin with, context and environment make an enormous difference in how a child approaches the testing process. Think about which of these kids will do well enough on an individually administered IQ test that the score might provide a reliable estimate of the child's ability:

- Milli loves puzzles and games and is enthusiastic about sitting for an hour or two with a strange adult who's giving her quizzes and puzzles to solve.
- Boris gets anxious when he has to talk to someone not in his family.
- Jonni doesn't see the point of working hard on games and puzzles that have nothing to do with school or anything else in her life.
- Boz hates to be wrong, so he answers questions only when he's 100% certain he's right.
- Robin loves solving puzzles but feels sick on the day of the test and proceeds anyway because the appointment was set a long time ago, and she doesn't want to inconvenience anyone.
- Samara didn't have breakfast the morning of the test—mornings are always hectic in her family, and sometimes there isn't time for breakfast.
- Banjara's parents are in the middle of a divorce, and he doesn't care about answering some stupid questions.

Clearly, Milli's test score is going to be a much better indication of what she's able to do (which is what IQ is supposed to measure) than any of the other kids' scores. I've outlined all these possibilities—and there are countless others—to illustrate the fact that there are individual differences in how people interact with the environment, as the APA task force report concluded. It, therefore, doesn't make sense to put too much emphasis on a single test score unless it is very high, in which case you know the child is exceptionally capable at doing whatever the test measures (which is not the same thing as whatever the test designers say it measures) and that the child is a good test-taker.

The second and third points on which the APA task force members agreed were that differences are not stable (i.e., IQ changes over time) and that test scores vary depending on which measures are being used. These were relatively new perspectives at the time, but they have both been borne out robustly in the decades since then.

Frances Degen Horowitz and Rena Subotnik are widely respected developmental psychologists and leaders in the fields of gifted education and talent development. I worked with them on a project at the Graduate Center of the City University of New York (CUNY) that resulted in a conference with experts who offered different perspectives on intelligence. Emerging out of that conference was a volume edited by the three of us (Horowitz, Subotnik, and me) called *The Development of Giftedness and Talent Across the Life Span.*[4]

Carol Dweck, the psychologist whose work on mindsets I discussed in Chapter 2, wrote the foreword to the book. She opened with

> This volume . . . represents a tremendous advance over past perspectives that simply categorized people as gifted or not gifted, that (erroneously) portrayed giftedness as a stable characteristic, and that sought more to measure giftedness and talent than to develop it. This volume, in stark contrast, recognizes that talent is often very specific, that it can wax and wane over time, and that one of the most exciting questions facing researchers today is how to encourage and sustain talent—across cultures and across the life span.[5]

The more we know about child development and the brain, the more we realize that intelligence develops in unique ways, in dynamic interaction with a child's social and emotional experiences and learning opportunities, as well as other environmental factors.

Frank Worrell is a renowned developmental psychologist who participated in the conference at CUNY Graduate Center. He took on the topic of differences by race and socioeconomic status in children's participation in gifted programming.[6] He described the systemic racism that leads to discrepancies in teacher expectations and children's academic achievement and argued for educational programming that supports and nurtures the development of giftedness and talent much more broadly across the population. Highly controversial at the time, this perspective has steadily gained ground to the point that it is a mainstream attitude among many involved in gifted education today.[7]

Not long ago, most people thought of intelligence as fixed and static. You could test a young child's intelligence and get an IQ score that was considered reliable across their lifetime. As more is known about the brain, however, and as intelligence is increasingly studied longitudinally across decades of people's lives, the more that neuropsychologists, developmental psychologists, and cognitive scientists emphasize that intelligence is dynamic, changing over time, depending on what's going on in a person's life. Is the person staying mentally active and alert? Are they staying healthy? Do they have a strong network of social support? It contradicts many people's "common sense" (or misconceptions), but all of these are important factors in a person's intelligence.

In two books I've written with Joanne Foster—*Being Smart About Gifted Learning*[8] and *Beyond Intelligence*[9]—we discussed the development of intelligence in some detail. We emphasized practical recommendations that help parents support the development of their children's abilities, from birth to young adulthood. We emphasized the key points mentioned here, including that intelligence reflects an individual's dynamic interactions with others and the environment.

Our bottom line is that the nature of a child's intelligence changes with opportunities to learn, and parents have a role to play in that process—especially in the relationship they form with their child—as I discuss through the rest of this chapter.

WHAT DO IQ TESTS MEASURE?

Countless tests describe themselves as tests of intelligence, from 20-minute quizzes you can take online to pencil-and-paper tests a teacher hands out to an entire class of students to highly reliable tests that a psychologist administers orally one-on-one as a series of quizzes and puzzles. Some tests focus on visual–spatial problem solving, others rely on memory or general knowledge, and still others attempt to assess a deeper level of comprehension. The scores generated on these different tests reflect distinctly different intellectual strengths. They don't all measure the same thing, although they all provide something they call an IQ, or intelligence test score.

No matter how good the test, an intelligence test score is not a good measure of how well a person does on real-world tasks. IQ can't take into account how well a child adapts to change, how well they learn from experience, whether they'll persist when faced with obstacles, or whether they'll invest the effort needed over time that's required for meaningful success, the persistence Einstein was talking about when he said, "It is not that I'm so smart. But I stay with the questions much longer."

When a child gets an unusually high IQ score, it confirms that they should be considered for special educational programming, but it doesn't provide any information about which subjects a child might need to be taught at a higher level or how advanced that programming should be. In combination with other assessment results, intelligence tests can help pinpoint where a child might be having trouble learning at a particular point or that they might be exceptionally advanced, but these tests shouldn't be used to permanently label abilities or problems such as giftedness or learning disabilities.

ABILITIES DEVELOP

A developmental perspective on giftedness results in two important objectives. The first is to understand the exceptional learning needs of children who are academically advanced relative to their same-age peers. These kids need learning challenges that match their ability so they can keep learning and growing. A fourth-grader who's ready for eighth-grade challenges in reading and English composition shouldn't have to do fourth-grade language work. A child who's in Grade 3 but ready for Grade 10 mathematical instruction shouldn't be expected to complete Grade 3 arithmetic homework (just as a kid who's working at the Grade 3 level shouldn't be asked to do Grade 10 work). These advanced-level kids don't need a more creative or enriched curriculum or more field trips—all things that all children benefit from—but they do need learning opportunities that are better targeted to their abilities and interests.

The second important objective is to take what we are learning about gifted development and make that information widely available to parents and educators so they can support a high level of intellectual development in all children, as recommended by Frank Worrell and many others. That means looking for each child's strengths and doing our best to give each child the challenges they need to keep learning and growing, so their unique form of giftedness gets the best possible chance to develop.

I am happy to report that educators are increasingly realizing that intelligence is dynamic, that it develops over time with motivation and opportunities to learn. More schools are providing a range of options to meet individual students' diverse kinds of advanced learning needs. They are also increasingly attentive to Frank Worrell's recommendation that giftedness be actively looked for and nurtured in all children across all sectors of the population.

The range of diversity-inclusive learning options is as wide as an educator's imagination, from high-quality universal prekindergarten to tailored single-subject acceleration (so a kid who's amazing in one subject area but not others gets to study at the appropriate level in their area of interest and ability but stays in their regular class otherwise); to summer courses such as the Academic Talent Development Program at UC Berkeley (where Frank Worrell is faculty director), which prizes motivation over conventional criteria like IQ; to mentorships with members of the community who share an interest with a given child; to online courses in areas of a child's interest, such as animation or electricity.[10] The objective of providing a range of learning options is to support children's learning in their areas of interest and strength, no matter what those interests are and where they're starting out in their knowledge, ability, and preferred mode of learning.

Joe Renzulli and Sally Reis have been sharing their ideas about providing wide-ranging interest-based schoolwide enrichment for decades now and have helped thousands of schools around the world diversify their approach to gifted education through their enrichment triad model.[11,12] Joanne Foster and I covered a wide range of possible options in *Being Smart About Gifted Learning*.[13]

THE EARLY YEARS: BIRTH TO 5

Healthy young children are curious and enjoy the learning process. If your baby or young child is interested in books, songs, artwork, building blocks, or something else, try to support their interest by way of age-appropriate tools, experiences, and materials, as well as encouragement, to learn what they want to learn.

Case Study: Theo

Theo was about 7 months old. It was naptime, so his father made sure Theo was dry and fed, read him some stories, sang him some lullabies, and put him into his crib. That day, Theo didn't complain about being left alone, as he usually did. In fact, he seemed uncharacteristically happy when his dad left the room. Once downstairs, his father—Noah—was surprised to hear thumping noises from above. Noah turned on the intercom viewing screen and saw a determined baby pulling himself up to standing and then dragging himself one step at a time the length of the crib, holding onto the guard rail. Every few steps, Theo would falter and tumble hard onto the mattress, which accounted for the thumping sounds. He'd pull himself up and repeat. He did this doggedly for the next 30 minutes before finally falling into a deep, long sleep.

Theo spent the next few weeks looking for opportunities to practice walking. He resisted sitting in his stroller and preferred that someone hold his two chubby raised hands, walking along behind him. By the time he was 9 months old, he was walking sturdily, and by the time he was 1, he was running.

Theo was an early walker—for most babies, this learning process happens closer to the 1-year mark—but his skill development process wasn't exceptional. In addition to physical strength, learning to walk takes enormous motivation, perseverance, and patience. It takes a solid belief on the part of the child and the adults around him that walking is possible and that, with lots of tumbles and scrapes along the way, it will happen.

Most parents understand that learning to walk takes time and effort and involves innumerable setbacks. They know their baby can and must master this skill and are justifiably proud when the first independent step finally happens. One of the themes of this book is that every skill worth having—from sitting up to talking to emotion regulation—is like walking: It develops one step at a time, with patience, intention, support, and many, many stumbles along the way. It is also dependent on the child's sense of agency. Babies decide for themselves when they want to work on walking and everything else. You can support them best by loving them and encouraging them in their curiosities and interests, not by deciding for them what they should be working on next. Once you accept that and see its application to pretty much everything, you are well on your way to providing everything your child needs for a healthy approach to learning.

Emphasize Play, Not Academic Learning

All the research I've seen and conducted on the development of children's intelligence and creativity has suggested that the best educational approach in early childhood, up to about age 7, should focus on play rather than academic learning.[14,15]

The mother of a child who was almost 3 asked me if she should worry about her daughter's academic skills. The mom said she was asking about this because "the teacher quizzed Sammi on letters, numbers, shapes, and colors and showed us the results. She didn't do very well. I think Sammi gave up at some point because I know she knows some of the letters she missed."

The mother didn't want her child to fall behind her peers. If there was a learning problem, she wanted to nip it in the bud. Some of the other parents had suggested she enroll Sammi in the extra classes their kids were in to get her up to speed.

"No!" I said. "Sammi isn't even 3 yet! Just as she's mastering personal hygiene, finding ways to safely explore her world, and learning to play nicely with others is not the time to introduce academic pressures."

In the early years, your child should be exploring and learning at their own pace, with an emphasis on their physical, social, and emotional development, not their academic mastery. The best long-term academic development happens when the child feels solidly secure in their family's love when the early years involve conversation, curiosity-driven exploration, imagination, relaxation, reflection, music, dance, and free play.

Read to Your Child

Reading to your child is a powerful brain builder. The growing evidence of the contribution of parents' reading to children's intellectual development is so compelling that the American Academy of Pediatrics (AAP) took action.[16,17] Now, when a parent visits a pediatrician, they get information about how important it is that they read to their child. Depending on the doctor and the neighborhood, they might also be given an age-appropriate, high-quality book. The AAP's policy advocates telling parents to "read together as a daily fun family activity" from infancy on.

One of the major reasons the AAP implemented this policy for their members was the research showing that parents were increasingly giving their kids screens for story time, not realizing there were so many other benefits associated with sitting down together with a book. When a parent reads a book to their child, they're spending close one-on-one time, showing the child they're interested in them as they tailor their comments and questions to the child's personality, mood, and imagination.

There are many benefits to reading to your young child, in addition to providing opportunities for bonding and relationship building. A book provides topics of conversation, even with a baby, and conversation stimulates their brain development. Reading a book can be a restful change of pace, a chance for some cozy quiet in the midst of stressful, busy lives. If you establish a regular reading time each day, it can be a reliable time for your child to have your focused attention. You're also inspiring a desire to read for themself and helping them develop important intellectual skills, including memory and attention. A reading session can be a happy change of pace for you, too, providing a bit of a rest in your busy day.

Intelligence Testing With Young Children

There are intelligence tests designed for young children, but in general, testing young kids makes sense only when there's a reason for concern. If you're worried that your child isn't grasping or retaining age-normal concepts effectively, or you wonder if the day care or primary school doesn't recognize your child's ability level, you might want to consider an assessment.

When interpreting test scores, you should know that before the age of 7, these scores are not statistically reliable.[18] Don't put much emphasis on them unless they're useful in finding appropriate interventions or allaying your concerns.

Case Study: Zachary

Many small children get bored by testing and would rather invent their own games than follow someone else's rules. I remember one delightful 5-year-old who came to my office for an assessment. His parents were concerned because his kindergarten teacher was complaining about behavior problems. The teacher said Zachary was talking in class, clowning around, and distracting the other kids with his antics. The parents knew him to be an intensely curious child who loved learning and was generally well-behaved. They hoped my assessment of him would show what was going wrong at school.

As part of the assessment, I gave Zachary an IQ test, which is a series of questions, puzzles, and games, delivered orally. On some of the subtests, he scored well into the gifted range (above the 98th percentile or 130+), but on others, he scored in the average range (within 15 points on either side of the 50th percentile, which is 100). Overall, his IQ score was in the high average range (125), but that didn't make sense to me. High average wasn't an accurate representation of the unusually lively and advanced intelligence I saw in my conversations with him. My observations suggested his score underestimated his ability by 20 IQ points or more.

So, after we'd finished, I went through some of the subtests on which Zachary hadn't done so well. He had fascinating explanations for what he'd done to spice things up for himself. One subtest, in particular, stayed with me: I had asked Zachary to put together a puzzle that showed a person's face. He put some of the puzzle pieces together quickly and correctly, but he put the other pieces into an odd and apparently random pattern, earning a low score. I wondered whether his visual–spatial perception was distorted. Or did he have an emotional problem that led him to misperceive human faces? Or did something else account for this anomaly?

When I asked him about the puzzle, he told me he'd put the face together the way Picasso would do it. He went on enthusiastically, talking about which of Picasso's pictures he liked best and comparing those with the work of Camille Pissarro, an artist of the same period he said he preferred to Picasso.

It was clear to me that what Zachary's teacher saw as misbehavior and disruptiveness signaled his need for more intellectual stimulation and learning opportunities. The teacher needed training and support that most teachers don't get and would also have benefited from reading Mona Delahooke's book on brain-based behaviors[19] or Chapter 5 in this book to understand that the best approach to misbehavior is to look for its cause rather than criticizing it and trying to change it.

I suggested to the parents that they look for extracurricular learning options and activities for Zachary that would engage his enthusiasm—maybe in art but also in science and anything else that interested him—so that he could feel fully engaged in some kind of learning process. I also suggested they share my report with the teacher, letting her know that Zachary had an exceptionally lively, creative, and well-developed intelligence, that he could be a classroom asset if she could find a way to channel that curiosity, energy, and intelligence.

I've told Zachary's story elsewhere, and I tell it again here because it's a memorable example for me of why test scores must be taken with a grain of salt. They're meaningful when they're high—they show the child is able to do what the test is measuring at a high level of achievement compared with others their age—but many factors get in the way of a true reading of a child's ability. There can be issues of maturity, temperament, mood, test-related experience, health, hunger, and so much more. These variables also affect test scores when assessing older kids, of course, but they make it impossible to give reliable estimates of young children's abilities.

CHILDHOOD: 6 TO 10

Play Is Still Essential, All Through Childhood

In Chapter 4, I talked about the importance of play in children's learning and brain building, as well as every other dimension of their lives, mentioning the fact that the AAP has recommended that doctors write prescriptions for play.[20] When playtime is sacrificed for school and homework, your child loses a lot more than they might gain in academic knowledge and skills.

Play strengthens your child's communication skills, working memory, creativity, attention span, self-regulation, and intellectual flexibility; reduces anxiety; and enhances coping skills and resilience. So, do your best to ensure your child has enough time for free, safe, unsupervised play in their day. Limit screen time and commuting time, as well as extracurricular activities.

Keep Reading to Your Child

Even after your child has become a good reader, try to make some time in your busy lives—maybe at bedtime—when you read to them. Reading to your child as they get older has many of the benefits it has in the early years: It can lead to interesting conversations about all manner of things; it supports the development of important cognitive skills, including concentration, memory, vocabulary, and language use; it engages their creative imagination as it expands their horizons; it deepens their empathy and tolerance for others; and it informs their ongoing journey of self-discovery. Take turns deciding what to read, including old favorites you remember as a child and books your child selects.

Reading to your child as they get older can provide opportunities for being close, something they still need but can get lost in the daily shuffle. So, get close and comfortable and enjoy a book together.

Welcome your child's questions and observations. Find the answers together if your child has a question, and celebrate their observations: "I hadn't thought of it like that!" Point out links to the real world of your child's and family's experiences, achievements, interests, and ideas. Look for books and other reading material that stretch their thinking, vocabulary, and life experience, books they might have trouble reading or understanding on their own. Read about people in situations they can relate to personally and also situations that are completely foreign to them, whether it's a multicultural family, an immigrant experience, a disability, a death in the family, the experience of prejudice or hardship, or something else, emphasizing the similarities, as well as discussing the differences with acceptance and empathy. Look for stories about people who prevail over adversity. Talk about why and how they've overcome their challenges and who the helpers have been. Help your child make connections to their own experiences and those of diverse others.

The best ways to encourage your child to enjoy reading as they get older are enjoying your own reading; making sure they have access to books they find interesting, whether that's through a library, a book exchange with friends or family, bookstores, or online purchases; and being patient. A love of reading—which can enrich them across their lifetime—grows with time.

Learning in the Elementary Years

While the focus in the years from 6 to 10 should be on play and social and emotional development, children do benefit from more structured learning as they go through these childhood years. Literacy is one of the most important skills; good readers have a head start in every area of learning, including academic achievement.

Once your child is ready to learn to read—usually by 7—how can you ensure their school is giving them what they need? You want your child to learn to make coherent sense of written material and find success in exploration, learning, and discovery across as many fields as possible. Some of the most common ways schools support kids' literacy have been proven not to work well, whereas others work much better.[21]

One of the frequently used but less effective ways to support children's literacy involves giving kids a list of words to define and use in a sentence. There's no obvious connection between this task and children's interests or anything else going on at home or at school, so it's not surprising that it feels more like an irrelevant chore than a productive learning experience. It's much better to engage children in reading for discussion, meaning, and interest. Let them read what interests them, and then discuss their reading with others.

Another ineffective literacy support is giving a prize for reading quantity. Some teachers create incentive programs, hoping to encourage their students to do more reading. It might be a publicly posted list of kids who read the most books or a candy bar to everyone who claims they've read a certain number of books. These programs not only don't work, but they also undermine kids' motivation to read. Something that does motivate children's reading is book clubs, where kids have time to discuss what they're reading with others who are reading the same book.

The weekly whole-class spelling quiz is another time-honored classic that doesn't work. For good spellers, it's a waste of time, poor spellers get a weekly reinforcement of their loser status, and average spellers don't remember the words for long. Instead, it's better to give children individually tailored assignments. Kids get the most out of reading assignments that match their interests and engage them in analysis, synthesis, and application of their reading to other contexts. This can easily be stepped up or down in response to an individual child's learning strengths and needs.

Good readers enjoy unstructured independent reading, but independent reading without structure, guidance, or support fosters neither reading mastery nor an interest in books. Instead, teachers can help children acquire strategies for choosing reading material and for reading more efficiently. Kids also benefit from constructive feedback and conversations about the books they're reading.

One last ineffective—even damaging—strategy is to cancel recess for kids who aren't reading well or completing their work. The kids who have trouble with literacy tasks are usually the ones who most need recess. All kids do better at reading, writing, and problem solving when they have lots of time for moving, playing, and stretching. It's way better to add outdoor playtime for kids having problems learning (and others) rather than taking it away.

Homework: The 10-Minute Rule and What to Do if There's Too Much

Your child's confidence, intelligence, creativity, and well-being depend on having lots of time for free play, so it's no surprise that many experts advise no more than 10 minutes of homework a day in the first grade, moving up 10 minutes a day per year, so children in Grade 2 have 20 minutes of homework a day, kids in Grade 3 get 30 minutes, and so forth. Before Grade 1, children shouldn't be asked to do homework; it's stressful enough just to last through a full day of kindergarten and/or day care.[22]

I have heard many emotional stories from parents who tell me that the 10-minute rule is not close to being followed at their child's school. They describe their family time as being eroded by homework demands, with their child showing signs of homework-related stress.

Malika, the mother of an 8-year-old, told me that her conscientious little boy, Jorge, was being asked to do way too much homework, to the point he was crying by bedtime every night, rarely having finished what he was supposed to do. Malika had no problem with the assignment of 10 minutes a day reading to one of his parents. "That's good for all kids," she said, "And Jorge and I both enjoy doing it." But she wondered about the additional 20 minutes of arithmetic problems every night, the demands of a project due the following week, and the requirement that he also complete three pages of reading comprehension questions nightly.

I agreed with Malika that that sounded way out of line for a third-grader, a young child who also needs plenty of fresh air, exercise, family time, relaxation, and sleep. I gave her some ideas for dealing with this troubling situation.

I suggested to Malika that she think about balance in Jorge's life and assess his homework demands in the context of the other demands on their time. Is Jorge spending too much time on screens and out-of-school activities? In this case, I think the homework demands are excessive, but in other cases I've seen, it's some of the other activities that should probably be curtailed.

I also suggested that she discuss the homework situation with other parents in Jorge's class and get a sense of how "normal" Jorge's experience is. Maybe he's more conscientious than other kids or slower in completing his work at school, or maybe the other kids are suffering just as much.

Another good suggestion anytime you have concerns about what's happening at school is to talk to the teacher. Maybe Jorge is bringing work home because he's not concentrating during school hours. Maybe he's holding himself to a higher standard than the teacher requires. You need the teacher's perspective before you can decide whether or not the homework allocation is a problem.

I told Malika that if she was satisfied that Jorge's understanding of the homework demands was valid and other parents agreed there was a problem, she could invite one or two of the other parents to go with her to talk to the teacher. They could use the meeting to listen and learn, an opportunity to find out the teacher's perspective. They could also let the teacher know their concerns calmly and respectfully. That might be all it takes to make the changes their children needed. Teachers often say they respect the expert opinion on the 10-minute rule and would love to follow it but are pressured by parents or the principal to give more homework than they want to.

When they hear from parents who want them to stick to the 10-minute rule, it helps them make the case to do that.

After the teacher visit, it was time to wait and see whether the teacher addressed their concerns. If Jorge's homework pressures were reduced to an acceptable level within a week or two, Malika would have succeeded as an advocate for her son.

However, if too-heavy assignments persisted, and Jorge was worried about completing them, Malika could discuss with him which assignments to do and which he could ignore. She could explain her concerns about too much homework (i.e., that she wants to make sure he grows up healthy and strong and that he has all the time he needs for playing, relaxing, and spending time with the family). She could also let him know she had spoken to the teacher about this and, if necessary, would sort out any problems if he doesn't get his homework done.

If Jorge continued to feel overwhelmed by homework demands, Malika could talk again with the parents who supported her initial advocacy efforts and see if she could find a few parents with whom she could go forward. From there, she'd be in a bigger advocacy situation, something I discuss in Chapter 10.

If Malika proceeds with care and respect—being careful she doesn't make things worse for Jorge at school—he will feel valued, secure, listened to, and supported. And that will stand him in good stead in the future.

I should also point out here that homework isn't inherently evil. Depending on the quality and quantity of it, homework can have important learning benefits, and some children thrive only when they have lots of time to do their work, as can happen when they take their schoolwork home. In other situations, however, as with Jorge, a heavy homework load can get in the way of essential childhood activities and interfere with health and well-being. Then it's time to think about what needs to change and what you and your child and your allies can do about it.

Learning Differences and Labels

Nobody is just gifted, learning disabled, or blind, just like nobody is just tall, red-haired, or anything else. Each person is a combination of many different attributes, strengths, and weaknesses, but when a child is labeled, many people—including the child—focus on the exceptionality and not the whole child.

Problems With Labels

An exceptionality label—an attention-deficit/hyperactivity disorder (ADHD) or learning disability diagnosis, giftedness, being hard of hearing—can be like the tail wagging the dog, becoming the dominant focus for parents, teachers, and the child themself. Other areas of life and learning can recede from attention, and any other exceptionalities or learning needs can be left unattended. Take Josh, for example. As a young child, he was insatiably curious and had an extraordinary capacity for retaining and making sense of most areas of science, but he had trouble learning to read and found writing impossible. He was labeled as learning disabled when he was 7 and, for the next 2 years, was given extra support and tutoring, using simple reading material that held no interest for him. He grew to hate everything to do with school and went from being an enthusiastic learner to a bored, unhappy child.

Another case where getting an exceptionality label masked other learning issues involved Mitzi, who had a zany originality. She was remarkably articulate and always on the go, moving from one interest to another. When she was 8, she was identified as gifted and put into a gifted program, where she couldn't keep up with the other kids. Her thoughts were scattered, and she found it impossible to sit down and write a whole sentence, much less a paragraph. After a year in that program, she was moved back to a regular class, which was a mixed blessing. She felt like a terrible failure, but it led to her having her attention problems diagnosed, which in turn led to her learning some coping techniques and beginning, after a year or two, to thrive again.

In both Josh's and Mitzi's cases, the exceptionality label was part of the problem because it masked the fact that the child's learning needs were more complex than the label suggested.

Another unfortunate consequence of giving a child a label is the built-in excuse it gives for not working hard or not doing well— "I can't do this. I'm learning disabled," "I don't have to do my homework. I'm gifted."

A child who is labeled often has to deal with misconceptions and prejudices: "If you're gifted, why can't you behave better," or "You're learning disabled, you'll never understand this." Sometimes it's a quieter kind of prejudice, as when a child with hearing problems is assumed to have cognitive deficits or a child on the autism spectrum is thought to be insensitive.

Finally, labels aren't always right. As I discussed earlier, there are many reasons other than actual problems that a child might be misidentified as having learning problems, including having a bad day on the day of testing, a difficult temperament, problems at home, or cultural attitudes that differ from the test designers'. Because assessment and identification processes are far from perfect and because each child is a complex whole person with many strengths, interests, and challenges, labels should always be taken lightly, used only as they make sense in the child's life.

BENEFITS OF LABELS

Although labels must be used carefully, they can have important benefits. When a child has exceptional learning needs, an appropriate label can help teachers adapt instruction to meet those needs. In many jurisdictions, the label is required to call in a special education expert to help design the best program for that child. A label can help parents gain access to resources and make connections that help them understand the situation, figure out how to proceed, and get the support they need.

A child who is different from others almost always notices that difference, and they can feel validated when their differentness is acknowledged. When the label is explained in growth mindset terms—"Everyone has strengths and challenges; this is an area of challenge for you, so let's figure out how to work around it or even make it into a strength"—it can help a child connect with their strengths as well as their challenges and help the child feel okay or even good about their difference from others.

A child with an exceptionality often feels lonely in their differentness and is happy to meet others with issues like their own. A label can help make the connection happen, sometimes through special educational programming and sometimes through parent or internet groups.

What Should You Do About Differences?

When it comes to learning differences, your attitude can change your child's experience dramatically. If you think your child may have some kind of exceptionality, start by recognizing your child's complexity. Your child has a range of attributes and abilities, both strengths and weaknesses. Don't overly focus on one to the neglect of others.

Once you've identified an area of possible difference, talk to your child's teacher. Most teachers aren't special education experts, but they do have a broader experience of children than most parents and are usually more objective. Be honest and direct with the teacher, letting them know what you've observed that makes you wonder about learning differences.

If you're still concerned about the situation after discussing it with your child's teacher, give serious consideration to what happens next. If you decide on an assessment, will you be able to manage any resulting label so it's more beneficial than problematic for your child? The best assessment questions are not about the label your child might be given but about your child's specific learning needs. So, if, after talking to the teacher and thinking about the implications of labeling, you want to proceed, request that the assessment address these questions: "What are my child's learning strengths and weaknesses?" and "What can I do to help my child learn?"

The best thing to tell your child about the assessment is something like this: "We want to make sure you're getting what you need at school to enjoy it and learn well, so we've called in a learning detective. Dr. Bock is going to ask you a bunch of questions and ask you to do some puzzles, and then she's going to help us figure out what's next." Keep the focus on getting information for creating a good educational match so you can fix something at school, not on finding something wrong with your child, something that needs to be fixed.

If an assessment supports your concerns and your child is given an exceptionality label, help your child understand the label in growth mindset terms. If it's a gifted label, you might say, "This means you find some kinds of learning easier than other kids do, and you need more challenging ideas and assignments in those areas." If it's a problem with attention, you might say, "ADHD means your brain is very active, and that's a wonderful thing. To help you enjoy doing your schoolwork, we need to find ways to help you control what you're focusing on." With a learning disability, you could say, "This means your learning process is sometimes different than other kids', and some things will be more difficult for you, but you might just have a creativity advantage." In all these cases, reassure your child you'll help them find some workarounds, but in the long run, the important results can be just as good or better.

No test, assessment process, or label can do justice to what your child is capable of over time, with the right supports in place. Regardless of the label, encourage your child's interests and abilities. Celebrate their achievements, small and large. If your child has a disability label of one kind or another, keep your primary focus on their strengths, and look for ways to use their strengths to motivate them to handle their problems. If, for example, you have a child with a reading problem who loves baseball, look for reading material about baseball—whether it's a graphic novel, a magazine, a book, or something else.

Finally, if your child is identified as having exceptional learning needs—whether giftedness or a problem with learning, attention, one of the senses, behavior, or something else—help them realize that the label denotes special learning needs at a given point, not innately and permanently superior or inferior ability. Remind them also, as often as necessary, that everyone has strengths and challenges and that it's great to discover your challenges early, as well as your interests and strengths, so you can get started working on them.

ADOLESCENCE: 11 TO 18

I talk in Chapter 5 about the important brain building that's happening through the years from 11 to 18. Adolescence is when the neural pathways that take your child into adulthood are being formed and strengthened. It's a time of vulnerability, volatility, and great possibility, particularly from 11 to 14. Your parenting role is a lot more important through these years than it might seem to be or your child may want it to be.

Depending on many complex interacting factors—family stressors and circumstances, your child's temperament and your own, the relationship you've built with your child in the years preceding adolescence, your network of social support—parenting an adolescent can also be a lot trickier than you expected.

In short, good-enough parents go easy on themselves as they navigate the unpredictable storms their teenager might create, doing their best to find a healthy balance between providing the support the young person needs to stay on course and the freedom they need for their growing independence. The importance of this balance applies to academic learning as to everything else: Support your young person in achieving academic success, but don't put that ahead of your relationship with them or their social, emotional, and psychological needs.

You may recall Suzy from Chapter 1 and then again in Chapter 5. She's Sara and Roy's daughter, a baby with a difficult temperament whose parents supported her in feeling secure in their love, a little girl who was mostly cheerful and cooperative by the time she went to kindergarten.

I met the family again when Suzy was 13. Sara had gone back to work when Suzy started school, and she and Roy had split up a year or so later. Roy had moved out of town and didn't provide any financial support. Sara enjoyed her work as a research assistant at the local university, but she didn't make a lot of money, and things were tight financially. She couldn't afford to take Suzy on the holidays some of her friends took or buy her the clothes and electronic devices she wanted. By the time Suzy was 11, she was openly resentful about what she didn't have that "everybody else" had.

It was Suzy's recurring truancies from school, her plummeting grades, her frequent overnight stays at friends' houses, and the building animosity they were each feeling toward each other that brought Sara and Suzy into my office when Suzy was 13. Sara was terrified because on Suzy's days of truancy and nights away from home, she was hanging out with kids who were using drugs or shoplifting. Sara was afraid that Suzy would drop out of everything she saw as important—family, education, her artistic pursuits—and never complete high school. Maybe she wouldn't even survive into adulthood.

I started seeing each of them for a weekly session on their own, with a joint session every 4 weeks. As Suzy began opening up with me, I saw the turmoil and conflict she was experiencing. She didn't like herself the way she was, but she didn't see how to turn it around. Although she'd always been a good student, she now found school boring and irrelevant. She was too young to get a job and support herself (which she said she wanted to do), but she found her mother's household rules intolerable. She needed stimulation and excitement, and hanging out with the "bad" kids gave her lots of that. She hated the way she was treating her mother, but she also hated the way her mother tried to control her.

My work with Suzy focused on helping her move toward attitudes of gratitude and self-acceptance. I thought that might start helping her find a way to keep herself safe and live peacefully with her mother. She knew her mother loved her, which I recognized as an enormous asset in helping this family turn things around. Suzy's real problems were with herself, and that's what we had to work on. As the weeks went by, Suzy began finding more things to be grateful for and more things to like about herself. I noticed her mood lightening. Sometimes she was almost cheerful as she entered my office, keen to tell me about something else she'd found to feel good about.

My work with Sara focused on helping her move past her fear-motivated attempts to control her daughter. I supported her in learning to connect with Suzy on a level of love and trust that had been missing for the previous 2 years. It was hard for Sara because there were genuine reasons to worry, but she had to get to the point of realizing she could no longer control Suzy's actions. She had to trust that whatever values Suzy had learned in her early years would come through to the surface if she could only relax. I suggested she find a photo of Suzy at her most wonderful best—maybe when she was 5 or 6, curious, engaged in learning and the world, filled with enthusiasm about so many things—and post that photo on the fridge, where both she and Suzy could see it. That photo reminded them both of the child they both loved but had lost sight of.

I helped Sara see that her job as a parent in the adolescent years was to support her daughter in developing her interests and abilities, whether or not they were academic. She had to pay more attention to what Suzy wanted to do, not so much what Sara thought she ought to be doing, and look for ways to help her do that. It was time to work on building more of a partnership than it had been when Suzy was little. Sara was still the parent, but it was time for her to relinquish some decision-making control so Suzy could feel respected and learn to make good decisions.

Our final group session occurred about 18 months after they started seeing me. I'd asked each of them to come to this last meeting with a brief report on where they were now and what they'd gained, if anything, from our work together.

Suzy and Sara came into the meeting together and sat on the couch. In our early days, they'd arrive separately at our joint sessions and sit as far away as possible from each other, one on the chair, the other on the far end of the couch.

Sara went first with her progress report. "I am so, so glad we did this," she said. "Suzy is doing great, and I feel like I have a daughter again. I think it's because I've learned to step back and let Suzy make decisions on her own."

Suzy groaned and said, "I wish."

Sara smiled and said, "It's a process, right? You keep telling us nobody learns anything all at once."

"So true!" I said. "If we're not making mistakes, we're not learning."

Suzy said, "And I must admit, Mom is doing a lot, lot better. She is no longer on my case about what I eat, when I go to bed, what I wear, whether I'm going to be on time for school—I could keep going, but she IS doing better. Thanks for that, Doc."

I asked Suzy for her progress report.

"I am definitely doing better. It was pretty bad when we started seeing you. I'm not feeling as angry as I was then. Sometimes I'm even happy now. I feel like I'm doing more of what I really want to do. I've started painting and writing again, and I am loving that. Mom and I visit art galleries—local artists and stuff—and sometimes we go to big art galleries. I'm thinking maybe I'd like to study art more seriously."

One of the changes they were both pleased about was that Suzy was no longer failing all her courses and was even doing well in two school subjects. She'd joined the school's writing club, which was open only by invitation, and had had some poems and short pieces published in the school's paper.

When I asked Suzy why she thought she was doing so much better academically, she said, "It helps that I'm in high school now. I was so sick of elementary school, and it was good for me to get away from some of the friends I had then. The teachers at my school now treat us more respectfully, less like little kids, and that helps. Most important, I think, is that Mom backed off her micromanagement. She needed to stop being so interested in my school stuff before I could become interested."

I congratulated them both for the work they'd been doing and the successes they were experiencing. I reminded them that even though they were doing well now, life keeps giving us obstacles. Next time either one of them experienced a problem, they should remember they'd dealt with some tough stuff and come through really well. Most important, I told them, they'd been able to go back to the strong relationship they'd established when Suzy was a little child: "This would have been a much tougher problem to solve if you hadn't had a deep well of love and concern for each other."

This story ended well partly because Suzy was now 15; she had moved into a more stable time in adolescence, a time when her hormones were beginning to settle a bit, and her brain was more mature than it had been 4 years previously when the problems began. But there's more to it than that. Suzy and Sara's story is a great example of how important it is to work on building a relationship with your child that will be able to weather any storm. That relationship can make all the difference in every area of life, including—perhaps surprisingly—academics.

It's also an example of imperfect parenting and that it's (usually) never too late to know better and do better. Sara had done a great job in Suzy's early years but had had trouble as her daughter became an adolescent. She was afraid of letting go of her parental control and letting Suzy grow up. But once she recognized that something needed to change, Sara sought the help she needed and made the changes she had to make to support Suzy in the next phase of her development.

YOUNG ADULTHOOD: 19 TO 24

Many parents expect their young adult to go directly from high school to the first stage of their career development. Whether that's an apprenticeship program, postsecondary school for training of some kind, university, or a job, many parents—and kids—think it's time to move toward supporting themselves when they reach the end of high school. Sometimes young adults are keen to do that, but sometimes they don't feel ready. Your child may need some time to consider the options, opportunities, and interests they haven't had time to explore during the busy years of high school. Some kids have no choice—there's no money for postsecondary education, and their family needs them to start contributing financially. Maybe there's a sick or absent parent or some other essential reason to go directly from high school to earning a living.

If your family is not in serious need of your young adult going directly to work from high school, and your child doesn't feel ready to choose a direction, you might talk to them about a gap year or a sabbatical. As you know, people's circumstances, temperaments, health, interests, abilities, and developmental timing are diverse and unique. That means there are many possible pathways to taking on adult responsibilities. One of them is to take a year off between high school and get serious about supporting oneself. Some kids travel during a gap year; some work; some get involved in volunteer work at home or abroad; some spend time actively exploring career options, doing internships or apprenticeships in areas that interest them; and some dive deeply into an area of interest they haven't had time to pursue until then—maybe music, art, or an entrepreneurship idea.

Some universities—Princeton, Tufts, Florida State, and many others[23]—offer gap year programs as part of degree programs, and many others recommend them as beneficial, leading to more mature students who are ready to learn when they come back to their studies.

If a gap year looks like a good option for your young adult, you can help them plan it so they can make the best use of that year. You might start by talking with your young person about how they see themself living their life 10, 20, 40 years in the future. Some high school seniors have a clear and realistic sense of what they want to do and how they want to get there. Many, though, don't have a clue, or their plans are unrealistic, either because they don't match their abilities or they won't yield much of an income. Many young people want to be rock stars, for example, but it's only a tiny percentage who make it. And that's one of the great things about a gap year—it can give your child a chance to find these things out for themself.

Another way you can support your young adult child is by reminding them as necessary that no career choice needs to be forever. One of the terrible pressures many young adults feel is that they have to choose their one best career right now because this is their only chance to do that. Increasingly, though, people are changing careers entirely, sometimes more than once. I know someone who started out as a lawyer, then became a teacher, and is now an educational consultant. I heard a radio interview with someone who had been a physics professor, who is now working for NASA as a space music consultant (yes, there really is such a job). Try to see your child's life as something they can create as they go, as they learn more about their strengths and interests. Seeing career choice as flexible, possibly changing over time, reduces the anxiety about making a wrong decision and frees them to find what they really want to do and how they want to spend their life.

What your late adolescent child needs most from you now is knowing that you love them, that you trust them to make the right decisions or to manage things if they make a wrong decision, and that you're there if they get into real trouble. They don't need you to make decisions for them or pressure them to make the choices you think they should. If you do your best to abandon your ambitions for your child and let them figure out what it is that they want to do, you'll be a safe harbor for them if the weather gets stormy.

TAKING IT INTO THE COMMUNITY: NEIGHBORHOOD READING CIRCLES

Frontier College is a Canadian volunteer organization committed to supporting literacy in those who are disadvantaged in one way or another, such as prison populations, remote communities, and high-poverty areas.[24] Recognizing that low literacy skills are linked to poverty, poor health, and high unemployment, Frontier College has fostered literacy across the country since the organization was founded in 1899.

One of the Frontier College activities that I've seen in action is the reading circle. This is a place where kids or families can drop in and read with enjoyment. Reading circles can be set up in schools, community centers, places of worship—anywhere that's comfortable, convenient, welcoming, and safe. They can be in any neighborhood, but most Frontier College circles are in high-needs areas, where literacy rates tend to be lowest. Volunteers are encouraged to establish circles of their own or attend a circle weekly at a set time, realizing that trust and predictability are important to the families who are coming to the circle. Volunteers can be older students (typically 12 or older) or adults who have an hour or more a week to donate to this activity.

Activities vary from one reading circle to another, with leaders and participants encouraged to contribute ideas and leadership. Some circles are strictly for kids who show up on their own after school, often attending the circle instead of an after-school care program. Others are mostly for kids, with parents and other caregivers invited to come and watch while volunteers help the kids with their reading. In other circles, parents have an active role in helping their children to read, working in pairs or small family groups. Parents are shown how to read to and with their children, so it's maximum fun and learning and minimum frustration.

In still other circles, kids participate in the reading circle time while parents have a circle time of their own, discussing issues they're having with their children or questions about access to various kinds of services—medical, dental, social, psychological, educational. There might be an occasional visitor to talk about frequently encountered issues in the community or current concerns, such as school funding, transportation, crime, or drug use.

A typical circle might involve a group time, where the leader talks about the day's books before breaking the larger group up into reading buddy groups of one to three children, each working with a volunteer. Some time is usually devoted to a volunteer reading aloud to the children, and time is also allowed for kids reading to each other or to their volunteer. Depending on the group, many children will have had reading problems at school and associate reading with embarrassment and failure, but the reading circle emphasis is on fun and engagement, making learning feel vital and interesting. There's always a healthy snack provided and an atmosphere of friendly inclusion.

Kids are allowed to choose a book to take home, sometimes using a lending library system and sometimes as a permanent gift, a contribution to their home library (which is often scanty or nonexistent). Some circles find sponsors that make it possible for children to choose a new book to take home every week.

I've seen children who can't believe their good luck that they're allowed to choose a book and take it home and keep it. I remember one little girl who spent several minutes trying to figure out which book she wanted. She'd lift up a book, holding it carefully in two hands and looking at it deeply. Then she'd set it down, nod, and pick up another book. After maybe five books, she chose the second book she'd picked up. She noticed me watching her, and she said, "I chose one I haven't read yet. We really get another chance to choose one next week, right?"

I said, "Yes. You can choose a new book each time you come to the reading circle."

She nodded and said, "Good. I decided to challenge myself this week with a new book. But next week I'm going to choose this one, *Good Night Moon*. I know it's too easy for me, but I've always loved it. I never thought I'd own it for myself."

If you have access to such a circle, you and your child might enjoy participating in it. You might also enjoy helping to start up a reading circle in your community or volunteering at one. It's a simple idea and a relatively small amount of time you'd be investing, with a big payoff, both for you and the families with whom you're working.

KEY TAKEAWAYS FOR HEALTHY LEARNING ACROSS THE LIFESPAN

- Intelligence is not fixed and innate. Instead, it develops in unique ways, in dynamic interaction with a person's social and emotional experiences and learning opportunities, as well as other environmental factors.
- Meaningful learning begins with curiosity and playful exploration.
- Test scores shouldn't be seen as reliable unless they correspond to what you see in the real world.
- Everyone has strengths and challenges. Things go best when the strengths are emphasized and used to motivate learning about the challenges.
- Loving your child and providing them with the guidance and security they need is the best way to support their ongoing learning.

CHAPTER 7

NURTURE YOUR CREATIVITY AND CREATIVE SELF-EXPRESSION

You can't use up creativity. The more you use, the more you have.
—Maya Angelou

You might wonder what creativity is doing in a book about being an imperfect parent and building a sturdy relationship with your child. As I see it, creativity may be at the heart of healthy parenting. There's nothing I can think of that requires more creativity than dealing with the everyday obstacles, calamities, and surprises that being a parent brings. And even when you have the perfect answer or execute the perfect solution, the questions and problems are constantly changing under your feet, requiring a creative attitude if you're going to do what needs doing while continuing to build your relationship with your child.

I argue in this chapter that creativity is more than and different from a person's ability to make beautiful art or music or flavors. Rather, it's a way of thinking and problem solving. Parents need to develop their creativity because perfection isn't possible. Taking care of daily business while being kind, loving, and caring with your child requires a creative attitude.

As with intelligence, there's a popular misconception that some people are born more creative than others. However, most experts now see creativity as a dynamic attitude and a valuable human activity, not an innate attribute you're born with. Also, as with intelligence, creativity is about what you do, not what you have. As you approach more activities creatively, your creative abilities strengthen, which is what Maya Angelou was talking about when she wrote, "The more you use it, the more you have."

That being said, some people's temperaments do lend themselves more easily to creativity than others. They find it easier to approach the activities, transitions, and people in their lives with an open and flexible mind. That doesn't mean that someone who is timid and resists new experiences is less creative, but it does mean they'll need more support in overcoming their resistance if they're going to find the joy, sparkle, and confidence that come from creative engagement. That's as true for you as it is for your child. As with pretty much every skill or attitude, it's never too late to discover the pleasures of creativity. What that means and how to do it is what this chapter is all about.

WHAT IS CREATIVITY?

There are as many definitions of creativity as there are of intelligence. Every expert who defines it puts their own spin on the definition. Some emphasize lateral thinking and speed, how quickly a person can generate different perspectives on the same thing. Others emphasize originality, how novel or far out of the box a person's ideas are. Others think of creativity as applying only to the arts, believing it's possible to be a creative musician or sculptor but not seeing the creative possibilities in mathematics and plumbing.

None of these approaches is entirely right or wrong, but each is limited in its practical applications for parents. Here are two approaches I've found useful for those who want to develop their creativity or support its development in the children in their lives.

Creativity as Multifaceted: Four Essential Dimensions

Daniel Keating is a developmental psychologist who once described creativity as having four necessary components: knowledge, divergent thinking, critical thinking, and communication.[1] This definition may seem disappointing, lacking the dazzle usually associated with creativity, but I've seen how it makes the idea of creativity more accessible, both for adults and kids. By supporting your child in each of these four dimensions, you nurture their creativity.

Domain-specific knowledge is the (perhaps surprising) foundation of creativity. Before you can create something new, you need something with which to be creative. A poet or a rap artist needs more than great ideas; they also need a broad vocabulary and a deep and complex understanding of how to use the language persuasively. A theme that runs through the biographies of people renowned for their creativity—people like Wynton Marsalis, Thomas Edison, Martha Graham—is a solid mastery of their particular area of expertise.

Divergent thinking is the next of the four building blocks. This is the dimension of creativity people often think about when they talk about creativity. This is where novel ideas come in, the ability to generate many possible solutions to a problem. Divergent thinking is original, surprising, and transformative. It's thinking laterally or out of the box. It's the sparkle of imagination shining through.

Next up is *critical thinking*. That's what you use to decide which ideas to abandon and which to take further. A person with deep domain-specific mastery and brilliantly divergent ideas can't be productively creative unless they can also think critically about the possible options and decide on one or two ideas to bring to fruition. If you have 10 ideas about doing something, they're probably not all practical or useful, and you almost certainly won't have the time or opportunity to pursue them all. Unless you whittle them down to the one or two with the most promise, you may waste a lot of time and end up with nothing valuable.

The final facet in Keating's definition of creativity is *communication*. You can have lots of great ideas and pursue one of them to beautiful completion, but if you can't share that idea effectively with others, you might as well not have bothered. You can write a symphony or design a building, but if you don't find a way to communicate the finished work with others so it can be played or built, it won't matter.

These four components apply to creativity across all domains—music, technology, cooking, carpentry, engineering, and everything else. If you want to nurture your child's creativity, look for ways to support each of these four facets in balance. If you focus too heavily on knowledge, you may inadvertently inhibit your child's originality and divergent thinking. If you over-prize divergent thinking, your child may scatter their time, effort, and energy. Too much critical analysis means your child will scrap every new idea they generate. And if you focus on communication at the expense of content mastery, innovative ideas, or critical thinking, you are fostering superficiality.

Creativity as a Decision: 10 Creative Thinking Habits

Psychologist Robert Sternberg made a case for creativity as something a person decides to do.[2] Arguing that everyone can choose creative attitudes and actions, Sternberg identified the following 10 habits for cultivating creativity:

1. **Redefine problems.** This is part of Keating's divergent thinking dimension of creativity. It means looking at situations with fresh eyes rather than accepting the normal way of looking at them. Little kids are often good at this because the world is still new for them. They see mud puddles as invitations to feel ooze between their toes rather than dirty obstacles to avoid. They see sticks as swords, dramatic props, and magic wands, not as garden debris. They see large packing boxes

as houses, forts, and hideaways, not as trash to be recycled. The boy I mentioned earlier—Zachary—saw the face puzzle as an opportunity to play with Picasso's perspective instead of a jigsaw puzzle to put together in the usual way.

2. **Analyze your ideas.** This is the critical thinking dimension that Keating discusses. No one's ideas are always good—not Elon Musk's, not Pablo Picasso's, not anyone's. Most people aren't naturally good at stepping back and critiquing their own ideas, so help your child learn how to decide which ideas to pursue and which are better abandoned or saved for later.

3. **Sell your ideas.** This is Keating's communication component of creativity. The more innovative an idea, the harder its creator usually has to work to gain acceptance. Oprah Winfrey and Steven Spielberg might have been unknowns if they hadn't persisted in trying to sell their work to others. Parents are sometimes irritated when their children's unusual ideas are not immediately accepted by teachers, but it's important your child learns how to make a case sufficiently compelling so others want to buy into it. By showing your child how to strengthen their skills of persuasion, you can help them develop their persistence, social intelligence, and communication skills, as well as their creativity.

4. **Remember that knowledge is a double-edged sword.** Content mastery is essential to creativity, but sometimes it's someone who is new to a field—like a child—who sees the innovative possibilities and opportunities. People who think they know everything can stop listening and learning and become blind to creative possibility.

5. **Surmount obstacles.** When you challenge how things are done, you're setting yourself up for opposition. Help your child realize that the important question is not whether people

with creative ideas will confront roadblocks but rather how they'll respond to the rejections they experience. My best work has generally been done in response to someone trashing my ideas. I've learned to indulge my sense of outrage privately—usually a rant to my husband—and then wait a few days until I'm ready to go back to it. Then I work furiously to make the work stronger, clearer, and more persuasive. I never look forward to doing that, but I have learned repeatedly that the finished product benefits from the process. Help your child discover that obstacles, failures, and rejections are opportunities to make their ideas better.

6. **Take sensible risks.** Too often, teachers penalize kids who take creative risks, so students usually do better when they stick with safe answers. You want your child to take creative risks, but you don't want them to experience damaging consequences. So, encourage your child in their creative risk taking, but also help them learn when to compromise. This means analyzing the risks associated with acting on innovative ideas and deciding which ones are worth taking. Once your child has proven themselves capable, they'll be freer to take creative risks, but they have to get there first.

7. **Keep growing.** Picasso said, "All children are artists. The problem is how to remain an artist once you grow up." Even for those who start off deciding for creativity, it's tempting to settle into more comfortable habits as time goes by. Across all fields, many of those who achieve success stop growing, sometimes even resisting others' new ideas with the same intensity they encountered. The best way to teach your child about continuing to grow is to look for creative ways to meet the challenges in your own life and work.

8. **Believe in yourself.** Proposing creative ideas means rejection, failure, and being wrong sometimes. One of the pleasures

of creativity is the thrill of taking risks, but a potential cost is losing confidence. Provide the encouragement your child needs to recover from their obstacles and failures. Help them learn that even if they're not coming up with good ideas right now, they will, as long as they keep learning, thinking, and generating new ideas.

9. **Tolerate ambiguity.** Tolerating ambiguity means being open to more than one simultaneous possibility. This is a tough principle to teach because children need certainty to feel secure. They need to distinguish between heroes and villains, friends and enemies, right and wrong, even though who or what might fit into each category can change from one moment to the next. As your child grows older, they become better able to see nuances and alternative possibilities.

One way to learn about the ambiguity inherent in complex ideas is to participate in a debate on a controversial topic such as animal rights, environmental protection, or homeschooling. Each person is assigned randomly to one side or another and then argues their assigned position. After a set time, the sides switch, so the person attacking the idea has to defend it, and vice versa. At the conclusion, each person is asked to formulate their position, including the strengths and weaknesses of each side. Then, each person is asked to reflect on the experience. Did the debate experience change your mind? Would you have reached as thoughtful an understanding if you'd defended just one side and not the other?

Although ambiguity is less comfortable than certainty, it's essential to creative work. Once your child is old enough to appreciate ambiguity—around 10 or 11—you can help them realize that one of the prices of creative work is the discomfort that comes from ambiguity. Be patient: Ambiguity is intellectually tough to master and can take a long time to grasp fully. Many adults never get there.

10. **Find what you love to do, and do it.** Help your child explore what they're interested in. Maybe your child needs music lessons and an instrument to practice on. Maybe they need a block of stone and a set of stone chisels or a membership in a science museum. Then again, it might be each of these over time, as the child experiments and decides what they want to take further.

Keating's facets of creativity and Sternberg's creative thinking habits are both built on the fact that creativity isn't a fixed ability or personality trait that some people are born with, while other people aren't. You can help your child decide for creativity and, in the process, arm them with one of the essential skills for success in a rapidly changing world. And perhaps—because the best way to teach anything is to live it—you can also decide for creativity for yourself.

Questions to Consider About Creativity

- Does anything in Keating's or Sternberg's approaches resonate for you or surprise you?
- Do you have any outlets for creative self-expression?
- Are there areas of your life that might benefit from a more creative approach—your work, your relationships, your parenting, your hobbies, your recreation, your self-expression?
- Do any of Keating's or Sternberg's ideas take you outside your comfort zone?
- Is there an idea you'd like to take further?
- Are you supporting your child in exploring and using their creativity?

SOME DIMENSIONS OF CREATIVITY

In addition to Keating's components and Sternberg's choices for creativity, there are other important dimensions to consider before thinking about how creativity manifests and develops across the years of human development.

In the Zone: Calm, Focused Energy, Engagement, and Creativity

For many decades now, creatively productive people in all fields—sciences, arts, sports, humanities, trades, professions, and whatever else humans do—have been talking about an experience called "flow" or "being in the zone." They describe total absorption in an activity, a feeling of energized focus, concentrated involvement, and loss of a sense of time. Those who experience it almost always want more, sometimes describing it as a euphoric drug that motivates deeper and ever-deepening engagement in the activity that prompted the sensation of flow in the first place. Flow has been described as an optimal experience associated with happiness, fulfillment, and serenity. It connects back to Eastern religions and can be seen as a state of mind that both results from engaging in creativity and also enhances creative possibility.

The term *flow*[3,4] was coined in 1975 by psychologist Mihaly Csikszentmihalyi—one of the founders of a movement known as positive psychology[5]—as he investigated happiness. He became fascinated by the fact that so many of the artists, athletes, and musicians he was interviewing described losing track of time when they were engaged in their work. Since then, flow has been intensively investigated, and researchers have drawn some conclusions about three components, each of which is essential to flow.

217

An Activity With Clearly Defined Goals

Those who experience flow have concrete short-term plans concerning the activity they're involved in, as well as reasonable long-term aspirations. For an athlete, this can mean working on a certain basketball shot and hoping eventually to join an elite team. For a writer, it might be writing a short story to submit to a contest and hoping to become a published novelist. For a chef, it could be mastering cake baking and aspiring to become a pastry chef. Although the flow activity is intrinsically motivated, the goals add direction and structure to the task.

Clear and Immediate Feedback

To achieve a state of flow, you need evidence that you are mastering your short-term goals, as well as supportive redirection when you're going off the track of your long-term goals. This feedback can be prizes, praise, or other kinds of commendation when you've earned them or constructive criticism that helps you get better. In some circumstances, direct, immediate feedback is built into the activity. If you're designing video game software, for example, you know if you're doing the technical part right because it works, whereas if you make a mistake, it doesn't.

Your Perception of Your Abilities Matches Your Experience of the Challenge

If you attempt something and find it too challenging to manage, you'll become frustrated. If you do something else and find it too easy, you'll be bored. To feel a sense of flow, the task must be hard enough that it feels challenging and easy enough that it feels doable. You have to feel confident that, with effort, you can complete the task at hand and that that effort will have been worth your while.

How Can You Nurture Flow in Your Child?

To encourage your child in experiencing flow, take their enthusiasms seriously. Talk about how they might take their interests further. Help them define realistic goals, both short term and long term. Help them find tasks that match their abilities. If you think your child is overconfident or if you think they're more competent than they realize, help them test and refine their perception.

The most flow-conducive tasks allow your child to see how they're progressing, but if that isn't possible given the nature of their interests and goals, think about how your child can get the supportive and constructive feedback they need.

Finding the Wonder in the Ordinary

Our kids' lives are often too busy for them to find out what interests them, much less pursue that with engagement and creativity. The joyful possibilities inherent in daily life—the wonder in the ordinary—are trampled in the rush to get things done. If you listen closely, your child's curiosities can provide the clues you need to help them discover the interests that motivate the engagement in learning—the persistence, focus, and effort—that are part of creative experiences.

In *The Parent's Tao Te Ching: Ancient Advice for Modern Parents*,[6] William Martin talked about the importance of slowing things down to allow creativity to flower. He wrote,

> Do you have agendas for your children that are more important than the children themselves? Lost in the shuffle of uniforms, practices, games, recitals, and performances can be the creative and joyful soul of your child. Watch and listen carefully. Do they have time to daydream? From your children's dreams will emerge the practices and activities that will make self-discipline as natural as breathing.[7]

219

Slowing things down enough to find the wonder in the ordinary doesn't mean changing everything in your life. Sometimes all it requires is taking a deep breath from time to time and making sure you're present in the moment with your child, listening to their questions, paying attention to their concerns. Sometimes it means cutting down on extra activities—either yours or your child's—and making a little space in your life for the magic to poke through.

Maybe instead of driving your child to school every day, 1 day a week, you walk with them to school. You point out things you notice in the neighborhood—people, flowers, changes, bugs—and stop for a minute and take a look at what interests them. Or 1 day a week, your mother or friend could pick them up early from school and take them to a neighborhood park or bookstore instead of going straight home. Maybe you do a special excursion with them on the weekend or 1 day a month when you go together to a local museum or art gallery or zoo, sometimes their choice and sometimes yours, and you leave time for dawdling and daydreaming along the way. And if they identify an area of interest they'd like to explore further, look for ways to help them do that.

When asked about parents' roles in supporting their children's creativity, neuropsychologist Rex Jung emphasized the importance of daydreaming.[8] He said, "The most important class when I was growing up was recess. You try different things, you make mistakes— it can't be all stuffing stuff into your brain. . . . The novelty generator needs a chance."

William Martin translated the scientific findings into parenting advice when he wrote, "And make the ordinary come alive for them. The extraordinary will take care of itself."[9] This is the true alchemy: With time, effort, persistence, and patience, curiosity is transformed into creativity, even genius. This magical process starts with the simple habit of taking the time to listen to your child as they find the wonder in the ordinary.

Creative Self-Expression for Healing, Coping, and Resilience

Everyone hungers to be seen and understood, but children don't have the cognitive or emotional maturity to recognize and understand their painful feelings or make sense of their confusing experiences. They may know something isn't right, doesn't feel good, or makes them sad, but they don't have the insight, knowledge, or communication skills required to share these complicated feelings with others.

Creative self-expression is one of the best ways to help your child gain access to and communicate their difficult feelings. Some good vehicles for self-expression include music, dance, painting, role-playing, writing, drama, and puppetry, but it's not limited to those areas. You or your child can also express yourselves through gardening, pottery, sandbox play, whittling, origami, or something else.

Observe, listen, and pay close attention to the feelings that might underlie your child's creative projects. Don't push too hard; instead, be still and listen. Don't try to interpret their productions for them, but instead, see if you can gently ask the right questions that will help them untangle their confusions.

Although creative self-expression helps children deal with small everyday confusions, it can be even more potent when helping a child manage serious trauma. When children experience any kind of abuse, are bullied, or live in a chronically stressful environment, creative self-expression can help them regain or retain their psychological well-being. Psychologist and artist Cathy Malchiodi described the actions of a Viennese artist named Friedl Dicker-Brandeis. In "Imagination and Expressive Arts as Antidotes to Adversity,"[10] Malchiodi wrote that Dicker-Brandeis was an inmate of Theresienstadt, a Nazi concentration camp during World War II. She smuggled art supplies into Theresienstadt and used them to teach hundreds of child inmates to see through the surface of the people and objects around them

221

and instead focus intently on the essentially positive nature of those people and objects.

Many decades later, Malchiodi interviewed the survivors of this experience. The survivors' consensus was that the creative self-expression experiences that Dicker-Brandeis had provided allowed them to achieve a postwar psychological resilience that would otherwise have been impossible. She'd helped the children see past the horrors of the concentration camp and remember the beautiful possibilities inherent in every person and any situation.

Traditional approaches to art therapy often use the creative process to understand and get past negative emotions. There's a growing body of research, however, suggesting the greater efficacy of using the imagination to attune to positive emotions, as Friedl Dicker-Brandeis did well ahead of her time.[11]

Creative self-expression has many important benefits as a wellness practice. It supports your child's well-being as effectively as getting enough sleep, eating the right foods, and spending time in nature. It's also a good stress-reduction activity, giving your child an effective mechanism for coping with challenging experiences, thereby increasing their resilience. The more troubling the circumstances your child is dealing with, the bigger the difference it can make for them to find a way to express themselves through creative outlets.

THE EARLY YEARS: BIRTH TO 5

Young children's natural curiosity and fresh eyes on the world give them a big advantage in creative attitudes. One of the best things you can do with your child (after love, patience, and security) is to nurture their budding curiosity and imagination rather than ignoring or extinguishing it. This supports them in exercising their creativity. Moreover, as early as 2½ or 3, you can be alert to signs of creative self-expression that are windows on what might be troubling them.

Sheri is a friendly and energetic 4-year-old. After kindergarten one day, Sheri brought two of her dolls and a teddy bear into the kitchen where her mother was making dinner. The mom, LaToya, watched and listened as the dolls and bear played happily together, Sheri giving each character a distinctive voice. After several minutes of noisy, friendly play, one of the dolls suggested in a loud, brash voice that she and the other doll should go somewhere else so they could play alone together without the bear. The two dolls went off laughing, leaving the bear sitting alone on the floor.

LaToya looked up and saw Sheri hugging her bear with tears in her eyes.

"How do you think that made Bear feel when his friends went off and played without him?" LaToya asked.

"Very, very sad," Sheri said solemnly, wiping away a tear.

"Has that ever happened to you?"

"No! I have lots of friends."

"Has it ever happened to one of your friends?"

Sheri looked defiant and said, "No!"

Her mother said nothing and looked at Sheri with a gentle question in her eyes.

After a minute or two of silence, Sheri nodded sadly.

"Was your friend sad, like the bear?"

Another small nod.

"Then what happened?"

"Recess was over, and we all went in."

"Is there anything you can do about this?"

"No! It already happened! It's over," Sheri shouted angrily.

"Yes. But there's usually a way to repair things after we've had a chance to think."

"There isn't."

"Hmmm."

"You don't know! There isn't anything anybody can do!"

"Okay."

"Maybe I can tell Ahmad I'm really, really sorry."

"Mm-hmm."

"He is my friend, and I shouldn't have listened to Annika."

"That sounds like a good idea," LaToya said as she gave her daughter a hug. "Now, let's get you a snack!"

This story illustrates how a parent's support for creative self-expression makes a difference to a young child's ability to understand and rectify a troubling situation. By listening deeply, asking a few simple questions, and giving Sheri her full attention, LaToya helped Sheri understand something important about friendship, loyalty, and integrity. Through this process, Sheri figured out how she felt and what she wanted to do about it and developed some tools for responding better to future situations.

CHILDHOOD: 6 TO 10

Two of the important developmental tasks of childhood are consolidating strengths and developing habits that will support the challenges of early adolescence. During the years from 6 to 10, ideally, your child is establishing the foundation of learning and behaving that will allow them to thrive over time. All the principles I've outlined in this chapter can be valuable during childhood—each of Keating's four factors of creativity, all of Sternberg's 10 recommendations for deciding for creativity, flow, finding the wonder in the ordinary, and creative self-expression. Here's an example of a parent supporting a child in experiencing flow.

Eight-year-old Joseph loves playing baseball. His short-term goals are to refine his aim in both hitting and pitching; his longer term goal is to make a select team that travels around the state to tournaments. His father has created a place in their small backyard where Joe can go out and practice hitting or pitching into a large net, so the ball isn't constantly going over a fence or into a window. He can see where the ball is landing and ascertain whether he's getting more accurate, helping him decide when to move back and make the task more difficult.

Every day after school, unless the weather makes it impossible, Joe has a quick snack and goes out to the pitching–hitting net. Within minutes, he's fully immersed in the activity. His parents say that he often spends a full hour out there, all alone, completely absorbed in improving his game. When he comes back inside, he's glowing, feeling good about himself, and wanting to show his dad or mom or anyone else who's there what he's been working on. His goals are tough enough to challenge him to get better and easy enough to be doable, and the task design is giving him the feedback he needs.

In supporting Joseph in experiencing a sense of flow, his father is giving him a priceless gift. Joe now looks for that experience of full immersion in other activities he values—drawing, science, and Minecraft. When he's in a state of flow, Joe focuses his abundant energy and intelligence on developing increasing levels of competence. He is experiencing the creative fulfillment that leads to achievement, well-being, and confidence.

ADOLESCENCE: 11 TO 18

Creative self-expression can be vitally important in an adolescent's life. It can make the difference between your child thriving and having serious problems. Creativity can help your adolescent establish an identity, one of the most important tasks of adolescence. If your child has a creative outlet, it helps them make sense of who they are and what they believe in, leading to positive self-esteem and giving them an outlet for self-expression.[12]

Suzy has come up in several chapters already. Most recently, in Chapter 6, I described a series of counseling sessions I conducted with her and her mother. Sara had come to me when Suzy was 13, worried about her daughter's truancies from school, the troubling behavior of her daughter's friends, and Suzy's overnight absences with those friends. Eighteen months later, when Suzy was 15, she was doing much better. She was attending school regularly and had a different group of friends. She and her mother were getting along better as they focused on strengthening their relationship and as Sara learned how to trust and respect her growing daughter.

Many complicated and interacting factors led to Suzy's problem behavior in her early teens, including her difficult temperament (which I addressed in Chapter 1) and her parents' divorce, which usually destabilizes things at least for a while (something I address more fully in Chapter 9). Another factor was Sara's needing to let her daughter grow up, something that many caring parents have problems with.

There were also other factors that led to Suzy getting on firmer footing. They included her brain maturation—15 is usually a more stable age than 11, when the problems began. Another was Sara's learning how to let go of her need to control and micromanage her daughter. Another was the emphasis they both put on reestablishing the relationship they had had during Suzy's childhood. Still another factor that was enormously important in Suzy coming to peace with herself—which allowed her to come to peace with her mother and find less destructive ways to spend her time—was Suzy's return to painting and other creative activities she'd enjoyed when she was younger.

Creative self-expression contributes to healing and mental health across the lifespan,[13] but it can be particularly valuable in the years from 11 to 18, when a young person is working hard on figuring out their identity and sorting out many other dimensions of life and relationships.

Support your adolescent in finding a vehicle for their personal brand of creative self-expression. It might be through any of the arts, a craft such as making jewelry or furniture, sewing, or some kind of entrepreneurship. Some teenagers get creatively involved in humanitarian, political, or environmental projects. Some invest their creative energy into raising consciousness and addressing social justice concerns, such as Black Lives Matter or a schoolwide rainbow coalition. Still others find an outlet for creative self-expression in Web design or software development. Your child might find a happy outlet for their creativity in coaching volleyball or tutoring younger children. There are opportunities for creative self-expression in practically any pursuit imaginable. It starts with your adolescent child finding an area of interest.

YOUNG ADULTHOOD: 19 TO 24

By the time your child enters late adolescence or early adulthood, they've probably identified some preferred modes of creative self-expression. Whether or not they've found an outlet for creative self-expression, do what you can to encourage them to invest time in activities that renew their spirit and keep alive the vibrant engagement in life that they had as a young child.

I met Clare and her mother, Margaret, when Clare was in her second year of university. She'd been an excellent student all the way through elementary and high school, winning prizes and rarely getting a grade below A. Her mother described Clare as having been an early reader and a keen learner from birth. Margaret said she'd occasionally worried through Clare's high school years because her daughter seemed too caught up in academics, too serious perhaps, and not much interested in a social life.

All that changed when Clare got to college. She discovered boys, alcohol, and drugs and became as intensely involved in her social life and substance exploration as she'd once been in her studies. She had a solid foundation of academic knowledge from her high

227

school studies, so her grades remained reasonably high that year, although not close to the top standing she'd had all through high school. Margaret figured that Clare was going through the usual first-year transition experience and didn't worry about it. She knew her daughter was a capable student and figured she'd get back to her studious habits in second year.

About 4 weeks into Clare's second year of university, she called home and told her mother that she couldn't get interested in her studies. She was staying out too late most nights, she said, drinking beer, smoking pot, and talking politics, philosophy, physics, and literature in a pub with other students and sometimes professors, and she was having trouble getting up in time for classes. She was enjoying some of the assigned reading and found some of the courses interesting enough to attend most of the time, but she was beginning to feel guilty about wasting Margaret's money.

Margaret was a single mother and had supported the family while her two children were growing up. Money had always been tight; they'd never gone on a holiday longer than the occasional 3-day road trip, and they lived quite simply in a modest rental apartment. The kids had started making their own spending money when they were old enough to babysit and cut neighbors' lawns, and Clare—who enjoyed working hard and making her own money— was continuing to pay for all the extras in her life, including buying her own clothes. Clare had won a scholarship that covered her tuition, but Margaret was paying the cost of her staying in residence. The deadline was approaching for getting a residence fees refund, and Clare wanted her mother to have a chance to get her money back.

Clare was remarkably honest, a tribute both to her innate integrity and her relationship with Margaret. She knew her mother wouldn't go ballistic, that she'd hear her out and respond reasonably one way or another.

When Margaret called me and described the situation, I first asked about sex, drugs, and alcohol. I wondered if Clare was getting into serious trouble.

Margaret laughed. She said, "Clare is solid. She reassured me that she's not going crazy, that she's being careful about everything, including sex: 'You don't have to worry about that, Mom. I'm only interested in one guy at a time, and it rarely gets to the point of an actual date, just the two of us, much less sex.'"

As for drugs and alcohol, Margaret said, "Clare told me she never drinks more than two beers a night, at a maximum of 2 nights a week. As for drugs, she said she's tried marijuana a few times but doesn't enjoy it or see the point of it, and she's had small-dose experiences with a few other drugs: 'I'm not trying to destroy myself, Mom, just exploring different parts of life.'"

I asked whether Clare had any vehicles for creative self-expression.

"Oh yes!" said Margaret. "Clare has been writing since she was a little girl. Her favorite courses in high school were the creative writing courses, and the teacher—who's a published novelist—told me that Clare was probably the best high school writer he'd encountered in his career."

"Is she doing any writing now?" I asked.

"I have no idea," Margaret told me.

I saw Margaret the following week. She told me that she'd called Clare and asked about the writing. She said Clare had asked, "How did you know? I'm spending a lot of my daytime hours working on a novel when I should be in class."

Margaret told me about the rest of the conversation. She'd replied to Clare, "That sounds good, actually. You've always been a good writer. Do you want to stay there, even though you're not doing much academic work, or would you rather come home?"

"I'd rather stay here. I'm really enjoying the people and the whole scene, and I'm getting some good writing done. But I know I'm not going to do well academically. I don't want you to feel like I haven't lived up to my end of the bargain. It's so expensive, and if I'm not even attending classes . . ."

"Are you learning anything?"

"Oh, yes! I'm finally learning about people and a whole other side of life I've never explored."

"It sounds like you're actually making good use of your time. It's a different kind of education than the one we'd thought it would be, but it might be just what you need right now."

"Really, Mom?"

"Yes. There are a lot of different ways to get an education. You've always worked so hard at learning your whole life until now. I trust your instincts. If this is what you think you need now and where you want to be, stay with it."

As Margaret had predicted, Clare's grades were terrible that year; she got only two of the five credits she'd signed up for in September. She spent the next several years traveling and writing and supporting herself in waitressing jobs and was a published novelist by the time she was 30.

Some parents will probably find this a terrible outcome, but I think it's just right. Clare never did go back to university, and she's making a life for herself that she loves. She's happily married with a delightful young child (who you'll meet in Chapter 8) and a writing career that is growing and changing.

As I reflect on the story, I think it illustrates many of the themes of this book, including the imperfect messiness of life; the uniqueness of every parent, every child, and every life; the value of creative self-expression; and—perhaps most important—the deep importance of establishing a bond of love and trust with your child, so you can weather the storms that will inevitably come along.

Your young adult child may not have that urgent need to express themself that Clare had, but things will go better for them if they have some kind of vehicle of self-expression that can help them figure out who they are and how they want to live their life. One of the best ways for you to encourage that is to model it in your own life. If you don't currently have an active mode of creative self-expression, think about what you might like to take up for the first time now or take up again, resuming something you left off doing years or even decades ago. Whether it's dance or art or environmental exploration, find something you can throw yourself into with abandon, and you'll increase the chances that your child does the same.

TAKING IT INTO THE COMMUNITY: CREATIVE PROBLEM SOLVING IN ACTION

At this time of widespread and well-justified fears for our well-being and the survival of the planet, we need creativity more than ever. We each need to do our part in nurturing our positive attitudes and creativity and also to do what we can to raise a generation of children who can tap into their creativity in solving the problems of survival.

Creative problem solving (CPS) is a proven approach to teaching children as young as 4 to approach and solve problems creatively.[14] It rests on a few basic principles,[15] including asking problems as questions. Children working alone or in groups are asked to identify a problem and then to think of a way of asking an open-ended question to address the problem—for example, "We're in the midst of a drought and I'm worried about water supplies and forest fires" (a frightening and potentially overwhelming, even disabling, concern) might become "What can I [or we] do to address the water shortages and fire risks this drought is causing?" (a positive and potentially energizing direction for the concerns). Other CPS principles include

231

suspending judgment about possible solutions until the brainstorming session is over and focusing on "yes" and "and" instead of "no" and "but."

Children who learn this process can become good at solving small problems in their lives and then move on to using this creative approach to identifying and addressing bigger problems in their communities. Some kids have become famous for finding creative solutions to consciousness raising about large problems that affect a lot of people.[16]

For example, as a young girl, Malala Yousafzai loved school. Her father was a teacher who ran a girls' school in their Pakistani village until the Taliban took over and prohibited the education of girls. At 11, Malala started speaking out publicly for the right of girls to go to school, which resulted in a Taliban soldier shooting her in the head. The story received global attention, and she woke up from the attack in a hospital in the United Kingdom. After months of surgeries and a difficult recuperation, she made a decision to continue her fight for girls' education. Since then, Malala has worked with many allies to find creative approaches to solving the serious problem of girls' educational restrictions, including establishing the Malala Fund Education Champion Network, which supports educators and activists in developing countries. She became the youngest Nobel laureate ever when she was 17, winning the Peace Prize in 2014.

Greta Thunberg is another young person who has drawn international attention to a global problem through her creative approach. At the age of 8, she became deeply concerned about climate change and wondered why nobody was doing much about it. Feeling hopeless about her concerns, she suffered serious mental health problems until she started taking action on her environmental concerns. At the age of 15, she initiated a school strike for the climate by standing alone outside the Swedish parliament with a sign that read, "School strike for climate." She posted a photo of herself on her first strike day to Instagram and Twitter; other social media accounts quickly took up her cause. Youth activists and environmentalists shared her posts, and on the second day, she was joined in her school strike by many other young people who shared her worries. This attracted local reporters, and within a week, her strike was getting international coverage. She argued that the climate is an urgent and immediate concern and tweeted, "I want you to act as if the house was on fire. Because it is." She has spoken at the United Nations and at huge climate rallies in Stockholm, Brussels, London, and New York, calling on international decision makers to commit to meaningful climate change action.

Malala Yousafzai and Greta Thunberg are examples of young people who have identified something they see as a serious problem in their communities and taken creative steps toward solving that problem. Although most people's creative problem-solving efforts don't get the kind of global attention these two have received, their stories illustrate the powerful possibilities inherent in reconceptualizing problems as questions that can be answered. These stories—and others like them—can inspire you and your child to take a creative problem-solving approach to issues you identify in your own community. Who knows—your child might be the next Greta or Malala.

KEY TAKEAWAYS FOR WEAVING CREATIVITY INTO EVERYDAY LIFE

- Like pretty much everything else, creativity is more about habits of mind and behavior—thinking and doing—rather than the innate qualities of a person.
- The more you exercise your creativity, the more creatively you will find yourself approaching every dimension of your life—relationships, work, play, health, and self-expression.

- Look for creative ways to express yourself across the full range of emotions—your sadnesses, joys, angers, disappointments, fears, and confusions. Some people find creative self-expression in writing, painting, music, or dance. Others find themselves connecting with their feelings and expressing them through making things with their hands.
- Listen to your child's interests and curiosities and support their passions. Ask questions. Help them take it further, supporting them in developing their curiosities and interests into abilities.

CHAPTER 8

CHOOSE LOVE, POSITIVITY, CARING, AND CONNECTION

Learning to stand in somebody else's shoes, to see through their eyes, that's how peace begins. And it's up to you to make that happen. Empathy is a quality of character that can change the world.

—Barack Obama, *A Promised Land*

Most people feel good when they encounter someone who exudes love, positivity, caring, and connection, and they don't feel so good when they encounter someone who's cool, negative, uncaring, and disconnected. They often don't realize that these attributes reflect the choices people make. We've talked in previous chapters about making choices and building habits into our lives that nurture our mindfulness, intelligence, and creativity. Similarly, this chapter is about the ingredients involved in being that first kind of person, no matter your history, temperament, or current habits.

Social skills are what allow you to interact successfully with others, making and sustaining healthy relationships.[1] Empathy is one of the key social skills at the foundation of all human connection. From a developmental psychologist's perspective, Barack Obama was right when he observed that empathy is a quality of character that has the power to change the world. Emotional skills allow you to understand yourself, regulate your feelings and behavior, and set meaningful goals.[2] Politics, religion, teaching, and writing poetry are some of the many fields that require well-developed emotional skills.

Social and emotional intelligences inform and interact with each other: Emotional skills emerge from interactions with others, and social skills develop along with self-awareness. So, although social and emotional competencies include different skill sets, they develop in tandem, each building on the other. As one develops, so does the other, and so, in this chapter, I discuss social and emotional development as an intertwined set of abilities.

Questions to Consider About Social and Emotional Strengths and Challenges

This might be a good time to take a minute to think about your own social and emotional strengths and challenges, as well as your child's. Your answers hold the key to your relationship with each other, as well as with others in your life, and to many kinds of fulfillment.

- How do you respond when you observe another person's suffering?
- Are you aware of your own moods?
- When you're having a conversation, do you focus more on what you want to say next or what the other person is trying to say?
- How do you cope with negative moods in yourself and others—fear, anger, irritation, sadness?
- Are you good at apologizing when you've hurt or offended someone?
- How do you think your family and friends see you?
- What are your sources of happiness? Confidence? Self-worth?

I'm going to start by discussing several of the building blocks of social and emotional intelligence—empathy, friendships, self-control, and more—and then come back to those elements later, describing how they are developing in each stage of your child's growth and what that means for your parenting.

EMPATHY: WHERE KINDNESS, COMPASSION, AND HAPPINESS BEGIN

If you visit a kindergarten class during a group activity, you might see the teacher smiling at the children and actively interacting with them as they laugh, move, and have noisy fun. At some point, the teacher will slow down, getting quiet and more serious, as they prepare for story time. Some of the children will notice what the teacher is doing and follow suit, settling down and getting quieter, too. Some of the other kids will see the first group of kids and slow down, too. Still others won't notice what's happening and will continue chatting and playing until the teacher asks them to settle. And one or two of the kids will be oblivious to what's happening, as well as to the teacher's requests.

Some people are born with a heightened tendency to notice what others are experiencing and respond appropriately, and some seem blind to others' feelings. Regardless of how you or your child feel or express empathy, you can learn to pay more attention to others and become more empathetic.

Empathy Types

Empathy is at the root of kindness and compassion and is an essential friendship skill. It contributes to academic and career success and is a critical dimension of leadership. It's the capacity to see what someone else is feeling, understand it, and sometimes feel it with them. Empathy encompasses imagining another's thoughts and emotions and providing a caring response. It is a highly complex set of abilities and responses that neuroscience is just beginning to figure out.

Writing for the Association for Psychological Sciences, Kim Armstrong interviewed several of the top neuroscientists working on the frontiers of empathy.[3] One conclusion from that research is that current one-dimensional models of empathy—where highly empathetic individuals are at one end of a scale and psychopaths are at the other end—are overly simplistic. We need to know more about the complex brain science of empathy before we can understand people who appear to be low in empathy.

People use the term *empathy* to mean different things, and it may surprise you to learn that empathy is not always a good thing. Daniel Goleman identified three types of empathy, and each type has drawbacks, as well as benefits[4]:

- **Cognitive empathy.** Sometimes referred to as perspective taking, cognitive empathy is the intellectual dimension of what is usually considered an emotional attribute: the ability to recognize what another person is feeling. Cognitive empathy enriches relationships, including parenting, but it's also the skill used for manipulative purposes by psychopaths and con artists, who take advantage of others' feelings.
- **Emotional empathy.** This comes closer to what most people think of when they think of empathy. This is what you're experiencing when you feel deeply connected to another, and that person's sadness or joy makes you feel sad or happy. It's a wonderful attribute in parenting and friendships, but it's a liability when it leads to being overwhelmed by others' emotions. It's an advantage for teachers, nurses, counselors, and others in the helping professions, except when it leads to burnout. It's also a problem when it distracts from an accurate judgment of another person's needs.
- **Compassionate empathy.** This is the empathy that leads to action, the desire to do something to help another when you perceive that they have painful feelings. It incorporates both of the other forms of empathy—identifying what another is feeling and feeling it with them—with the added dimension

of a desire to change the other person's predicament. It's the transformative world changer Obama was talking about in this chapter's opening quote, but it can also lead to someone being an intrusive do-gooder or to burnout.

These different types of empathy are all beneficial when used intentionally and appropriately for good, but each one can cause problems both for the empath and their target when they're misused. When I was training to be a counselor, I heard a great story that has stayed with me all these years.

Imagine a person is at the bottom of an emotional well. No matter how much you feel for them (emotional empathy), that person doesn't want you to climb down to the bottom to be with them in their suffering. They'd much prefer you to stay at the top and figure out what they're experiencing (cognitive empathy). Then, they'd like you to lower a rope down to them (compassionate empathy), so they can climb out of the well. Feeling another's feelings builds connection, but sometimes it's not what's most needed.

How Does Empathy Develop?

Empathy is a complex and nuanced attribute, and it develops one step at a time, just like other complex skills. According to research done by Jean Decety and others, empathy builds on many of your child's other experiences, achievements, and skills.[5]

To begin with, a child needs to experience a secure, strong, loving relationship with at least one adult—usually a parent, most usually the mother—to develop empathy in all its complexity. If your child didn't have that attachment experience as a baby for one reason or another (such as their mother experiencing substance dependency or mental or physical health problems), it's possible to build the attachment later, but it will take an enormous investment of time and effort.

No matter how naturally empathetic your child seems to be, they can learn to see a situation through another person's eyes and respond with compassion. To help your child learn about empathy, be warm, respectful, and empathetic toward your child. Acknowledge and value other people's feelings, especially in your child's presence. Be understanding when someone is sad, upset, distressed, or frustrated.

It also helps if you talk about your feelings with your child in an age-appropriate way. When their parents are out of sorts, kids usually worry; they wonder if they'll be safe, and they think it's probably because of something they've done—they've disappointed you or made you angry somehow. So, starting when they're young and continuing into adulthood, talk to your child about what you're experiencing if you're having a hard day or you're feeling something strongly, whether good or bad: "I'm feeling sad today, Benjy. I don't know why; I just am," or "I didn't do very well on the last assignment I handed in, Tomma, so I am not feeling good about myself today," or "I had such a good sleep last night! I feel like a million dollars!" You may sometimes be surprised by your child's wisdom and kindness, and you'll be helping them recognize their own emotions, as well as those of others, at the same time as you strengthen your relationship with them.

Another important empathy-building action you can use from your child's birth through to adulthood is to acknowledge and solicit their feelings. Show your child you notice and care how they feel: "Are you disappointed we aren't going to the park after school today?" "It looks like you're enjoying your dance class," "I'm sorry it didn't work out for your friend to come for a sleepover."

Empathy develops across the lifespan, but the foundation is set for it in the early years, from birth to 5. In The Early Years section of this chapter, I go into some detail about how empathy builds in those years and how you can nurture your child's empathy skills.

FRIENDSHIP

Meaningful relationships are important at every age across the lifespan, but they're essential to children's healthy development, and they build on empathy, as well as self-regulation skills. According to the National Scientific Council on the Developing Child at Harvard's Center on the Developing Child, children's friendships have many important advantages.[6]

It's through friendship that your child discovers who they are—their interests, personality, and abilities. No matter how often you or other adults might remark on your child's strengths, when a friend tells them they're good at running or math or painting, they know it's true. Friends can also help your child through a bad patch, whether it's momentary, such as a failed test, or momentous, such as the loss of a family member. Through friendships, your child will deepen their understandings of sharing, kindness, and empathy.

Friends can bring cognitive and academic benefits, too. Having a friend with similar interests stimulates your child's learning in the areas of shared interest. Children who experience greater peer acceptance enjoy school more and do better academically.

Friends expand your child's experiences and enhance their mental and physical health. They can motivate your child to participate in activities they might otherwise avoid or not think of. When your child has friends, they want to play with them and be active together. This is good for their physical and mental health now and into adulthood. It's through friendship that your child learns most about how to address and resolve disagreements. In their interactions with others, your child figures out what ethical behavior is and learns about their own values.

The nature of friendship changes from early childhood into adulthood; I address friendships in each stage a bit later in this chapter.

SELF-CONTROL: STAYING CALM, FOCUSED, PRESENT, AND REASONABLE

We all know what poor self-control looks like: a hot quick temper, low frustration tolerance, short attention span, restlessness, distractibility, and more. One of the biggest gifts you can give your child is helping them gain control of their emotions and behavior, which will allow them to remain calm when challenged, retaining their capacity to respond intelligently, wisely, and well to whatever situation presents itself.

If you have more than one child, you probably know that self-control comes more easily to some people than to others. One child in a family might be remarkably good at staying calm, processing their emotions constructively, and staying on task. Another might have a more tempestuous temperament and find it challenging to control their immediate reactions to things. They can both go on to experience happy relationships, interesting careers, and fulfilling parenthood, so don't despair if you have a child who doesn't take easily to learning to manage their responses. With love, time, and attention, even a wild child can learn enough self-control to function well in the world.

Self-control is "the ability to manage or regulate impulses and desires in a socially appropriate way, rather than be managed or regulated by them," according to Jay Belsky and his colleagues.[7] As I mentioned in the Introduction to this book, in *The Origins of You*, Belsky and his coauthors described their findings from four different large longitudinal studies. One of those was the Dunedin Study, which involved 40 years of intensive research with 1,000 children as they grew into middle age. The research team found that self-control in childhood predicted many dimensions of life decades later. Good childhood self-control didn't necessarily lead to better functioning later, but it was a good predictor of it.

Belsky and colleagues assessed self-control by looking for its absence, including low frustration tolerance, restlessness, impulsivity, impulsive aggression, distractibility, and lack of persistence. Observations were made of each child by trained observers, parents, and teachers at the ages of 3, 5, 7, 9, and 11. There were also self-evaluations at 11 and a variety of other measures at 13, 15, 18, and 21, followed by interviews and real-world measures such as health and police records at 26 and 32. The research team found that poor self-control in childhood persisted well into adulthood, predicting behavior problems in adolescence and health concerns, poverty, and criminal activity in adulthood.

Belsky and colleagues concluded that childhood self-control is enormously important, affecting health, wealth, and happiness in adulthood. They also emphasized that development is an ongoing, dynamic process, open to environmental factors, including support from adults. Interventions teaching self-management skills can make a long-term difference to a child's development. These interventions are best when implemented in early childhood, but they can also be effective later.

The findings reported in *The Origins of You* suggest that adversity might interfere with the development of a child's self-control, and that is exactly what Liliana Lengua found.[8] As a child clinical psychologist who runs the Center for Child and Family Well-Being at the University of Washington, Lengua, with her colleagues, demonstrated how early adversity—whether poverty, family disruption, illness, or something else—disrupts children's attention, stress hormones, and adjustment. It's not surprising that children experiencing adversity—as so many children are now—can have a harder time achieving self-control and social–emotional well-being.

Researcher Stuart Shanker distinguished between self-regulation and self-control.[9] He called it *self-control* when a person inhibits their strong impulses; they still have those impulses, but they keep them under control. A person using *self-regulation* reduces their strong impulses by managing their stress. This may be a valid distinction, and certainly, Shanker has a large following of people who have benefited from this perspective. He tells parents to listen calmly—and not respond with impatience, irritation, or anger—when their child is in distress. Almost always, he said, an out-of-control or misbehaving child responds better to patient soothing than to punishment. In Chapter 5, I wrote about *Beyond Behaviors: Using Brain Science and Compassion to Understand Children's Problem Behaviors.*[10] In that book, Mona Delahooke made the same recommendation as Shanker, in her case, based on a distinction between top-down (consciously regulated) and bottom-up (unconsciously driven) behavior.

Whether you think of it as self-control or self-regulation, managing your emotional reactions has a major impact on every area of your life and every person in your life. We all know people who never learn to do that, and many people believe that's just the way they were wired—"I feel the way I feel, and I have to act on it," or "My moods are bigger than I am." How you behave is a choice you make, and you can learn to do better or different if you want to.

Although young children can begin to develop some of the prerequisites for self-control, the major work happens a bit later, so it's in the Childhood: 6 to 10 section of this chapter that I discuss how you can support your child (and yourself if applicable) in the challenging task of learning to manage emotions and behavior.

A POSITIVE ATTITUDE

Most people prefer to spend time with people who are cheerful and cooperative rather than critical and difficult. Marilyn Price-Mitchell is a parenting expert who has written about the neuroscience of negativity and the benefits of supporting kids in finding a positive attitude.[11] She discussed the research of Andrew Newberg, Mark Waldman, Barbara Fredrickson, and others who have found that people with positive attitudes experience more happiness, social success, academic achievement, and career success than those who tend to be gloomy. On the other side of that equation, negativity is stressful, both for the negative person and those they spend time with. Although some people are blessed with more optimistic temperaments than others, positive attitudes and habits can be learned, as can negative ones.

You want your child to learn to be positive and cooperative, but you don't want to break their spirit. That's a hard balance to strike with any child and even more challenging if your child is intensely confident in their opinions or has a difficult temperament. Regardless of your child's temperament, though, learning to be more positive will make it easier for them to live with themself and easier for you to live with them, as well as help them with other important dimensions of life. I share some ideas for supporting your child in becoming more positive in each of the age-related sections next.

HAPPINESS

Some children—and some parents—seem to go through life with smiles and laughter. Others tend more to worry and negativity, sometimes judging other people's apparent happiness as phony, lucky, or superficial. And sometimes, a not-so-happy child will ask their mom or dad or someone else a question such as, "Where does happiness come from?"

In *Understanding Emotions*,[12] the authors discussed the pitfalls of happiness. Striving too hard for happiness or trying to maximize it in every circumstance puts one at psychological risk. They wrote that instead, "It is a complex matter to find meaning and happiness, one that requires patience and the acceptance of life's complexities and difficulties alongside its delights and joys."[13] On the basis of a review of the research on happiness, they concluded that happiness is made up of pleasure, engagement in one's activities, and a sense of the meaningfulness of one's activities. They pointed out that engagement in meaningful activity, whether social, intellectual, artistic, or something else, has a stronger influence on happiness than the pursuit of pleasure.

The research on happiness is conclusive in showing that it doesn't result from wealth, talent, athleticism, or appearance. Poverty, racism, sexism, and other systemic inequities make it harder—but not impossible—to experience happiness. But people who have nice clothes, cars, or other possessions aren't happier than others. Whether you're rich, middle class, or poor; divorced, single, or married; tall, short, or somewhere in between, you can help your child make choices that are more likely to lead to happiness. In circumstances where happiness seems like a stretch—during times of illness, financial reversals, or family breakdown—there are still ways to increase your happiness quotient and that of your child. The strategies for doing that aren't age specific, so I'll review them here rather than breaking them down by age.

One of the best ways to be happy is to be kind. That makes you feel better and helps your child feel valued. The child—of whatever age or circumstance—who is confident of at least one parent's love and attention and who can count on that parent to be understanding when they mess up has a head start toward happiness. Happy people usually treat others with kindness, and it also works in the opposite direction: Treating people with kindness helps you feel good about yourself. You might suggest that your child find an opportunity every day to do something good for someone else, something unexpected that doesn't have any obvious benefits for themself.

A mother I was working with was having a rough time in a number of ways—divorce, financial troubles, and other worries. Janice told me that in addition to everything else, her kids were increasingly angry and grouchy with each other and with her.

"I'm having trouble keeping my head above water," she said. "I really can't handle my kids arguing all the time, being mean to each other, treating me badly."

"Why don't you suggest a daily mitzvah?" I asked. "I tried it with my kids when we were going through a rough patch, and it really worked."

"What does that mean?"

"Ask each of your kids to find a situation every day when they can perform a random act of kindness, with no hope of personal gain, other than knowing they've helped someone out."

"They'll say no. Why would they want to do that?"

"Listen patiently and calmly to each of their objections. Nod as if you think it's a reasonable objection. Don't argue with them. Tell them it's an experiment. Say you heard that being kind can make people feel happier, and you thought they might enjoy giving it a try."

The next time I met with Janice, she said, "That daily mitzvah is a lifesaver! It worked like a charm!"

"What happened?" I asked.

"The older two kids thought it was a stupid idea, but 6-year-old Jili took to it immediately. The day after I suggested it, she couldn't wait to tell me about her mitzvah. I picked them all up from after-school care, and Jili said, 'Mommy! I helped Clifford with his math today. I noticed he hadn't learned something from last unit, and it was keeping him stuck. So, me and him stayed in for recess, and I showed him, and he got it, and he was SO happy!'"

"I ignored her grammatical error and asked her how it made her feel," Janice said. "Jili thought for a minute, and she said, 'Really proud and happy.' I told her that made me proud and happy too. I didn't ask either of the other kids about mitzvahs."

"That's great!" I said. "You validated Jili's effort and put no pressure on the other two. You gave them a chance to think about it and wonder if it might be a good idea."

247

Janice smiled and said, "Then, the next day, when I picked them up, it was 8-year-old Jayden who came bursting into the car: 'I did a mitzvah, Mom!' She'd picked one of the kids nobody usually picked for an after-school softball game. 'I thought he deserved a chance,' she told me. 'After the game, he came up to me and very quietly said thank you. I could tell it was really important to him.' Jayden was glowing, and I could see she felt happy and proud, too, like Jili the day before. And then, of course, Jili had to tell us all about her mitzvah that day."

"And Jett?" I asked. "He's 12, right?"

"Yes, 12. A tough age. He's still a kid, but he's trying so hard to be a man. When Jayden talked about her mitzvah, Jett said nothing, and none of us asked him about it. But the next day, it was Jett who couldn't wait to share. He did it in a bored voice, like he was too cool to be kind, but I could see he was feeling good about himself for it. He'd noticed that one of the kids wasn't eating at lunchtime. Jett sat down beside him and shared his lunch. The other boy had forgotten his lunch and didn't have any money to go out and get something to eat."

From time to time after that, I'd ask Janice about the mitzvahs. She'd always grin and shake her head. "It has changed my family life," she said once. "My kids' attitudes are not always great, but they don't grumble so much, and they're more cooperative with me and each other. I think all of them are happier just because they've learned to look for random acts of kindness. It's not every day, but at least once a week, I'll hear a report from each of them about some mitzvah they've done."

Being kind is a great start, but being happy also depends on doing what needs doing to take care of yourself, something we talked about in Chapter 4. Nobody's happy when they're tired or hungry or not getting enough exercise. So, do your best to ensure you and your child work toward healthy habits for food, sleep, outdoor exercise, and free play, as well as getting the intellectual, artistic, spiritual, and physical stimulation you need. Think also about the activities that make you happy, whether it's cooking, dancing, writing, watching movies, or reading books. Share that with your child. Talk with them about your enthusiasms and theirs.

Gratitude is another happiness accelerator. I mentioned this in Chapter 3 in connection with mindfulness. Feeling grateful shifts your focus from what's wrong in your world to what's right. As with being kind, expressing gratitude has a positive effect on your brain chemistry and your social environment, and grateful people find they have more and more to feel happy about.[14] Mindfulness itself increases happiness—as you learn to manage your mind, you don't focus so much on what's wrong, and there's more room in your consciousness for what there is to feel good about. And gratitude is a useful tool to use when you notice your own happiness or your child's needs a boost.

We talked in Chapter 2 about all the benefits of growth mindsets. One of those benefits is that it increases your experience of happiness. If you or your child learns to welcome problems as chances to discover what you need to learn more about, you'll take more interesting risks and meet more creative challenges head on. Not only does this attitude lead to increased happiness, but it also leads to greater success in every area of life, from friendships to academic achievement to career fulfillment.

And finally, happiness depends on your learning to accept the dark times as well as the bright ones. As Dacher Keltner, Keith Oatley, and Jennifer Jenkins observed in *Understanding Emotions*,[15] happiness requires the patient acceptance of life's complexities and difficulties.

There's an alchemy to these simple practices. You can help transform your child's negativity—and your own—into a golden feeling that will illuminate all aspects of their life. I have learned through challenging times of my own that by using these strategies to intentionally increase my happiness quotient, regardless of the circumstances, I also increase my child's chances of creating a happy life for themself.

SELF-CONFIDENCE

As with all other social and emotional dimensions, temperament plays a role in the development of confidence. People who have an easier temperament are happier entering new situations and meeting new people and are reinforced for their positive attitudes, so they're likelier than others to exude optimism and confidence. This leads to easier friendships and builds social confidence, which feels great and which most people find attractive. Helping your child achieve this kind of confidence is more challenging—and more urgent—with difficult or spirited children, but no matter your child's temperament, you have an important role to play in your child's developing confidence.

Misconceptions About Self-Confidence

Some widely held misconceptions interfere with many parents' attempts to support their child's developing confidence. The first is that people are either confident or they're not across all areas. Most people have areas of life in which they feel confident—sports, for example, or mathematical reasoning, friendships, or professional expertise—and other areas where they have little confidence. Your child may feel good about their appearance or their artistic ability but terribly insecure about other areas.

Another widely held misconception is that praising your child helps them feel more confident. In fact, hollow or unspecific global praise—"You're the most beautiful little girl ever!" "You're a natural athlete!" "You are so smart!"—actually undermines a person's self-confidence. The biggest contributor to a person feeling good about themself is a sense of competence in areas that matter to that person. It doesn't matter what those areas are—juggling, academics, athletics, social popularity, appearance, dog walking—as long as the person values expertise in that area and feels they have attained a reasonable degree of it. Praise your child for specific and measurable actions— the effort they invested in solving a math problem, the colors they used in a painting, how fast they ran a race—rather than global attributes such as intelligence, artistic ability, or athleticism.

A third misconception is that confidence is always a good thing. Earned confidence is great, but it's best to go into a new situation with humility, wondering how to proceed, and looking for the right kind of help. True confidence is built on competence, which takes time, support, and effort to achieve.

How to Encourage Your Child's Confidence

As part of their work with mindsets, Carol Dweck and her colleagues have made many pioneering discoveries in the past 2 decades, and many of them apply to supporting people's confidence.[16,17] The recommendations emerging from this work apply across the age spectrum, from early childhood into adulthood.

One of their recommendations is to encourage the awareness that everyone has strengths and weaknesses. Help your child appreciate what comes easily for them and also what's harder for them to learn. Regardless of any diagnoses or identified special needs they might have, help them see themself as just like everyone else in having a profile of abilities; everyone has strengths in some areas and challenges in others. As I discussed in Chapter 6, feeling "special" because of strengths or problems in one direction or another can undermine your child's confidence, so acknowledge their areas of difference from others, but keep your emphasis on the ways they're just like everyone else.

Another way to increase a person's confidence is to emphasize the incremental nature of all accomplishment. Everything worth doing is built one step at a time, so strength builds slowly and systematically on strength. Support your child in identifying their big goals, then breaking the goals down, one step at a time. To a child who is seriously interested in painting, say, "I admire how you stayed with that picture, working on it until it was just right. What are you thinking of painting next?" To a child who wants to qualify for a softball team, say, "You've hit all the balls I've pitched. What do you want to work on next?" You can acknowledge their long-term goals—becoming an artist or professional ball player—but refrain from focusing on those. Instead, keep your focus on mastering each of the necessary steps along the way.

Your child's confidence builds through participating in activities they enjoy and can get better at. When planning their extracurricular activities (keeping in mind their need for ample free time), look for classes or groups that support their continued progress. Making progress toward competence and confidence in any field—music, sports, academics, anything—usually means a series of transitions over time across learning situations. Be ready to support your child as they consider their options, review their goals, and adjust their efforts to adapt to changing demands and circumstances.

As I discussed in Chapter 2 with respect to mindsets, show your child—from the time they're very young and into adulthood—how to see difficulties as chances for learning what they need to pay attention to and work harder at, not as dead ends or impossible hurdles. Remind them as necessary that problems are inevitable, a necessary part of the learning process. Teach them to welcome and overcome setbacks, and you'll be supporting their growing confidence.

THE EARLY YEARS: BIRTH TO 5

Most experts on children's early years emphasize children's social and emotional development. For example, the National Scientific Council on the Developing Child (NSCDC) is a multidisciplinary, multi-university collaboration hosted by Harvard University's Center on the Developing Child. Their first working paper, "Young Children Develop in an Environment of Relationships," opened with this paragraph:

> Healthy development depends on the quality and reliability of a young child's relationships with the important people in his or her life, both within and outside the family. Even the development of a child's brain architecture depends on the establishment of these relationships.[18]

Empathy Develops

Empathy—a fundamental component of social and emotional development—provides an excellent illustration of the NSCDC's emphasis on relationships. For most children, empathy starts in infancy with an attachment to the adult who makes them feel cherished and safe, most typically their mother. By 6 months old (and sometimes sooner), the baby actively pays attention to their mother's reactions to other people and gauges their own reactions accordingly. If the baby sees that their mother feels comfortable with someone, chances are good they'll respond well to that person. If the mother is apprehensive about a person or a new situation, the baby may show signs of fear or agitation.

As the child approaches their second birthday, they begin to realize that others have thoughts and feelings and that these are sometimes different from their own. At about the same time (between 18 months and 2 years), the toddler will recognize themselves in a mirror, showing that they understand themselves as a person separate from their mother and others.

253

By about 3, your child can recognize common feelings and see how they are connected—how disappointment leads to sadness or anger, for example, or happiness results from a pleasant surprise. By the age of 4, they can learn to see a situation from another person's perspective. They can look at a particular situation (such as watching a classmate say goodbye to a parent) and imagine how they—and therefore their friend—might feel in the moment.

During your child's fifth year, they can learn to imagine what response might be appropriate and comforting, such as offering a sad friend a favorite toy or an invitation to join a game. Most emotionally healthy 5-year-olds like to talk about their feelings, often in some depth. You can use this to build a bridge to their emerging understanding of the feelings of others. Your 5- or 6-year-old is also ready to learn how to read social cues about other people's thoughts and feelings through paying close attention not only to their words but also their actions, gestures, and facial expressions.

And also starting at about 5, your child is ready to see themself as a valuable member of a group. By modeling and encouraging empathy, you can help your child learn how to become a compassionate member of a caring community at home, school, and elsewhere.

As with pretty well everything in children's development, this progress toward empathy is not uniform or reliable. A young child may show deep compassion for another child, being the first to see when a classmate is emotionally needy, for example, and soothing them effectively but then go home and laugh when a young sibling has a bad fall. Knowing how to handle big feelings and reliably translating observations of others into empathetic behavior requires maturity and practice, practice, practice.

CASE STUDY: CLARE AND ALIX

You may remember Clare from a story in Chapter 7 about her dropping out of university to continue her education in the real world and follow her creative instincts. The focus then was on the way her mother, Margaret, supported her daughter in figuring out the best way forward at an uncomfortable juncture in her life. Clare and I have stayed in touch through the years since then, and she is now happily married, a published novelist, and the mother of a spirited 4-year-old named Alix. She recently shared a story with me that illustrates a parent's role in the development of empathy.

Clare wrote, "Alix is working on a challenge that she designed for herself. Before Christmas, I bought more things for her than I wanted to give her all at once, and she found one of them. She asked if she could have it. I said I was saving it for a challenge, and she asked what the challenge was. I said I didn't know yet and asked her what she's having trouble with that she'd like to work on. Her dad suggested she work on not talking when he and I are trying to talk to each other or when one of us is on the phone. Alix didn't like that idea and said, 'How about if I work on helping kids at school when they're crying?'

"I asked what she normally does when a friend cries. She shrugged and said, 'Sometimes nothing.' So, I said, sure, she can work on a compassion challenge. She asked what compassion is, and I said it's seeing that someone needs your time or attention and then giving it to them. She said, okay, that can be her challenge. We agreed that if she helps people when they're crying at school all week, she can have the gift on Friday after school."

A few days later, I asked Clare how things were going with the challenge. She told me it was going amazingly well: "Alix took it upon herself to notice when other kids needed help, like when a younger girl needed help with her coat buttons, and a couple of other times when friends were crying, she went to them and offered comfort. Her teacher, who had no idea about the challenge until afterward, told me when I arrived to pick Alix up from school how helpful Alix had been with other children all day."

Clare is helping Alix learn that it feels good to notice what others are feeling and be kind to them when they're hurting, the foundation of empathy.

Nurturing Your Child's Empathy

It hurts to feel someone else's pain, so it's natural for your child to want to back away from feeling others' pain, as Alix had been doing before she took Clare's challenge. The better your child is at managing their emotions, the easier they'll find it to overcome the impulse to back away from others' suffering.

When your child is quite young—maybe 3, sometimes younger—you can teach them the language of empathy. Stand together in front of a mirror. Take turns making faces and naming the emotions you're representing: sadness, anger, surprise, disappointment, happiness, anticipation, and so forth. Take pictures of you and your child making different faces. Make a book of emotions together, using these photos or pictures you've found elsewhere. Don't correct or criticize your child if you have a different opinion about the meaning of a certain facial expression or behavior but rather state the way you see it, and tell them there isn't a right answer. One of the cardinal rules for building good relationships is to realize that the only way we ever know how someone is feeling is to ask them.

It's also empathy building if you encourage open dialogue with your child. If they're distressed, ask them what would make them feel better. Do some problem solving together about that. When others are distressed, ask open-ended questions that encourage your child to think about meaningful ways to help them. Clare's questions and her subsequent conversation with Alix helped Alix see the importance of comforting friends when they're experiencing some difficulty.

You can also point out your perception of others' feelings, making sure you own them as your perceptions and not necessarily the truth. Even better, ask your child how they see it: "Do you think maybe Janine is sad because she lost her ball?" "Did you think Ibrahim was happy when his mother arrived early?" "Issie looked like she was having a good time at the party—what do you think?" You can do this with characters in books and movies, as well as with people in your life. Help your child see the common humanity we all share.

When talking about feelings, connect them with behaviors so that your child can see a cause-and-effect relationship—for example, "Maybe Joey's feeling sad because Oscar took his truck?" You can also do this through stories and role-playing, both in fiction and real life. Make connections between emotions your child observes in others and experiences they've had.

Work with your child to build an atmosphere that encourages every member of the family to be empathetic with each other. Point out how kindness begets kindness and helps everyone: "I was proud of how you let Robin use your blocks when she was feeling sad. Maybe she'll let you use her paint set tomorrow." When you're reviewing the day with your child at bedtime, in addition to asking about their achievements and experiences, ask them about acts of kindness they might have observed or participated in that day.

Under certain circumstances, people who are otherwise kind can be unkind or stand by when others are badly treated. Help your child see the importance of keeping their empathy response on active alert. Point out instances where that is important in everyday life, as well as in fiction and nonfiction stories you encounter.

Finally, in helping your young child become empathetic, think about ways you might expand your circle of concern. Volunteer, attend community meetings, and do what you can for people in need, across lines of culture, race, sex, religion, and political affiliation. When possible, include your child in these activities. Talk with compassion about events in the news and ways you might be able to help.

As your child gets older, you might look at advocating at their school for a school-based program that supports children's empathy because it fosters a climate of kindness, working against bullying, sexism, and racism,[19] a topic I address more fully in Chapter 9.

Friendship in the Early Years

As early as 12 months—and sometimes even sooner—your child may be showing a preference for certain children. They can play simple games, such as imitating each other or peek-a-boo, engaging in early friendship activities. By 2, your child can sometimes be kind to another child and demonstrate concern when the other child is showing distress. In spite of these emerging signs of maturity, however, you can expect occasional aggressive acts and social missteps until your child is quite a bit older.

As with adults, some children seem to make friends easily, marching happily into social situations and getting energy from being around people. Others do well in social situations only when they've had time to watch what happens before joining in. Still others can find it tiring, overwhelming, or even frightening to spend time with people outside their family.

Just like other skills, friendship skills need to be learned. These skills include listening, sharing, taking turns, cooperating, resolving conflicts, showing an interest, soothing hurt feelings, and negotiating different ways of thinking about things. Young children are just beginning to learn about self-regulation and social interaction, so you can expect occasional social disasters when they get together with other children.

Aggression

Disputes are normal and healthy, but when a child behaves aggressively—hitting, pushing, kicking, and so on—it's time for an adult to step in. You might say something such as, "People have different ideas sometimes, and that's okay, but it's not okay to hit or hurt other people." Be clear, specific, and calm. It takes a long time and many experiences for a young child to learn not to use the weapons at hand (e.g., fists, feet, teeth) to get what they want.

SOLO PLAY

There are many reasons a child might opt to play alone when potential playmates are available. As with adults, sometimes a young child just needs some time and space alone to recharge. If, however, your child always seems to be on their own, they might need your help with friendship skills.

HOW TO HELP YOUR YOUNG CHILD MAKE FRIENDS

Eileen Kennedy-Moore has written a delightfully helpful blog series and books that provide practical recommendations for parents who want to support their kids in making friends.[20] She suggested starting with teaching your child about greetings. Initiating a greeting is hard for most children and especially challenging for shy children. If your child is too shy to respond to a greeting, much less initiate one, they need your help. You might do some role-playing. Show your child how to make eye contact, smile warmly, say the person's name (if they know it), and speak loudly enough to be heard. Do some practicing, with each of you taking on different roles—you playing your child to begin with and your child playing a sibling, relative, teacher, and (finally) a prospective friend. Then switch roles so that your child plays themself, and you take on other people's roles. From there, you're ready to take it live. Start slowly by greeting family members, and then move on from there.

Everyone likes appreciation, so another way to signal an interest in friendship is to comment favorably on something. Brainstorm with your child about ways they like to be complimented: their artwork, fashion sense, athletic prowess? Then help them think about what a prospective friend might like to hear. Your child can practice this skill by complimenting family members.

Noticing what another child needs and offering that is a great way to demonstrate openness to friendship. Show your child how lending a crayon, saving a seat, or offering to help carry something can break the ice. You might initiate a nightly bedtime question about acts of kindness in your child's day: "Was anyone kind to you today? Were you kind to anyone?"

Kennedy-Moore observed that young children sometimes believe they have to be amazingly wonderful for others to like them. That can result in bragging, which most prospective friends will perceive as off-putting. Help your child realize that kids simply want to spend time with kids who share their interests or experiences. Instead of proving they're wonderful, suggest they look for ways they can connect on an equal footing.

To have fun with a peer, your child needs to behave in ways that the other child enjoys, communicate respectfully about their likes and dislikes, and avoid or resolve disagreements. They need to learn that fun gets wrecked when they ignore or walk away from the other child, refuse to share, or grab toys. It's also not fun when they boss the other child around, yell at them, or hit them. If your child has problems keeping friends, these are areas to look at helping them with.

Once your child has made contact with another child they want to be friends with, you can facilitate the process by helping your child plan a one-on-one, activity-based playdate. Talk with your child ahead of time about what's involved in being a good host: ensuring their guest feels welcome and has a good time. If your child has special toys they will have trouble sharing, put those away before the guest arrives. Talk about snacks and activities they might both enjoy. When the playdate is in progress, don't hover, but do remain close enough to intervene with a change of activity if needed, so they can regroup and go back to having fun.

Supporting a Positive Attitude in the Early Years

Although a positive attitude goes a long way toward making friends, feeling happy, and getting what you want in life, it's healthy and natural for young children to be difficult, at least some of the time. Here's a conversation with an almost 3-year-old:

"Time to put your boots on, Jackson."

"No!"

"We have to leave soon."

"I am not putting my boots on."

"Not an option, Jackson."

"No!"

We want our kids to have minds of their own and assert their individuality, and that's what's happening in this exchange between Jackson—who is usually reasonable and even-tempered—and his mother, even though they mostly get along well. Children have so little power, so little control over anything that matters to them. Saying "No!" is one way they can feel a little bit of power. So, how does Jackson's mother support his developing independence while moving him toward a more cooperative attitude?

She should start with herself. When your child begins to be negative, take a deep breath and remind yourself you have choices here: You can manage the situation so it goes well, or you can escalate the negativity. Too often, adults find themselves saying "no" to kids: "Not an option, Jackson," or "No, you can't have a cookie, Brooke," or "No more television, Essie!"

Try a positive spin on your "no." As much as possible, tell your child what you do want them to do: "Boots on feet, please, Jackson," or "You can have a cookie after lunch, Brooke," or "Hey, Essie, it's time to get out the blocks and build a tower."

Your child will feel more respected and included in the decision making if you share your reasoning with them: "You want your feet to be toasty warm and dry when we're outside, right, Jackson?" or "First, you need something healthy to make you big and strong, Brooke. Cookies come later," or "Too much TV isn't good for your brain, Essie, but playing and building help you learn to think."

To help your child feel respected and help them move toward positivity and cooperation, you can frame your demand as a choice. Instead of "Time to put your boots on, Jackson," try "Are you going to put your hat on first or your boots?" Instead of "No, you can't have a cookie, Brooke," try "Would you like a cracker now or a cookie later?" Instead of "No more television, Essie!" try "Do you want to build something with your blocks or have a dance party with me?"

Another approach that can flip things from negative to positive is to create a contest they can win: "Let's see who gets their boots on first, Jackson," or "I'll race you to the kitchen, Brooke," or "I feel like making the tallest block tower ever."

If none of those approaches seem appropriate at the moment, you might try thinking about something silly. That can help your attitude, as well as your child's, and prevent things from getting (more) confrontational—for example, "Can you hop on one foot when you're wearing boots, Jackson? I can!" Wobble precariously while you do it. Or "No, Brooke, you definitely can't have a cookie. I ate them all up." Then pretend you're Cookie Monster, gobbling up lots of cookies. Or "I'm building a dragon to barbecue the television into charred nothing. Watch this!"

Try to catch your child being good, not bad. Reward cooperation and a positive attitude whenever they show up. When your child does what you ask without arguing, give them a tangible reward related to the act of cooperation—for example, "Thank you for getting your boots on, Jackson. Now we'll have time to stop at the park on our way home." Or "You didn't even ask for a cookie, Brookie! You get a bonus cookie after lunch today." Or "You turned off the TV when I asked you to, Essie. Next TV time, you get 5 bonus minutes for cooperation now."

In *Pig Will and Pig Won't*,[21] children's author Richard Scarry shows the Pig family going about their usual routines, with one cooperative child, Pig Will, and one child who says "NO!" to everything, Pig Won't. Pig Will ends up going on happy outings with one parent and the other and even getting ice cream, all of which Pig Won't misses out on. At the end of the book, Pig Won't intelligently decides to change his ways, and they live happily ever after.

> *Jackson:* No! [I won't put my boots on.]
> *Mom:* Hmmm. Are you Pig Will today or Pig Won't?
> *Jackson:* Pig Won't!
> *Mom:* Okay. So, we'll stay home. If we're not going to the grocery store, we won't be able to make cheesy noodles for lunch. And of course, we won't go to the park on our way home.
> *Jackson:* [No comment, just a glower]
> *Mom:* [After a pause] Are you Pig Will and putting on your boots or Pig Won't and staying home?
> *Jackson:* [Begins to put on his boots]

CHILDHOOD: 6 TO 10

During the childhood years, your child is strengthening their social and emotional skills as they build other areas of competence, too.

Supporting Your Child's Friendships

Friendships affect your child's happiness, health, and success, so take it seriously when your child talks about problems with a friend. Turn off your phone and give your child your full attention. Avoid being judgmental; just communicate that you know how much it hurts. If they ask for advice, ask questions that help them find a solution.

Another good way to support your child in this important dimension of their life is to model respect for others' emotions. Be warm, respectful, and empathetic with your child, as well as with other people. Speak about others with kindness and respect. You can point out others' feelings: "I think Ethan is sad because he lost his thermos," "Sergio looked happy when he saw you." Help your child see the common humanity we share, regardless of differences. Do this with fictional characters, as well as people in your life.

Be sure to create a friendly atmosphere in your home. Model friendly greetings and concern for each other member of the family. When visitors enter—whether it's a delivery person or best friend—stop and greet them warmly, and ask that your child do the same if they are present.

If your child needs help finding friends, look for others with similar interests. It's easiest to make friends with those who share interests and hobbies. Look for clubs and groups focused on activities your child might do well at: a choir, sports team, dance class, robotics club, anything where your child can develop the confidence that comes from competence and interact with others who share their interests.

If your child has persistent friendship problems, consider getting professional help. Perhaps you or your child would benefit from counseling that focuses on relationship building. If so, this is the time to do that; it's important to address any issues before the problems get embedded in their self-concept.

Be careful, though—not all people want to spend a lot of time on social activities. If your child has one friend and is happy with the situation, social skills counseling might make them think there's something wrong with them when there isn't, making a problem out of a nonproblem. This can be a dicey judgment call, requiring you to listen carefully to your child and observe their moods and behavior before deciding to call in an expert. Depending on your personality and how sociable you are, what you see as a problem might or might not be a problem. Talk to the other adults in your child's life—teachers, friends, and others—and then make up your mind about this, knowing you can always choose a different path—professional help or not— if something changes.

Self-Control

One of your child's important developmental tasks during the years from 6 to 10 is learning to regulate their reactions to life's inevitable setbacks and problems, so they can make good decisions and act from a place of thought, not instinct. Managing one's emotions and behavior is particularly challenging and also particularly important in circumstances of poverty, racism, dangerous neighborhoods, and other stressors.

The best way to help your child with self-control is your own example, so do your best to regulate your own emotions and behavior. When feeling stressed, especially when it comes to your child, take a deep breath. Take another breath. Get enough sleep and exercise. Eat nutritious meals.

When your child misbehaves or overreacts, be calm, kind, and supportive, which models what self-control looks like and soothes the child's turbulence, which needs to happen before they can regulate their emotions and reactions.

Michael Ungar is known for his work on resilience.[22] He recommended that parents use chores to help kids acquire the self-regulation skills they need to survive stressful times. He argued, based on decades of international research, that having responsibility for chores supports kids' cognitive, emotional, physical, and social development at the same time as it helps parents cope with their stressors.

Physical activity is another way to help your child with both stress reduction and self-regulation, as are regular family routines—meals, chores, bedtime, and other schedules. Having a reliable schedule provides your child with a sense of control and trust.

There are many other techniques you can use to support your child in learning to control their emotional and behavioral responses to disappointments and setbacks, many of which we've already considered in this book. Mindfulness practices can be great, even with young children; kids from 6 to 10 often enjoy the self-mastery these practices give them. A growth mindset is another approach that helps with self-regulation. Support your child in learning how to welcome obstacles as learning opportunities and approach every challenge as a chance for creative problem solving.

Role-playing is a technique a lot of kids enjoy and a powerful way for your child to discover important truths about behavioral choices people make. You might wait until something happens or ask your child to name a situation that challenges their coping skills. Take turns, each of you playing different parts as you reenact the situation. Use props if appropriate—maybe a pair of glasses when playing one character, a scarf or jacket or hat when playing another, a broom when playing another. Do it with good humor, laughing together if your child finds something funny (and, of course, never laughing at them, only laughing together with them).

A Positive Attitude

I talked earlier about the importance of having a positive attitude—the way it changes our brain chemistry, allowing for possibilities and pleasures we can't see when our mind is focused on negativity. The childhood years are a good time to consolidate positivity as a mental habit that will serve your child well throughout their lifetime.

Children who appreciate what's good in their lives take pleasure in helping others and make friends at the same time. Helping your child develop an attitude of gratitude rather than entitlement increases their chances for well-being, happiness, energy, optimism, empathy, and popularity. Say "Yes!" whenever possible, and try to catch your child being cheerful and cooperative more often than you comment on their misbehavior.

You'll get more positivity from your child—and increase their sense of well-being—if you find ways to avoid the predictable negativity times. For one thing, that means trying to keep to a regular schedule. Just like adults, kids are grouchier when they're hungry, tired, cold, too sedentary, or otherwise uncomfortable. So, do your best to give your child a reasonably predictable schedule of naps, meals, snuggles, playtime, outdoor time, and rest. Also, kids quite reasonably resist moving from fun activities to meals, bedtime, bath time, and so forth, so give your child lots of warning. You might start with "Five more minutes to bath time!" and move down in 1-minute increments to "One minute to splashdown!"

Unfamiliar experiences (meeting new people, moving to a new house, starting a new school year) can be extra stressful and more so for some kids than others. Help your child anticipate the possible pleasures of what's coming and focus more on the gains than losses where that is possible.

You can prevent some negative experiences by remembering that some kids are bothered by noise, crowds, or too many requests all at once. Respect your child's temperament and sensitivities and avoid overstimulating them as much as possible. Your child doesn't enjoy being negative, so help them make the choices needed for positivity.

ADOLESCENCE: 11 TO 18

By the time your child is 11, you want them to have a foundation of social and emotional skills. Their empathy skills should be pretty firmly in place, they should be enjoying making and keeping friends, they should be doing pretty well at self-control most of the time, they should be reasonably positive, and you hope they're finding sources for happiness.

There are many reasons for one or more of these skills not being solidly in place yet, including a disrupted childhood, family illness, a temperament mismatch with a parent, a dangerous environment, parental stressors, inadequate nutrition, and many more. Happily, there is a window of opportunity in your child's adolescence to help them develop these skills. No matter where your child is on the temperament and social–emotional skills scales, some solid attention and support from you now can make a life-changing difference. It's not too late for your child to acquire these skills if they're not yet part of their repertoire. And if your child is socially and emotionally mature at 11, you can support them in strengthening and further developing these important skills.

If you have a preteen or teenager, you know that friends can be sources of solace, inspiration, motivation, pain, temptation, and torture. Lydia Denworth is a science journalist who has investigated the history, purpose, and meaning of friendship across species, disciplines, and the lifespan and who has written about the importance of social connection to wellness and longevity. In one recent article, Denworth discussed new findings showing how teenage friendship problems can cause long-term brain damage.[23]

Laurence Steinberg is a renowned psychology professor who has written about the impact of friends on brain development and adolescent decision making.[24] The new findings Denworth described confirm Steinberg's analysis of adolescence as an "age of opportunity," a critical brain-building period during which social experiences are sculpting the brain, changing the brain's architecture. Steinberg showed how adolescence is a period of enormous brain activity, second only to early childhood in its activity and volatility.

One of the new sets of findings that Denworth discussed is from rodent studies, showing how social isolation in adolescence leads to less efficient brain development, resulting in immature adult brains and decision-making skills. Rodents who experience social isolation during adolescence are more prone to addiction and exhibit social anxiety in adulthood. It's a long way from rats to human adolescents, but these early findings underscore the importance of friendship during adolescence.

Although your teenage child, from 11 to 18, needs to choose and keep their own friends, there are still many ways you can support their friendships during adolescence. To begin with, no matter how badly they behave, do your best to be warm, loving, and respectful. Take your child's problems with peers seriously. Don't pry, but be alert to the possibility that your teen might want to talk with you, and be ready to problem solve with them if they ask for that.

Try to create a home environment that your child wants to invite friends into, and welcome your child's friends if they arrive. Be warm, parental, and available, but stay in the background unless they invite you to participate in a conversation or activity. You can also look for opportunities to include your child's friends on outings or for family meals.

Remember, too, that peer pressure is a serious force at this stage. When your teenager is with friends, they are susceptible to genuine pressures that can override their normal judgment. They don't yet have the neurological maturity to delay gratification and can be attracted to risky behavior. So, as much as possible, keep your young person safe from the dangers of this age—alcohol, drugs, sex, teenage drivers—by being available as much as possible, making rules about curfews, doing your best to ensure they go where they say they're going, and so on. You can do this with kindness and respect, understanding that your child is not willfully "bad" if they break the rules but is in the process of growing up.

YOUNG ADULTHOOD: 19 TO 24

By the time your child is 19, your active parenting for social and emotional development is pretty much finished. You still have an essential role to play in their life by way of ongoing love, guidance, and support, but what they haven't learned by now from living with you all these years, they're going to learn from their interactions in the world—or not. As I mentioned in Chapter 2, this is a potentially vulnerable stage where your support can make a big difference to the outcome,[25,26,27] so stay ready to help if your child asks for that or is experiencing serious problems they can't handle alone. But don't try to change their behavior or "fix" them in any way. Instead, love them just the way they are, live your own life with empathy, kindness, self-control, and positivity, and be available as needed if problems arise.

In Chapter 1, I introduced you to Elizabeth. She and her husband, Neil, had a baby named Ezra and had some early problems responding to their son's spirited temperament. Over time, they moved from being authoritarian parents, demanding that Ezra comply with their rules, to being authoritative parents, working with Ezra to support him in feeling safe.

What I didn't mention in Chapter 1 was that little Ezra came by his sensitivity and need for extra reassurance honestly—Elizabeth had always been unusually sensitive herself, although she hadn't seen it that way. When she was let go from jobs or overlooked for promotions, she blamed her coworkers or bosses for being stupid or unreasonable. When people seemed happy, she wondered how real it was.

Elizabeth was innately kind, but her kindness was hidden behind a thick wall of cynicism and irritability. All that changed when she met Neil. They shared a quirky sense of humor, and Neil was able to ignore Elizabeth's short temper. She loved his nonjudgmental nature and adventurous spirit and enjoyed his company enough to start controlling her temper better. He brought out a softness in her that no one had seen since she was a little girl.

Feeling secure in that relationship gave Elizabeth what she needed to begin to relax and develop some of the social skills she hadn't acquired during childhood and adolescence. Having a baby with a difficult temperament was more stressful than she could handle and caused her to relapse into some of her old habits. But with time and counseling and ongoing support from Neil, she began to strengthen the social and emotional skills she'd never valued. Over time, Elizabeth learned to take better care of herself and regulate her moods. By the time Ezra was 10, Elizabeth had a friendly, positive quality that people were drawn to. Instead of others avoiding her—which she'd always perceived but not understood—they were drawn to her.

It's best for everyone if your child has well-developed social and emotional skills by the time they're 24, but if they don't, there's still a chance they'll acquire them as they build a life for themself. There's not much you can do about it at this stage other than live your own life with love, positivity, caring, and connection.

TAKING IT INTO THE COMMUNITY: TAKING SOCIAL AND EMOTIONAL SKILLS TO SCHOOL

Social and emotional skills are enormously important in making a happy and fulfilling life. They have an impact on every dimension of life—friendships, school, work, relationships, parenting, and so much more. Unfortunately, for one reason or another, some children don't get much of a chance to learn these skills at home. That is why some educators, psychologists, and social justice advocates have come together to create school-based programs to help kids learn to care about each other and the common good.

Earlier in this chapter, I mentioned two of the many programs that work toward teaching social and emotional skills and establishing a climate of kindness in classrooms, thereby working against bullying, sexism, and racism. You and your child might be interested in taking one of the dimensions of one of these programs into your child's classroom or school.

Roots of Empathy described its mission as building "caring, peaceful, and civil societies through the development of empathy in children and adults ... to change the world, child by child."[28] The program has been proven to reduce levels of aggression in children from age 5 to 13 by increasing their social–emotional competence, with an emphasis on empathy. It originated in Canada and has been adopted around the world, including in the United Kingdom, Germany, the United States, Costa Rica, South Korea, and many other countries.

If you want to get a Roots of Empathy program going in your child's school, you'll need the school on board, and you'll also need to have an infant or find one in your neighborhood. If you find one, you'll also need their parent, whose job will be to bring the infant for a series of classroom visits. You can become a Roots of Empathy volunteer instructor yourself or ask Roots of Empathy for help with that. There's a detailed curriculum with different activities each week. The instructor visits the classroom before and after each family visit to prepare the students for what to expect that week and reinforce the teachings. This program yields many important cognitive and psychological benefits in addition to social–emotional learning and has been covered by CNN, BBC, and other local, regional, and national media around the world.

Making Caring Common is another approach to helping kids learn social and emotional skills that enrich their own lives, as well as enriching the community. They described their vision as

> a world in which children learn to care about others and the common good, treat people well day to day, come to understand and seek fairness and justice, and do what is right even at times at a cost to themselves. We believe that young people with these capacities will become community members and citizens who can strengthen our democracy, mend the fractures that divide us, and create a more caring, just world.[29]

Making Caring Common is based at the Harvard Graduate School of Education and has many different research initiatives, "with the goal of helping children develop the capacity to care for and value others—particularly those who are different from them— to treat people well day to day, and to understand and seek fairness and justice."[30] In their Caring School Network, they provide K–12 schools with a simple and relatively inexpensive process for building caring and inclusive school communities.

As a parent, you can learn more about Making Caring Common and become an advocate for it at your child's school, or—if you're really excited about it and have the time and energy—you could offer to coordinate the program or one like it at your child's school. As with Roots of Empathy, your child and other children at the school will reap many benefits in addition to the social and emotional learning, as will the teachers and other parents. These programs can change the trajectory of kids' lives, communities, and, yes, even the world.

KEY TAKEAWAYS: IT'S ALL ABOUT CONNECTION

- You can choose to be loving, positive, caring, and connected or choose to be cool, negative, uncaring, and disconnected from others.

273

- Empathy is a key dimension of social and emotional intelligence. It is more complex and multifaceted than many people realize, and it is not always a force for good.
- Friendships are enormously important in children's development, and there are ways that parents can support their children in forming and maintaining healthy friendships.
- Good self-control does more for your child than just help them behave better. It has important implications for success and happiness in every dimension of their life, well into adulthood.
- There are ways to support your child in feeling confident, starting with encouraging their enthusiasms and curiosities, and supporting them in becoming competent in areas they value.

CHAPTER 9

BE THE ADULT IN THE ROOM: NOT PERFECT, BUT WISE

Turn your wounds into wisdom.

—Oprah Winfrey

Once you become a parent, you take on serious adult responsibilities, whether you feel ready or not. And even if you do feel ready— you've been yearning to be a parent for years, you've prepared the baby's sleeping space and everything else, and, finally, your dream is realized—there are bound to be moments—or years—when it's all a bit overwhelming.

Those are the moments (and years) when you most need the ideas in this book, when you most need the self-care and self-soothing techniques that can help you be the adult in the room and continue to strengthen your relationship with your child no matter the challenges. That does not mean being perfect because no one ever is, but it does mean aspiring toward wisdom. This chapter is all about doing what you can to turn your wounds into wisdom, as Oprah so wisely recommended.

Nobody arrives at parenthood without wounds. Some have been lucky enough to have received the support and resources they needed along the way to (mostly) recover. Many of us, however, arrive at parenthood with wounds still fresh and bleeding or damage as yet unacknowledged, wounds that parenthood will soon rip open. No matter how damaged we might be, though, our challenge is the same: to be the adult in the room no matter the circumstances we encounter with our child. Your child needs you to be a grown-up, whether you feel ready for that or not. In this chapter, I discuss approaches and ideas for responding as wisely as you can to some of the complicated situations you might encounter.

Each of these complications is infinitely more complex and personal than this brief discussion allows and is the topic of entire books and research agendas. Just as each of these concerns develops in complex ways and over time, I describe how their solutions also develop over time, with understanding, patience, and the necessary supports in place. This chapter, then, is a starting place for thinking about some of the complications you may experience and how you might approach them with a degree of wisdom as an adult.

Complications Quiz

Before considering some of the challenging circumstances that require parents to be the adult in the room, you might want to think about your current perspectives on these topics:

1. My child would never bully another child. T/F
2. My child would never stand by and watch while someone else is bullied. T/F
3. If my child experienced racism or any other kind of bullying at school, I'd figure out whose fault it was and make sure there were consequences, whether it's a teacher, another parent, or a child. T/F
4. I always have my phone on and handy. I never know when someone will need to get in touch with me, and I enjoy checking my social media feed and playing video games while my child is occupied. T/F
5. I protect my child from knowing anything about the outside world. There are too many horrible things happening, and they're too young to know about them. T/F
6. If my child were to hear about a school shooting or some other terrible thing, I'd insist on finding out where they heard about it and

---

Complications Quiz (*Continued*)

make sure that information source was no longer available to them. I would not talk to my child about the situation; that would only make things worse. T/F

7 Children of divorce always have problems. T/F

8. Children who grow up with a single parent don't have the same chances as other kids at a good marriage or a good education. T/F

9. Same-sex parents can never do as good a job as a mother and father. T/F

10. A child who goes to day care or has a nanny has a permanent disadvantage. The mother—or maybe the father—is the only person who can take good care of a child in the first 3 years of life. T/F

I've put these questions a bit starkly, without much by way of nuance, to stimulate thought. I'll come back to them at the end of the chapter, and you can think then about whether any of your answers have changed.

BULLYING

Bullying is one of the most ubiquitous and potentially damaging childhood experiences. Depending on how it's defined and measured, estimates vary, showing that from 25% to 90% of children experience some form of bullying or harassment in any given year.

By the time we reach parenthood, most of us have experienced bullying in one form or another somewhere along the way. Some people are lucky and had protections in place when the bullying happened to provide the support they needed for resilience, but many of us have felt alone and carry the scars into adulthood, even into old age. So, naturally, we want to protect our child from being bullied. That is easier said than done. What we can do is make sure they have the supports in place to avoid it, if possible, and be resilient if it happens.

Bullying has many definitions, but there's a consensus that it includes ongoing harassment, humiliation, or harm inflicted by a bigger, stronger, older, or higher status person on someone who can't easily defend themself. It runs the gamut from small, deniable actions such as pretending not to see or hear someone to mockery and flirtation to larger, more obvious, and more damaging actions that can lead to deep humiliation or even suicide. Over the past decade, cyberbullying has become an increasingly serious problem, sometimes ending in tragedy. Too often, the perpetrators are children or teenagers who hide behind the sense of invisibility afforded by social media to gang up on classmates or even strangers who appear to be vulnerable or different.

Bullying is one of the topics addressed in *The Origins of You*,[1] a book that reports on four large studies of children as they grow through adolescence and into middle age and which I mention elsewhere in this book. Using their database of over 4,000 families studied over several decades, the researchers investigated bullying as one aspect of peers' roles in children's and teenagers' development. Although I wasn't surprised by their results, I found them enormously alarming: A child who is bullied can experience damage that lasts a lifetime, affecting every dimension of their life. Bullying during elementary school can lead to emotional, social, academic, and behavioral problems well into adulthood. The authors concluded, "Bullying can be part of a downward spiral of developmental functioning, cascading to influence many aspects of development."[2]

Kids who are bullied are more likely to engage in acts of self-harm, gain weight to the point of obesity, and experience distress. The more long lasting and worse the bullying experience, the more serious is each of these symptoms.

These findings are disturbing, but there is good news. The research also showed that parents have considerable power to influence the outcomes. When bullied children live in supportive families with caring parents and siblings, they are more resilient to the harmful effects of bullying. Bullied kids do better when they have a warm and caring mother, supportive siblings, and a positive home climate. As with the harmful consequences of bullying, the protective factors also operate on a continuum: The cooler the mother, the less supportive the brothers and sisters, or the more negative the home climate, the greater and more lasting the damage.

These research results show how important it is to include the families and peers of bullying victims in attempts to intervene or reduce the impact of bullying experiences. They also show how the danger is doubled for kids who are both bullied and whose home or school situations are uncaring. The peers and family of the bullying victim are interacting factors, working together to affect the child's resilience and vulnerability.

Bullies rarely realize that their actions constitute bullying. Instead, they see their behavior as harmless fun or as self-protection. Actions that bystanders might interpret as bullying can result from a number of possible factors, including the bullying child misreading the intentions of others and interpreting neutral actions to be hostile or aggressive. Victims of bullying are sometimes fearful, submissive, or conflict averse. They're usually perceived to be lower in status, whether because of a lack of confidence, their weight, height, parents' economic status, race, popularity, or some other factor.

You can't entirely prevent the possibility that your child will be bullied, become a bully themselves, or stand and do nothing while others are bullied. However, you can reduce the likelihood of all these things and ensure your child has the resources and resilience they need to thrive in spite of any of these experiences.

To begin with, do what you can to make sure your child feels loved. If you're able to convey warmth and your child feels secure in your love, they're more resilient and better able to resist bullying. Establish an atmosphere of loving acceptance in your home. Your child gains a layer of protection against bullying if they experience their home environment as warm, encouraging, and inclusive.

You can also listen and be available. Bullying is often confusing and humiliating, so your child will only tell you about any worries in this area if they feel safe in your willingness to listen to them with love. If you're present and caring and respect their smallest concerns, they're more likely to trust you with bigger worries like this.

If you have more than one child, teach them to be respectful and kind to each other. Show your children how to be good to each other—compassionate, kind, respectful, and patient. Supportive siblings can help each child resist bullying or make the difference that a bullied child needs.

Strengthening your friendships and family support network also helps protect your child against the dangers of bullying. Similarly, do what you can to strengthen your child's network of social support. When your child is alone, a bully is more likely to target them, and if your child has several friends, as well as adults who they feel comfortable talking to, they're less vulnerable to bullies. A child who feels they're part of a strong network of supportive relationships is more resilient in the face of bullying, as well as many other problems.

Finally, if you think your child might be experiencing bullying and you're not able to take care of it yourself, it's time to get help. The sooner you do this, the better the chances of a good outcome. Possible helpers include your child's teacher, a school social worker, or a child psychologist.

Many organizations have good bullying prevention resources available free online. These include Roots of Empathy[3] and Making Caring Common,[4] two organizations I discussed in Chapter 8. Their resources are mostly directed at creating schoolwide bullying prevention programs, but they also have helpful resources for parents and children.

TECHNOLOGY: USE MINDFULLY

Technology is another complication of life today that many parents have trouble navigating. There's been an alarming increase in anxiety in young people, and many observers are blaming social media. For example, one journalist quoted a psychiatrist as saying, "Anxious teenagers from all backgrounds are relentlessly comparing themselves with their peers, and the results are almost uniformly distressing."[5] According to the same article, most kids agree with this analysis and take it further. One teenager said, "Social media is a tool, but it's become this thing that we can't live without and that's making us crazy."[6]

Some writers argue for avoiding certain kinds of technology. In *America the Anxious: How Our Pursuit of Happiness Is Creating a Nation of Nervous Wrecks*,[7] the author suggested that anxious people avoid apps that promise enhanced well-being. Instead of signing up for a happiness app, she said, spend time with other people.

And then there are experts who argue that, rather than turning away from technology, we should learn to use it mindfully and help our children do the same—for example, Personal Zen[8] is an app for monitoring and regulating anxiety, developed by Tracy Dennis-Tiwary, codirector of the Stress, Anxiety, and Resilience Research Center at Hunter College, City University of New York. Dennis-Tiwary observed that rather than blaming information overload for technology's impact on anxiety, we should think about "filter failure" resulting from not being sufficiently attentive or thoughtful in our use of technology.[9]

The technology that surrounds us is brilliantly designed to capture and hold our attention, Dennis-Tiwary pointed out, so we're at a disadvantage when we try to establish ownership of our attention. She concluded that mindfulness is the best answer:

> A rich inner life protects us from the constant siren call of "the grass is greener on the other side," and "everyone but me has a perfect life," which is the natural consequence of living super-connected, exquisitely-curated, social media-driven lives.[10]

Benefits of Technology

When wisely chosen and used well, technology can have many benefits for children and adolescents. Video games and interactive online activities can provide enjoyable learning opportunities that expand a child's world. This can be particularly important for kids who live in rural communities (if they have access to high-speed internet) or are otherwise restricted in other kinds of activities, as many families have been through the global pandemic. A bit of time watching television can provide welcome relaxation at the end of a challenging day. There are some excellent programs available that inspire, educate, and amuse children and adults. And technology-based learning options can be life changing for a child with special learning needs, whether giftedness, learning problems, or something else.

When Is Technology a Problem for Kids?

Technology can distract your attention or your child's from what matters most in your life, leaving nothing in its place other than wasted hours and a mild sense of unease, much like you feel after eating too much junk food. When a child or adult is paying attention to an electronic device, they're not paying full attention to the people they are with, and opportunities for true connection can be lost. When it goes too far, people stop paying attention to their health and well-being and the social relationships, friends, and activities that nourish their well-being.

When kids spend too much time on devices, they're usually not spending enough time on healthier activities, including social interactions, family time, physical activity, playtime, outdoor time, and sleep. Not surprisingly, then, increased technology use can sometimes lead to increased stress and anxiety in kids.

Kindness can be another casualty of technology overuse. The feeling of anonymity in video games and social media can lead to children and teens becoming rude and disrespectful online, which sometimes spills over into negativity—and even cruelty—in real life. In its extreme, this results in cyberbullying, which can have serious, even fatal, real-world effects.

Parents are right to be careful about which online games they allow their kids to play and to what extent. Many of the games marketed to kids are violent, have hypersexual avatars, contain foul or aggressive language, or include elements of gambling that can be addicting for certain kids in certain circumstances. If your child wants to play a video game, and you're not sure about it, you can check its age rating and read experts' reviews of the game on Common Sense Media.[11]

For some children, the technology-mediated world becomes more interesting or less painful than the real world. While that can sometimes be a good thing, these children risk addiction, with all the attendant damage that can bring. Factors to look for if you're wondering how serious the problem is include a decline in your child's academic grades; sleep problems; increasingly negative behavior, language, moods, and/or attitude; loss of interest in activities your child used to enjoy; or consistently preferring video games over time with friends, family, and activities. If you can check off one or more of these factors, it's time to moderate your child's technology use, and if you can't do that, think about getting professional help.

Reasons to Turn Off Your Phone

I'm saddened when I see adults using their devices and ignoring the children they're with. On the street, in parks, in restaurants, at friends' houses, I see adults engrossed in their texts, email, video games, or phone conversations while the child they're with looks blankly off into space, plays half-heartedly with a toy, or works to get the adult's attention by misbehaving. Maybe it's just a momentary lapse on the parent's part, but sometimes it's habitual, and the parent has no idea how valuable the opportunity is that they're wasting or the damage they're doing both to their child and their relationship with their child.

In infancy, your child depends on your attention for their survival, and although their urgent need for it decreases over time, your attention continues to be enormously important to their sense of security, well-being, and confidence. There's increasing evidence that from birth until adulthood, parents' and caregivers' attention to their portable electronic devices is harming children's development.

Tracy Dennis-Tiwary and her colleagues assessed children from 7 months to 2 years on a variety of issues, including social engagement, interest in exploring their environment, temperament, and resilience.[12] The infants and toddlers in the study were less likely to engage in exploration and showed more evidence of distress when their mothers used their phones. They also observed that those infants and toddlers whose mothers used their phones habitually when outside the lab were more negative than other kids and took longer to recover their emotional equilibrium after an upset. The researchers concluded, "Like other forms of maternal withdrawal and unresponsiveness, mobile-device use can have a negative impact on infant social-emotional functioning and parent-child interactions."[13]

In another study, an international research project focusing on children between 8 and 13, 32% of the 6,000 kids surveyed described themselves as feeling "unimportant" when their parents used mobile devices while sharing meals, having conversations, and spending family time together.[14] Many of the children described feeling they had to compete with their parents' phones for their attention. Over half of the young people felt that their parents used their devices too much.

An experiment conducted on rats showed that distracted mother rats can damage their babies' capacity for pleasure and social engagement.[15] The rat pups were given everything they needed, except that their mothers were on fragmented, unpredictable schedules. The experimental pups' weight was no different than that of pups raised normally, and their time with their mothers was the same. The only difference was the quality of maternal attention they received. Compared with the normally raised pups, their mothers' focus on them was unreliable, inattentive, and unpredictable. The researchers concluded that brain development is disrupted when maternal care is fragmented, leading to subsequent emotional problems. This team is now testing how well their findings apply to human development.

Jenny Radesky is a Boston pediatrician who became distressed as she observed parents ignoring their kids while using mobile devices.[16] She and her colleagues designed a study focused on cell phone use in fast-food restaurants. They observed a lot of parents pulling their phones out as they sat down at the table. In most cases, the parent used their devices while they were there and often seemed more interested in their phones than their children.

Radesky found that when parents were engaged in using their smartphones, the children were noisier and sillier, and the parents on devices were often impatient and irritable with their kids, which of course, escalated the noise and antics. The researchers concluded that parents' use of devices interfered with their parenting. Children "learn by watching us how to have a conversation, how to read other people's facial expressions. And if that's not happening, children are missing out on important development milestones."[17]

Finally, in *The Big Disconnect*, Catherine Steiner-Adair described her study of 1,000 children, who she asked about their parents' smartphone use.[18] She reported that many of the children, aged 4 to 18, described themselves as "sad, mad, angry, and lonely" when their parents used their devices. Several of her interview subjects said they had damaged or hidden their parents' devices. Steiner-Adair concluded that parents are giving their kids a terrible message when they pay attention to their phones: "We are behaving in ways that certainly tell children they don't matter, they're not interesting to us, they're not as compelling as anybody, anything, any ping that may interrupt our time with them."[19]

I've described here only a few of the dozens of studies on this topic. I haven't found any that suggest that your cell phone use doesn't matter or is good for your child. Instead, the findings show that using a smartphone when you're with a child is a form of psychological withdrawal and nonresponsiveness and that it has real, serious, and long-term consequences for your child.

Distracted parents—those who keep their devices close and frequently check them or respond to phone calls and messages— tend to be less predictable, reliable, and attentive. These findings show that fragmented and chaotic maternal care disrupts babies' and young children's brain development, which can lead to emotional disorders later in life.

That doesn't mean you should be off your phone all the time you're with your child—more like 80% or 90% of the time. It's okay to answer an urgent text or make a quick call, especially if you explain to your child what you're doing, as you would with a friend. But do your best to put away your phone and spend this valuable time paying full attention to your child. And if your child is spending a lot of time with another caregiver, discuss with them the importance of staying off their phone as much as possible, too.

Responding to Terrible Events in the World

Tamsin and Michael have three children: Mika, who's 3; Marni, who's 7; and Thor, who's 11. They're a mixed-race family—Tamsin is White, and Michael is Black. For a few years now, Tamsin—a social worker—has been active in her kids' schools, as well as professionally, teaching about racism awareness. In addition to a demanding day job counseling families, she does talks and workshops on anti-racism topics. She's frequently interviewed by local media on this topic and mostly enjoys her fast pace of life. She's long since stopped attending Pilates classes and playing tennis, both of which she used to love. She thinks she gets all the exercise she needs running around to her various activities and taking care of her busy family. She feels she does fine on the 5 hours of sleep she gets most nights.

Michael is a dentist. He has a calmer personality and a less stressful schedule than his wife. He's supportive of Tamsin's anti-racism work but less involved in it than she is. Recently, he's been helping Thor learn to be careful to avoid attracting police interest. Thor has reacted with anger to this, telling his father it's not fair that he has to be careful about what he wears, how he walks, who he hangs out with. "None of the White kids have to do this," he complains.

And then George Floyd was murdered. The family was devastated, especially Thor, who was outraged. He watched media coverage of the Black Lives Matter marches and felt the emotions he saw on people's faces. It was hard for him to understand their mix of grief and positive excitement about speaking out together—he mainly picked up on their anger. He started following the same YouTubers as his friend's older siblings, and the best he could make out from what they were saying was that White people were the enemy. Thor absorbed a lot of information, but his parents and other adults in his life weren't filtering any of it for him, so he had to work out its meaning on his own. Even little Mika was upset.

All Tamsin wanted to do was watch CNN and see what was happening in Minneapolis. For a few days, she let everything go. She was horrified at this latest atrocity and ashamed to be White. She went into work but was only partially able to attend to her clients. She continued doing her after-hours talks, workshops, and media interviews—it was more important now than ever to talk about racism, wasn't it? She'd often stay late, talking to the people who attended the events, trying to give them the support they needed. She was always exhausted, but she persevered.

At home, in addition to being gone from the house more than usual, Tamsin was distant and disconnected. She ignored the kids' fighting and crying. She agreed with Thor's accusation that White people like her were to blame for this and many other atrocities, but she wasn't interested in helping him process his feelings. She let the kids watch as much TV and play as many video games as they wanted to. Normally attentive to good nutrition, she had no energy for shopping or cooking and bought junk food at the local pharmacy when she was passing by. For dinner each night, Michael ordered in fast food. He cleaned up and took care of the kids while Tamsin continued with her activities or was glued to the television.

The fourth day after the murder, Michael said to Tamsin, "Honey, I know how upset you are about this. We're all feeling wrought up about it. But we need you to pull yourself together."

She shouted at him, "Pull myself together?! You must be kidding! My whole career is about fighting racism, and this happens! Why do I bother? Nothing's ever going to change!"

"We have three kids, Tamsin. They need you now, more than ever."

"You blame me because I'm White, don't you?"

"Nothing could be further from the truth, Tamsin. I know you are a strong antiracist."

"You have no idea how I feel!"

"Honey, I know you. I know all too well how you feel. But right now, our own house is on fire, and you are doing nothing about it."

"How can you say that?!"

"Look around you. Or, please, maybe you can just listen for a minute? And then you can get back to CNN."

Tamsin stopped and listened. She heard the TV on loud in the family room, with a YouTube video of teenagers arguing about a hair product. Mika was crying, and Marni was shouting at her. They were fighting over control of the remote and about who had eaten more than their share of the chips and chocolate bars whose wrappers were strewn on the floor around them. The TV was on just as loudly in the adjacent kitchen, where Thor was watching the relentless coverage of Floyd's death while he polished off a big tub of ice cream.

Tamsin looked at Michael and burst into tears. He gave her a long hug while she sobbed. After several minutes, she breathed out hard and said, "Thank you, Michael. I'm sorry."

"You don't need to be sorry. I love you, and I love it that you feel things so intensely. But we need you back in action here."

Tamsin is a social worker and knew exactly what Michael was talking about. She knew what she needed to do about it, but she's also a highly sensitive human being whose emotional response to what she'd seen in the news had triggered trauma from her past and overwhelmed everything else. Her childhood experiences of abuse—which she'd never properly dealt with—meant that she was retraumatized by the video footage of Floyd's death.

She took a leave of absence from work and canceled her upcoming weekend and evening workshops, as well as her media interviews. She told her boss, the event sponsors, and her media contacts, "I need time to process what happened and also to take care of my family. I have to get strong and centered again before I can continue."

Everyone was sympathetic to her situation and more than happy to give her the time she was asking for. "We know what you're like, Tamsin," her boss said. "You give your all to everyone—more than your all. We appreciate that and love you for it, but now you need to take care of yourself. Take as much time as you need."

Tamsin set up an appointment with a therapist she trusted. She spent the next few months dealing with her issues of childhood abuse and repairing the damage of those 3 days with her children. She learned something for herself that she'd always counseled her clients: You have to take care of yourself first before you can respond to your kids about terrible events in the world.

Tamsin's therapist told her, "A child worries when they hear about a dangerous situation they have no control over, whether it's a racist murder, a deadly virus, a devastating hurricane, or a mass shooting."

Tamsin nodded. "I know. I feel so terrible that I didn't handle it better for my kids."

"But please remember, Tamsin," her therapist told her, "it's challenging for parents, too: In addition to being there for your kids, you're coping with your own responses to the situation. You have to start there."

Tamsin realized the therapist was right. As with so many of the complications that parenting brings, successful navigation through terrible events begins with taking good care of yourself. One of the lessons Tamsin learned in the aftermath of her response to the George Floyd murder was that she hadn't been taking good-enough care of herself before this event. She'd been ignoring hints that she had issues of her own she needed to deal with—snags that had come up with friends and clients, trouble sleeping, binge eating, moments when she wasn't coping as well as she might be—and had let go all her self-care practices in the interest of getting in one more talk, one more workshop, one more media interview. She vowed to prioritize her health and well-being in the future so that she could take the advice her therapist gave her.

What Tamsin learned from therapy applies to each of us. It's wise to do your best to get yourself in good psychological and physical shape so that when you're hit with a terrible event in the world or something closer to home, you can be as calm and available as possible, as responsive as possible to your family's needs. At the same time, remember that you are human and experiencing your own worries; you can't do everything perfectly. You don't want to exacerbate any concerns your child has, so remember to think about your own feelings before you try to address your child's worries.

Talk to friends, family members, and others about what is happening. A strong network of social support is invaluable at a time like this. Security and predictability can provide comfort in times of trouble for you and your child. Try to keep to the usual routine of meals, bedtime, and everything else. Make sure you're there when you tell your child you will be.

Second only to your providing a model of calm, loving, reliable strength, your child needs your honest reassurance that you'll do what needs doing to keep them safe. Some children are easily able to express their concerns, and some are not, so listen carefully to what your child isn't telling you, as well as what they are telling you. Ask whether they're okay or they're maybe worried about something, and be available to talk about it, whether or not their worries seem related to the current situation.

But don't insist on a conversation. For some children, a few quiet moments with you or a long, close hug can be more comforting than a conversation. Your child may be more needy than usual, start wetting the bed, or need extra reassurance before falling asleep. Help them feel okay about that. Let them know this is normal in times of stress.

Be as honest as possible in an age-appropriate way. Don't lie to your child or underplay the situation. Don't pretend there is no problem or provide false reassurances. Your child may not be intellectually sophisticated, but they are intuitive and exquisitely sensitive to your emotional undercurrents. If you're worried and tell them there's nothing to worry about, that will only make them worry more about what you're not telling them. So, acknowledge the facts your child needs to make sense of what they're hearing. Be available to discuss the details, as appropriate to your child's age and as your child asks for them.

There is a limit, however, to which details your child can make sense of and in what form those details are presented. Your calm but serious words describing the situation are usually better than graphic images in the media. It isn't helpful for your child (or you) to hear and see horrible images repeated, so keep media exposure to a minimum.

No matter your child's age, talk to them about the helpers, the people working to protect those who are or might be affected, including rescuing, responding, and rebuilding. This is a good time to be with friends and family, people you love, and those whose company you enjoy. Help your child see the importance of maintaining a network of social support. Look for stories of real or fictional people who've found love, courage, and resilience as they've navigated tragedy.[20]

As Tamsin's story illustrates, horrible events in the world can be particularly stressful for someone who has experienced other traumatic events, is highly sensitive, has a history of emotional problems, or doesn't feel connected to friends and others. That's at least as true for children as for adults, so watch for changes in sleep patterns, activity levels, eating habits, and moods, both yours and theirs. Consider professional help if your strong reaction or your child's persists, and you or they stay deeply troubled.

Another good coping strategy for exceptionally stressful times is artistic self-expression. Get out your art materials, and help your child find an artistic medium they enjoy, whether drawing, music, writing, drama, or something else. As I discussed in Chapter 7, creative self-expression is good both as an emotional outlet and as food for discussion. In particular, emphasize the value of positive self-expression, ideas for moving forward from the tragedy. Once Tamsin had pulled herself together a bit, she encouraged Thor to work on a mural commemorating George Floyd at his school. He found enormous solace in doing that and, at the same time, consolidated friendships with the other kids at school who were working on the mural, as well as one of the teachers he'd always liked but never had much cause for interaction with.

Over the next few months, Tamsin and Michael helped Thor reconcile himself to the fact that although White people had been responsible for inflicting horrible damage on Black people for centuries, not all White people were bad. Some even want to be anti-racist, but they need to educate themselves about how to do that and how to see those areas of their lives where racism isn't as obvious as how we treat our neighbors and classmates. And perhaps even more important to his developing sense of himself, it was okay to be biracial. That did not make him part of the victimizing class, nor did Tamsin's Whiteness make her an evil person. He was at a tough age to accept these apparent contradictions, but with his parents' help—informed by Tamsin's work in this field—he got there.

In times of trouble, let your child know it's okay to have fun, that they're not hurting the victims of misfortune when they forget about them for a while and enjoy themselves. Help them realize—and remind yourself—that if they play and take care of themselves, they're getting strong enough to be one of the helpers themselves when the time comes for that. This was a message that Marni particularly needed to hear. At 7, Marni had been feeling guilty for wanting to have fun when her family's world seemed to be falling apart.

At times of vulnerability, people can feel particularly powerless. Don't treat your child—or yourself—like an invalid who needs delicate treatment. Instead, look for ways you can be productive and active together. If you ask for help with laundry or cooking or cleaning right now, something you can do together, your child will feel less powerless.

As Tamsin strengthened, she realized she'd been carrying too much of the household management load herself and that that had been part of the burden that led to her collapse. With Michael's support, she gave away some of the chores that everyone—including her—had always assumed were hers. Thor discovered an interest in cooking, and he and Michael started making a healthy dinner each night. Mika began helping Tamsin with the laundry and felt proud when she managed to do a great job of matching up all the socks and folding the dishtowels and washcloths. Marni took responsibility for setting the table and clearing it afterward. She created a different centerpiece each night—sometimes a single flower in a water glass, sometimes a few pretty rocks she'd collected and put into a clear bowl, and sometimes something more elaborate she'd assembled from bits and pieces of things. She was particularly happy with one she made from buttons and marbles and small pinecones, arranged in a small basket. "I like it when the table's pretty at mealtime," she said. "It feels more like a special family time then."

No matter how young your child is, they can be part of a solution or response to the situation. If the tragedy has affected other children, you and your child can learn about relief efforts or get active in preventing future similar events by participating in anti-racism protests, joining an environmental action group, writing to a lawmaker about gun control, or starting a blog. And if your child is a bit older, you can ask them if they have any good ideas for things you might do together to help your family and others move forward past the trauma.

SEPARATION AND DIVORCE

If you experience more conflict than happiness in your marriage, you may have some troubling questions. Should you stay together for your child? How much harm will you cause your child if you leave your partner? If you decide to separate, what do you tell your child about what's happening? How can you ease the transition? As with everything else, there can't be stock answers to these burning questions. Every story is complicated and unique, so that means thinking about it from different points of view and then making as informed a decision as you can based on your particular circumstance. That being said, some parameters can help you make sense of what probably feels like a terrible muddle of competing interests and points of view. And it doesn't hurt to know something about the research.

Should You Stay Together Only for the Kids?

In an article in *Scientific American Mind*, Hal Arkowitz and Scott Lilienfeld reviewed decades of research and concluded that the short-term answer is usually that you should stay together for the kids.[21] Kids do best in two-parent families where they feel secure in the love of each of their parents and know that the parents love each other. When parents separate, children experience it as stressful, unsettling, and destabilizing, except in circumstances of serious abuse or conflict.

During the first 2 years after separation, most children experience some degree of distress, anger, and/or anxiety.[22] They feel needy, and their behavior often regresses. Many kids feel guilty, believing they're to blame for the change. They're more likely to have problems with academics, behavior, substance abuse, emotional equilibrium, and risk taking.

That sounds like a lot of good reasons to stay in a bad marriage. Stepping back a bit, though, divorce can lead to better long-term outcomes for children.[23] If their parents were arguing a lot or deeply incompatible, divorce can be freeing, as they leave behind the chronic stressors of an unhappy or combative relationship. When parents handle the process well, divorce brings a temporary disruption to the children's lives, but it also brings long-term advantages, including greater resiliency.

Mavis Hetherington is a coauthor of a landmark longitudinal study investigating the after-effects of divorce.[24] Similar to others' conclusions, she and her colleagues found that although many children have short-term problems, most kids do well in the long term. How you handle the divorce matters, they observed, but divorce itself doesn't leave children with long-term damage.

How to Tell Your Child You Are Splitting Up

Children thrive on predictability. They feel more secure when they have dependable routines. That's why it's wise to approach upcoming changes carefully and with a plan, whether it's a new caregiver, a new home, a new school, or a change in your family structure. If you and your partner have decided to separate, what do you say to your child? What can you say and do to help them get through the process as healthy and resilient as possible? As you read through this list, you might realize that the answer is the same for divorce as it is for pretty much any difficult conversation you have with your child.

- **Share the information soon.** Even very young children are remarkably perceptive and will know something is going on. Secrecy can be more damaging than troubling knowledge because your child knows you're holding something back from them, and that leads to all kinds of worries, most of which are worse than the impending reality.

- **Talk as a family.** When you decide you are separating and have established a plan for moving forward, tell your child or children together with their other parent.
- **Choose a good time.** Don't have the divorce discussion when one or more family members is tired, hungry, or needing to be somewhere soon. The conversation may turn out to be a brief one—your child might not have any questions and just want to get on with doing whatever they were doing—but you should be available in case they want to talk, shout, argue, cry, or snuggle.
- **Keep it simple.** In your first conversation about it, the simple facts of their changing life are enough—where you'll all be living (if you know that), who'll take them to school and pick them up, how often they'll spend time with each parent, the fact they will still have two parents who love them.
- **Emphasize your abiding love and protection.** One of your child's biggest fears is that they'll lose one or both of their parents. Reassure them as many times as necessary that you will continue to love them forever, no matter what, and that you will keep them safe.
- **Be loving, calm, and confident.** Don't burden your child with your anger, resentment, worries, or issues. They need you to be strong and confident in your assurances that everyone will be fine. Save the drama for your friends or therapist.
- **Be kind and respectful with and about the other parent.** Treating the other parent with respect will help your child feel safe in the world. No matter the problems you may have with your partner, your child will be happier, healthier, and stronger if they feel they can count on you working together on their behalf.

- **Take ownership.** Be on the lookout for signs your child blames themself (most kids do). They might become excessively good and compliant, for example, or antagonistic and contrary. Reassure them that it is you and the other parent who needed to make the change and that it is not their fault.
- **Wait and listen.** Be alert, attentive, and available for the next several days, weeks, and months. Some children explode with immediate questions, and others take months to process the information and ask a single question.
- **Answer your child's questions as honestly as possible.** Don't try to sweep their worries under the rug. Be sympathetic, patient, and as honest as you can.
- **Be patient with regression behaviors.** Common reactions to parents' divorce include fear, anger, temper tantrums, tears, clinginess, emotional instability, anxiety, whininess, and general irritability. Depending on their age and temperament, your child might have trouble getting to sleep, start bedwetting, or have nightmares that require your calm, reassuring presence, night after night.
- **Maintain the old routines and schedules.** Consistent care and nurturing are more important than ever in any transition, including divorce. They reassure your child that the world is safe and predictable. Meals, outdoor play, bath time, and bedtime routines are more important than ever now.
- **Prepare the other adults in your child's life.** If your child is young, ask their teacher to look for possible mood changes and questions. Ask the other adults in your child's life to be sensitive and understanding. In most cases, they should avoid asking your child about it unless the child introduces the topic.
- **Be patient with your own emotions and your ex-partner's.** The more mature you and your ex-partner can be during the process of separation, the better for your child. But this is a challenging

time for most parents, physically, emotionally, and financially, so if you or your ex-partner is angry or upset in your child's company, accept that and apologize to your child, explaining that change is always difficult. Emphasize your confidence that you will get through it and everyone will be fine but that it will require some adjustments.

- **Don't drag it out.** Once you've told your child it's happening, get on with the practical business of establishing new situations and routines.

Change is stressful, but it doesn't have to damage your child. If you can be kind, loving, confident, mature, and trustworthy, you and your child can make it through the process stronger, with better coping skills and strengths.

How Can You Buffer the Impact of Divorce?

Every situation and every child is unique, and divorce—like any other change—can affect any aspect of a child's life and development. Some kids' grades plummet; others become super-focused on academics. Some children become depressed or angry; others become unusually helpful and cheery. Some kids become antisocial; others become excessively social. Some become mistrustful of close relationships; others become hypersexual. Some children experience eating disorders or sleep problems; others seem to sail through, apparently unaffected by their parents' divorce.

No matter how your child responds to the changes in their life, remember that two-parent families have problems, too, and that your parenting behaviors through the disruption and afterward can make a difference to their long-term development. Divorce might turn your world and your child's upside-down for a while, but the basic rules of parenting still apply. If you can be good to yourself and strong for your child and stay attuned to their emotional, social, physical, and intellectual needs, you'll find you'll both emerge stronger in the end.

ALTERNATIVE FAMILY COMPOSITION

Fewer children today live with two biological parents than children who live in other family configurations.[25] Although each approach to creating an alternative type of family has its own challenges, there is no family composition—including the mother–father–kids format—that is free of problems. What matters most to your child's long-term development is love, kindness, security, and chances for exploration, not how your family is structured. Two mothers, a blended family, or a single father can give a child everything they need to thrive. With the right kind of loving support, a child who has had a rough start in life can thrive after adoption or once their parents have sorted out their issues.

So why am I including a section on family composition—something that's more about who you are—alongside information about how to act or behave in complicated situations? I do not believe that certain kinds of family relationships need fixing or troubleshooting the way that nonmindful use of technology does. Rather, I included this section because other people in your life—strangers, neighbors, sometimes even family members—might see your family composition as a problem when it doesn't conform to what they think is traditional or healthy, and also because, as with racism, bias against single parents and same-sex parents is baked into larger systems that affect your life. Your family composition is not a "complication" in and of itself, but biased systems can stack complications in your way, adding stress to your life.

Next, I briefly mention two of the family types where parents often experience stress, and I then describe some of the practices that work for all parents but can be especially important if your family doesn't match the traditional model that includes a biological mother, a biological father, and one or more children.

Single-Parent Families

Feeling overloaded is almost guaranteed if you're a single parent. Finding enough patience, energy, time, and/or money can feel overwhelming. It's tough when there isn't another adult at home to help with the worries and joys of parenting and with all responsibilities of daily life—getting the kids to and from school, appointments, and extracurricular activities; doing the grocery shopping, cooking, and kitchen clean-up; keeping the house clean and the laundry done; paying attention to what's happening with the kids; reading bedtime stories—all on top of self-care and work.

One of the most important things to do if you are a single parent is to strengthen and depend on your social support network. Friends and family members can help you care for your child and provide another adult for both you and your child to talk to. It can seem impossible, but you'll be a better parent if you find ways to attend to your social, physical, spiritual, and intellectual needs, as well as everything else. That's true for every parent, of course; it's just a lot harder to do when you're running the household solo.

Same-Sex Parents

After decades of research, it's clear that same-sex partners can do just as good a job of parenting as mixed-sex partners.[26] In some communities, however, children of same-sex parents can still be subjected to social pressures that other kids don't experience. They can be bullied or treated differently from others, so same-sex parents can sometimes have extra pressures to help their child feel safe. But

301

the factors that lead to your child's thriving are the same, no matter the family composition: Feeling loved, secure, and supported is what matters most in the long run.

WISE PARENTING PRACTICES FOR ALTERNATIVE FAMILIES

The foundation of thriving for all kids is the love they feel at home. If your family looks different from other families in one way or another, it's more important than usual to be present to your child—patient, loving, and engaged. As frequently as you can through the day, make time to listen to your child with love. That goes a long way to ensuring you weather the storms and make it through strong, together, and intact, with the resilience you need to weather the storms that will come along in the future.

It also helps your child feel safe if they have a reasonable structure of rules they can rely on to be enforced. This is particularly important in alternative family situations, where you might be tempted to break the rules to compensate for extra challenges your child might be experiencing. I wish I'd done a better job of this when I was a single parent. There were times I allowed my guilt and empathy to lead me to be too permissive, and that wasn't good for any of us.

Make sure there's ample time for play in your child's life. Free, unstructured play is always important for kids: It supports them in being imaginative, curious, healthy, self-aware, and happy. For a child growing up with extra stressors, things can feel too serious for play, but (as we saw in Tamsin's family) it's especially important then because it connects them to what's happy and good in their life and supports their growing skills in making friends, resolving conflicts, making good decisions, and regulating their emotions and behavior.

And pay attention also to all the other recommendations throughout this book about self-care, mindfulness, and creative self-expression. Support your child in exploring where their enthusiasms lie and discovering their strengths. That can sustain them through some tough moments. Encourage downtime for yourself and your child; it's more necessary than usual in stressful situations. Make sure your child has ample time for all the activities that matter: playing, reading, exercising, sleeping, spending time with friends and family, exploring nature, and being creative.

At times and in situations of extra stress, it's particularly important to approach problems positively, not as signs of defeat or failure but as chances to figure out what needs attention to do better next time. Show your child how fulfillment and confidence are built on working hard over time with patience. This can be particularly important for a child growing up in a nontraditional family or a stressful situation, where there can be more challenges than usual.

And finally, one of the best ways to relieve stress or move beyond grumbles is to look around for what's good. Teach your child to notice what there is to be grateful for. Gratitude is a wisdom practice that frees up energy, optimism, happiness, and empathy, making room for a sense of well-being, even in the midst of trouble.

THE EARLY YEARS: BIRTH TO 5

The early years can present some of the thorniest problems a parent faces. In this section, I focus on two of the problems requiring a special order of wisdom: child care decisions and bullying.

Making Good Decisions About Child Care

The National Institute of Child Health and Human Development (NICHD) conducted the largest and most comprehensive study of child care ever, the Study of Early Child Care and Youth Development. In 1991, NICHD identified over 1,000 infants from a variety of places and circumstances across America. Over the next 15 years, the research team collected data on the growing children's cognitive abilities, behavior, and health. Jay Belsky was one of the principal investigators; he and his colleagues described the study and its findings in *The Origins of You*.[27]

Highly trained observers spent several hours observing each child's day care experience, focusing on the extent to which caregivers interacted with the child in an attentive, sensitive, responsive, stimulating, and affectionate manner. This careful analysis was repeated twice at each of five different ages when the child was 6 months, 15 months, 2 years, 3 years, and 4½ years old. These intensive observations were repeated when the child was in Grades 1, 3, and 5. In addition, each child's family was carefully studied at each observation period through questionnaires, interviews, and videotaped interactions between a parent and the child. In addition to this labor-intensive data collection process, multiple aspects of each child's development were assessed at regular periods until the child was 15.

The breadth, depth, and longitudinal nature of this approach allowed the researchers to assess the impact of day care in more complexity than has been done in any other study. They found, not surprisingly, that quality makes a difference, at least into adolescence. Higher quality care leads to better cognitive, linguistic, health, and emotional outcomes. In addition, children who participated in lower quality day care as infants and young children were more likely to show aggressive and delinquent behavior in adolescence. When thinking about day care options for your child, look for well-trained caregivers who are attentive, warm, and responsive and settings that provide high adult-to-child ratios in a good balance of stimulation and calm.

They also found—not surprisingly—that smaller groups are better than larger ones. Children whose child care experiences included fewer children did better over time than those whose child care was spent in larger groups. Try to find day care settings with small groups.

One of the more controversial findings was that children before the age of 3 do best at home and not in day care. They do best across all outcome measures—they behave better, are healthier, and are less stressed—if they're cared for at home and if one of their parents is home with them a lot of the time. Allied to this is that less time in day care before the age of 3 meant more sensitive mothering. Detailed analyses of mothers interacting with their child showed that the more time an infant or young child spent in day care, the less sensitive the mother's response to the child.

The amount of time spent in day care had other consequences, too. The more time spent in care in the first 4½ years of life, the more aggressive and disobedient the child was likely to be, no matter how high the quality. As average hours of child care increased, so did the child's likelihood to score in the at-risk range. Children who spent more hours per week in day care until the age of 4½ were more likely to engage in sex, drugs, and other risky activities and were more likely to act without thinking once they moved into their teen years.

The good news for parents who have been sending their young child to day care or for whom that seems to be the best option is that family matters most. The researchers found that the effects of both quality and quantity of care were surprisingly small, compared with what's happening at home. In predicting child and adolescent outcomes, a warm, loving, supportive family made a much bigger difference than the amount or quality of early child care experienced. Overall, the NICHD study findings showed that quality and quantity of day care have implications for subsequent development and that quantity matters more than quality but that what's happening at home matters most.

This research supports you in creating your own best approach to child care, with the understanding that what's best depends on your child's personality and needs, as well as your family's circumstances and requirements.

A Bullying Case Study: Clare and Alix

Even the most socially competent child can have bullying problems, sometimes as a victim and sometimes as a bully. Your reaction to these problems can make a difference in how successful your child will be in dealing with them.

I introduced Clare in Chapter 7 as a young woman who dropped out of university to follow her creative interests. She came up again in Chapter 8 in connection with supporting the development of empathy as the mother of Alix, an imaginative and spirited 4-year-old. I bring Clare and Alix back for this chapter with a story that illustrates how parents can work with teachers to prevent bullying.

Alix loves playing with other children, but she's also shy and needs alone time. Things seemed to be going well for her at preschool until the teacher told Clare that Alix had been excluding other children from games. Ms. Simmons told Clare, "The other kids love Alix and always want to play with her. I understand why this might feel overwhelming for a shy child, but she needs to learn that excluding kids isn't okay."

Clare felt terrible when she heard this, thinking maybe she'd been letting Alix get away with bad behavior. But then she told me, "We broke it down to the root and turned it into a challenge, and it became fun for us both."

In response to Clare's gentle questions, Alix told her mother that she likes everyone in her class and is happy to play one-on-one with any one of them. But Alix also described feeling overwhelmed when too many people joined in, changing the dynamic of the game.

She said she reacted to that bad feeling by telling the next child who wanted to join that they couldn't play. Clare could see that Alix was doing what she needed to do to feel okay. Her daughter intended no malice, but her behavior resulted in the excluded child feeling bad.

Alix loves princess stories, particularly the movie *Frozen*, so Clare told her that Alix is like Queen Elsa in *Frozen*. She has a superpower (everyone likes her), but her power is also her biggest problem because she has to learn to control it to live the life she wants. Alix liked that idea, and together, she and her mother created a challenge. At school, the rule is that everyone is always included. If it gets overwhelming and Alix feels the need to exclude someone, she can exclude herself. She can recharge somewhere in the classroom, then join up with the others again when she's ready. If she gets through a whole day without making anyone feel excluded, she can have a friend home for a play-date and have the one-on-one play she craves.

So far, Clare says, their solution is working well. She told me Ms. Simmons is thrilled with how hard Alix is working to be kind and cooperative. Alix feels proud and happy with how well she is doing and loves the frequent playdates at home. Clare is relieved to have passed this parenting hurdle and is getting ready for the next one.

Alix is young, and her behavior couldn't be classified as bullying, but the way she used her popularity to exclude other kids could, if left unaddressed, have led to the "mean girl" variety of bullying.

How to Help Your Child Deal With Bullying, Racism, and Other Big Problems

Clare's response to Alix's behavior illustrates several of the important principles to keep in mind if your child is dealing with something serious such as bullying or racism. Most important is the solid relationship Clare had built with Alix. Clare's first action when she learned about the problem was to talk it over with Alix to get a sense of her perspective. As with so many childhood problems, when it comes to bullying and racism, kids do best if they think their parents believe in them. They need to know that conflicts are a natural part of life, that acting out is not acceptable, and that there is someone they can talk to when things aren't going well.

Another reason this situation was resolved happily for everyone is that Clare didn't look for who to blame. Many parents in her situation would have blamed the teacher for allowing the problem to happen or the other children for pushing into her daughter's games. Alternatively, they might have blamed their daughter for being mean to other kids. Clare didn't judge the teacher, the other kids, or Alix; instead, she put the emphasis on understanding and solving the problem.

Another strength in Clare's problem-solving process with Alix was her commitment to ensuring that everyone has their needs met, including Alix, the other children, and the teacher. If your child is having trouble, you might try a collaborative problem-solving approach, as Clare did with Alix. Together they came up with a creative solution to the problem, grounded in Alix's love of *Frozen*. That allowed Alix to own the solution and be invested in making it work.

If you're experiencing something like this, something requiring a wise response, you might start as Clare did by asking gently prodding questions that help your child figure out what's wrong and the best way to resolve their problems. Focus on listening with an open heart and helping your child find the best solution, the one that allows them to be kind to others, build relationships successfully, and feel good about themselves.

Alix's teacher made it easier to resolve the problem by emphasizing Alix's strengths, but many parents become adversarial when teachers raise problems. If you think there might be bullying (or something else) going on, approach the teacher respectfully, in a spirit of collaborative problem solving.

If these strategies don't work to eliminate the problem, it's time to consider counseling or even changing the school environment for your child.

CHILDHOOD: 6 TO 10

As children move out of early childhood, their problems can get more complicated. They don't have the constant adult supervision they had when they were younger and are more often expected to take responsibility for what's happening, even though they don't yet have many of the necessary skills for doing that. Being the adult in the room also gets more complicated—you're not always in the room when the problem happens, and you want your child to be able to take care of themselves.

There are situations where a potential victim's behavior is enough to stop a bully before too much damage is done. For example, your child can sometimes surprise or shame a bully into backing down if they push back verbally at early attempts to bully them. Sometimes it's as simple as saying, "Hey, that is not cool. Please leave me alone."

Depending on your child's personality and presence of mind, they might be able to surprise a bully or racist into backing down by being funny or grinning at them. That's not always easy to manage, of course, but you can practice possible witty responses with your child. Just knowing that's an option can help.

Bullies are not always easily deflected, however. They can do real damage, so help your child learn when it's best to walk away and when it's time to consult a friendly grown-up. Bullying, by definition, involves a power dynamic, so sometimes a child really can't manage it alone. This is where the relationship you've built with your child makes a big difference. If you don't yet have a strong, easy, warm relationship, invest your time and energy now in making that happen. It can make the difference between things going well from here and things going badly off the rails.

If your child shares a concern with you, take it seriously. Don't say anything suggesting they might be responsible for the bullying or the racism. Instead, look at it as a chance to do some problem solving together, just as Clare did with Alix. And if the bullying or racism is happening at school, it's time to talk to your child's teacher.

ADOLESCENCE: 11 TO 18

Technology and bullying are two of the complicated issues parents have to navigate. They come together in cyberbullying, which can be a problem at younger ages but becomes seriously problematic in early adolescence, as kids are more likely to have unsupervised time and independent access to their own electronic devices. It's also a time when social connections become enormously important, and kids are intensely sensitive to others' opinions of them, so the harm this form of bullying can do is very real.

Cyberbullying is a serious and growing problem. In a recent study, 4,500 middle school and high school students aged 12 to 17 responded to a questionnaire on bullying.[28] The researchers defined *cyberbullying* as "when someone repeatedly threatens, harasses, mistreats, or makes fun of another person (on purpose) online or while using cell phones or other electronic devices."[29] Just over a third of the students (34%) reported they had experienced cyberbullying at some point in the past, and 17% said they'd been cyberbullied within the last 30 days. Most (80%) of the respondents who reported having been cyberbullied said that it was in the form of "mean comments" posted about them online, and 70% reported that other kids had spread rumors about them online. About two thirds of those who reported having been cyberbullied described themselves as having been strongly affected, both in their ability to learn and feel safe at school. As with other kinds of bullying, kids are cyberbullied for many reasons, the most common being appearance, race, intelligence, sexuality, religion, and financial status.[30]

It's important to talk to your child about cyberbullying, so they will recognize it if it happens to them or if they see it happening to someone else. Teach them also about the importance of standing up to it and speaking out against it. The role of the bystander is enormously important both in condoning cyberbullying and condemning it. Help your child see they have more power than they realize and that if they act against cyberbullying when they encounter it, it gives courage to other bystanders to follow their lead.

The National Crime Prevention Council has a great cyberbullying tip sheet for kids.[31] They recommend that kids tell a trusted adult as soon as they suspect cyberbullying might be happening and that they don't delete any suspicious tweets or messages. Make sure your child knows they can and should talk to you about something they think might be a problem, and do your best to be calm and reasonable if that happens. Your child doesn't want to be a troublemaker or get known by classmates as a tattletale, so be sensitive to their social worries, and work with them to make sure they feel good about a solution that benefits everyone. As always, remember that whatever is happening is far more complicated than it appears at first, so do your best to approach cyberbullying with wisdom and caution.

Your child can also become active in antibullying and bullying prevention information sessions at school and elsewhere, along the lines of the Making Caring Common and Roots of Empathy programs. There are many other programs available[32] to help kids and parents get involved with schoolwide antibullying campaigns.

YOUNG ADULTHOOD: 19 TO 24

One of the hardest things a caring parent has to learn is how to let their child grow up, release control, and trust their child to make the decisions they need to make. Every adult I know—including myself—has made serious mistakes along the way, mistakes we want

311

to save our kids from. Sometimes we forget that all of us—including our children—have to make our own mistakes and figure things out for ourselves.

As hard as this is, know that your child will make mistakes, and don't try to save them from them. Offer your wisest counsel if you're asked for it, but otherwise, you've done your parenting job. Your child has learned what they're going to learn from you in all the years you've had together before now. You have nothing more to teach them, other than through your ongoing example of how you live your life and respond to your problems. They will make better decisions in the long run if you've learned to back off and provide support but not pressure.

In Chapter 7, I wrote about Margaret's support for her daughter, Clare, who found herself disengaged from her university studies. Margaret realized that Clare had to figure it out for herself, and Margaret put no pressure on her to buckle down to her schoolwork. She trusted that her daughter was an independent person with a unique life history, personality, and set of talents and challenges, a person who had to make the decisions she needed to make. Margaret couldn't possibly know what those decisions should be—nobody ever can. She recognized that she could only provide the love, respect, and support that helped Clare do what she needed to do.

COMPLICATIONS QUIZ DISCUSSION

At the beginning of this chapter, I suggested you think about a series of true/false statements. I come back to them now (in a somewhat shortened form), after you've read the chapter, and ask you to think about whether you might answer them differently. I should start by acknowledging that I was a bit tricky with the way I wrote the quiz:

Each of these statements (other than Item 9) is too complicated to be slotted into true or false categories.

1. *My child would never bully another child.* It's probably not useful to think of bullies as "other," an alien form of bad human. Even kind, good little kids like Alix can be bullies in the right circumstance. It's better to understand that all children need help learning how to get along with others, and they need the adults in their lives to be wise, nonjudgmental, and compassionate in that learning process.

2. *My child would never stand by while someone else is bullied.* Again, it's wise to avoid thinking that your child is in a special category of perfect human being. They're like every other child—they need your help and guidance if they're going to learn how to be brave and noisy when they see bad things happening.

3. *If my child experienced racism or any other kind of bullying at school, I'd figure out whose fault it was.* You would have to take quick action, but I'd recommend doing your best to avoid blaming anyone. That usually becomes angry and confrontational and causes more pain to everyone without solving anything. Instead, I'd recommend taking a calm, respectful, problem-solving approach, the way Ms. Simmons did with Alix, working with your child and their teacher to sort it out in a way that leaves the perpetrator, your child, and the school culture richer, better, and wiser going forward.

4. *I always have my phone on and handy.* This is a bad idea. I'm rarely so definite on a topic, but on this one, the research is solid and unequivocal: Spending time on your phone when you're with your child makes them feel unimportant in your life, undermining their sense of security as well as your

relationship. Answer urgent calls and texts that can't wait, but generally, when you're with your child, be with your child. In the end, you'll be glad you did.

5. *I protect my child from knowing anything about the outside world.* It's a good idea to be careful about how much your child learns about the tragedies and horrible things happening, but I wouldn't go overboard and become overprotective. Instead, you can trust that with a solid connection with your child, you can help them cope with whatever they do learn. What's most important for your child is a sense of warmth and security at home.

6. *If my child were to hear about a school shooting, I would not talk to my child about it.* It's important that you do talk to your child about what they hear, reassuring them that you're doing everything you can to keep them safe. They need to talk to someone, and it's far better that it's a wise and loving parent than a kid at school whose sources and information are questionable. There are many other ways to help your child process terrible events in the news, and I discuss many of them in this chapter.

7. *Children of divorce always have problems.* Most children do experience turbulence in the first 2 years after their parents divorce. Some kids have serious problems in the first 2 years, although most don't, and after that—as long as at least one of the parents has supported their child through the process— most children don't have lasting problems.

8. *Children who grow up with a single parent don't have the same chances as other kids.* Growing up with a single parent carries more potential stressors than growing up with two parents, including a higher likelihood of poverty and a dangerous neighborhood, as well as less support for the parent. However, the long-term outcome depends not on family

structure but on the warmth of the home the single parent provides and the nature of the parenting. If the parent is authoritative and wise and the child grows up feeling valued and secure, the outcome can be just as good as for any other situation.

9. *Same-sex parents can never do as good a job as a mother and father.* Unlike most of the items in this quiz, this item is simple to answer: There's a lot of research on this, and it shows conclusively that same-sex parents can do just as good a job as others, with outcomes that are just as positive.

10. *A child who goes to day care or has a nanny has a permanent disadvantage.* While it's true that the best thing for a child in the early years is being at home with a parent, what matters most to their long-term outcome is the warmth in the family, not whether they go to day care or have a nanny.

TAKING IT INTO THE COMMUNITY: ACKNOWLEDGE YOUR WOUNDS, LOOK FOR HELP, AND REACH OUT TO OTHERS

Turning your wounds into wisdom requires an openness to acknowledging your wounds, as we saw Tamsin do after George Floyd was murdered. And then it requires you looking for the right kind of help, as she did. Wisdom isn't something some special wise people contain inside themselves but is something anyone can gain from being mindful as they go through life, acknowledging their pain and learning from it and strengthening and diversifying their networks of social support.

Whether you're dealing with bullying, cyberbullying, racism, technology, divorce, or some other complicated and disturbing issue, you will do a better job of it if you stay connected to your friends, neighbors, extended family, and other possible helpers. As a parent, there will be times the problems feel insurmountable. More than ever, that's when you need to reach out and find the help you need.

Then, when you're stronger, you can look for ways to reach out and provide opportunities for others to form healing connections. I've mentioned antibullying programs such as Making Caring Common and Roots of Empathy a few times. It's great to advocate for programs like this at your school, but there are also many other ways of sharing wisdom ideas more broadly in your community. A Girl Scout leader who is warm, wise, and inclusive can be a healing force in her community, as can a Big Sister or Big Brother. If there is a cause that interests you, you might decide to become politically active at the local, state, or national level. Perhaps your best contribution is with the parent–teacher association, leading nature walks, or starting up a community garden. Maybe your faith group has a choir you can join. Maybe there's a local bowling league that welcomes people across age, race, income, and sexual orientation.

What matters here is not the intended purpose of the community group you're reaching out to, initiating, or joining but rather the spirit of your participation. Do it with the idea of strengthening and diversifying your network of social support and, at the same time, strengthening and diversifying connection opportunities for others. Share your activities with your child, and include them to the extent that that's possible and they are interested.

KEY TAKEAWAYS: CLEARING A PATH TOWARD WISDOM

- Nobody arrives at parenthood without wounds. People differ in the amount of support they've been given along the way to recover from their wounds and in the ways they respond when parenting inevitably reopens the wounds.
- Every parent has to navigate through rough or particularly thorny patches—bullying, racism, technology, divorce, alternative family composition, and more. You can choose to handle these complications wisely or not.

- You won't handle every challenge with perfection. Nobody does. But you can be the adult in the room for your family, and that is good enough.
- Your social support network is a critical dimension for getting through the complications as wisely and well as possible.
- Your family's situation is unique because it pulls together your various dynamic resources, experiences, attitudes, and temperaments. That means your challenges and your solutions are unique to you.

CHAPTER 10

WE'RE ALL IN THIS TOGETHER: LISTEN, CONNECT, AND COLLABORATE

Alone we can do so little, together we can do so much.
—Helen Keller, quoted in J. P. Lash, *Helen and Teacher:*
The Story of Helen Keller and Anne Sullivan Macy

One of the things we've learned about from the COVID-19 pandemic is the interconnectedness of all life on the planet—human life and animal life, all of us around the world. Although it so often appears otherwise, in the end, there is no privilege that protects some of us more than others. For one of us to be safe, we must all be safe, and the air we breathe and water we drink must also be safe. So, it's in every person's self-interest to start by taking care of ourselves and our children and then think about how to reach out and connect to diverse others in creating a safer world for us all. In the first nine chapters of this book, I discussed ways of reaching out and being part of the village that raises each child, but my emphasis was mostly on taking care of yourself and your child. In this final chapter, I emphasize how listening to, connecting with, and collaborating with others enriches your life and your child's.

Sometimes it's best to take care of yourself and your child before reaching out to connect with others, and sometimes the best way of taking care of yourself and your child is to reach out and connect with others, getting help as needed. But more often, I think, it's a back-and-forth process, where healing yourself is the best way for you to heal your child and others and also where healing your child and others is the best way of healing yourself. It's when this all makes a seamless circle that you're in just the right place. You're in the place of accepting your human imperfection, building a relationship with your child that will weather any storm, and collaborating with your child in making connections with the wider world that will sustain you both. Helen Keller was so right when she said, "Alone we can do so little, together we can do so much."

You may have noticed that throughout this book, I talk about you and your child, not you and your family or you and your children, even though "family" and "children" have the benefit of being more inclusive. It could have been any of these, but I intentionally stayed with "child" because I want to emphasize that the relationships we forge are always singular. Child by child we create a family and build a strong neighborhood and a healthy world. If your child feels your devotion and connection to themself as an individual, knowing you love them exactly as they are in all their unique imperfection, they have a better chance of thriving.

Working together, we can put the supports in place to increase the chances for each of us to become confident and fulfilled citizens of a rapidly changing world. Just imagine the benefits for each child, each adult, and the planet we share.

Questions to Consider About Your Community Connections

Before I talk about ways people connect with others outside their family and how doing that benefits everyone, you might want to think about the ways you're already doing that and whether you want to expand your connecting activities or maybe pull them back or change them.

- Have you ever participated in activities that strengthened community connections? Maybe it was helping neighbors with chores, participating in environmental or political causes, using social media or signing petitions to raise racism awareness, attending parent–teacher association meetings, teaching Sunday school, helping out at the library, initiating a pride parade, volunteering at a community center, participating in a bowling league, or something else.

• Whether past or present, who benefits from your community activities? What do those activities give you back by way of satisfaction, fulfillment, or something else?

• How do your community activities fit into the balance of your life? Would it be good to scale them back for a time? Is there something more or different that would have a greater impact or feel better for you? Do you include your child as you can, sharing with them what you're doing if they're too young to join you or they're not interested?

ADVOCACY: MAKING CONNECTIONS FOR MAKING A DIFFERENCE

Most of us have at least one cause, one aspect of society we care about and would love to see changed. Maybe yours is immigration policies, antiracism, or environmental sustainability. For many parents, there'll be times in your child's education when you'd like to see something changed so your child is better able to learn and thrive at school. Advocating for school change is one example of collaboration in action, a great way to connect productively with others, working toward a shared objective.

There are many reasons for wanting to see a change in your child's schooling experience. Maybe you're concerned about a rowdy lunchtime environment, insufficient opportunities for outdoor play, or incidents of bullying, or maybe your child needs more challenging work to reduce behavior concerns. Although school policies and practices might seem resistant to change, they're frequently revised, and parents usually have more power to make changes than they realize.

Parents of kids with special needs have long realized the necessity of advocacy. In many cases, their advocacy efforts have led not only to improved circumstances for their own children but also to system-wide changes that improve the school experience for all kids dealing with challenges like theirs. One great example of this can be found in "Parent Advocacy With Schools: A Success Story," where three parents described their work with families dealing with autism spectrum disorder.[1]

Two Case Studies: Jarel and Janine

In my decades of work with children, families, and schools, I've been involved in many advocacy attempts. Some have worked quickly and well. I remember a seventh-grader whose parents came to me because their son had developed a behavior problem at school to the extent he was at risk of being expelled. Although Jarel's parents described him as increasingly unhappy and difficult at home, when I did my assessment with him, I found him delightful. Jarel enjoyed the challenges I presented and was chatty and cooperative throughout 5 hours of testing. I had no problems with his attitude or behavior, and his test scores were off the chart. His math skills, in particular, were well beyond the 12th-grade level, so I wasn't surprised that it was math class where his behavior was the biggest concern. It's often in a child's best and favorite class that they experience the most frustration if the work they're given to do is something they've long since mastered.

Jarel, his parents, and I met with the principal and the homeroom teacher, as well as the math teacher. I reviewed my findings. The principal asked for my recommendations. I suggested an online mathematical acceleration and enrichment program, which Jarel could do in the library during the regular math class he'd been disrupting.

The homeroom teacher thought it might help. The math teacher liked the idea and said he would be happy to organize and supervise it.

With the principal's approval, the school implemented my recommendation, and it worked like a dream. Jarel rocketed through the online math program and, with the math teacher's help, began participating in—and frequently winning—international math contests. The school also benefited in that the principal got together with the teachers and decided on a range of learning options (subject-specific acceleration, extracurricular enrichment, and online opportunities like Jarel's), which they offered to other students who needed advanced work in one subject or another. A few years later, Jarel went on to do graduate work in physics at a top university. That advocacy effort was a highly gratifying success.

At another school, I encountered what began as a similar situation. The child—a third-grader named Janine—was exceptionally advanced in her language skills. She was reading, understanding, and reasoning at a 10th-grade level and increasingly showing frustration with the teacher's insistence on her completing Grade 3 work and homework, which she experienced as an annoying waste of time. At our meeting with the principal, Janine's parents and I (the principal said Janine was too young to participate) were met with a hard wall of resentment, including angry rebuttals, the principal saying that the school was already doing a great job of meeting every student's every need and that it was Janine who had to change, not the school. That advocacy attempt was a failure, except that Janine ended up changing schools and found herself a lot happier socially and academically than she'd been at the first school.

What Do You Need to Know to Be a Good Advocate?

Most of my efforts have landed somewhere between these two experiences, and I have learned a lot in the process about what works and what doesn't. Although, as Janine's story shows, not every advocacy attempt accomplishes what the advocates hope to achieve, parents have a lot more power to effect school change than most of them realize.

Another lesson is that the school principal makes a big difference. In what might have been my best advocacy experience—where Jarel was given work that matched his abilities and interests, and he not only stopped misbehaving but also started thriving, and other students also benefited—the principal was open, confident, flexible, and creative. Instead of responding defensively—as some educators do—she thanked the parents and me for helping make her school better for gifted learners. In what was probably my worst experience— where Janine's parents and I were met with rude disinterest, and no changes were made—I later learned that the principal had been working hard to maintain control over a fractious group of teachers and a board that wasn't happy with his performance. He didn't have the confidence, vision, or energy to realize we could help him do his job better.

In Chapter 6, I discussed Malika's problems with Jorge's excessive homework load and reviewed how she might advocate for getting that changed. Here, I describe an advocacy process that can apply to a variety of concerns, including but not limited to excessive homework. Putting my varied experiences together with others' experiences with effective advocacy,[2] I've identified some steps to consider for getting the changes you think your child needs.

It starts with watching and listening. You may have a genuine grievance, but you need to understand the school environment and listen to all the players before you ask for change. Learn about your child's teacher, the principal, and the school climate. Gather all the relevant information. The defenders of the status quo may trip you up if you've been careless at this stage, so be resourceful in searching out as many facts as possible, making sure they're up to date and accurate. If I'd known more about the politics of Janine's school and the principal's precarious situation, I might have approached our request for accommodations differently. Perhaps we could have found a board member who would sign on as an advocate for our cause, which would help ensure that the principal would listen to us more openly. Maybe the school culture was just too embedded in the way it had always been done, and it wasn't going to be possible to make any changes, but we would have had a better chance if we'd known more.

No matter how wrongheaded you may find some educators and other parents, behave with humility and respect, remembering that nobody's perfect, and most of us are just doing the best we know how. A school is a complex and interdependent community with its own history and a culture that includes parents, teachers, kids, administrators, and support staff, each of whom may have a legitimate stake in maintaining the status quo. Try to be mindful that your talk of change might elicit emotional reactions in some stakeholders, so do your best to understand their point of view before offering yours.

Once you have a sense of the situation and the players, look for like-minded others. Approach other parents, as well as teachers, principals, counselors, community leaders, and anyone else who might be interested in your cause. Advocacy is a whole lot easier and a lot more effective when done collaboratively with others.

As you go through this process, work on keeping an open mind. There are many possible solutions to every problem. Don't decide on one option as the only acceptable one; instead, be open to others' ideas and solutions.

One of the secrets of successful advocacy is pinpointing objectives. Identify the core of the issue. Discern what needs to be addressed and why as clearly as possible. It's easy to get sidetracked or divided in your efforts, so spend time establishing clear and simple objectives, revising them as you get more information. One of the reasons the advocacy effort with Jarel worked so well was that we were able to identify a serious mismatch between what his math teacher was asking him to do and Jarel's abilities and interests. We didn't say, "This kid is gifted. He needs gifted education," which would've been vague and problematic for other parents at this school, which did not have a gifted program. We simply wanted him excused from a math class that was ridiculously easy for him and to be given math to do that challenged him, and the school was able to figure out how to do that. Other parents didn't clamor to have their child also do work at much higher grade levels, although the school did begin paying more attention to who else might need accommodations like this.

Once you know what your objective is, make a plan. Define simple goals, a reasonable time line, and specific responsibilities. Put your ideas in writing. Make sure your suggestions for change are focused, meaningful, and clear and that you have a consensus among your collaborators. In both my stories, it was just the parents and me (a psychoeducational consultant they'd hired), but I made sure to follow this step, putting in writing the nature of the problem as I saw it, my recommendations for a solution, a reasonable time line, and specific responsibilities. I then consulted with the parents to make sure we were on the same page with how we wanted this to proceed. That way, we were a harmonious unit when we attended school meetings.

As you are formulating your plan, consider community and other resources. Are there relevant connections that might help in your advocacy efforts? Think about the public library, the internet, local businesspeople, volunteer groups, retired educators, or others. In Jarel's case, the school was able to find some terrific online solutions that meant they didn't have to invent a whole new curriculum for him. In another similar case I worked on, a local math professor who had recently retired was delighted to start up a math club and tailor a curriculum to meet the learning needs of the school's advanced math students. This concept doesn't work only for kids with advanced math abilities; it also applies to mismatched learning needs in every other subject area—music, languages, science, and the rest.

Include your child in the advocacy process to the extent their age and maturity allow. There is no more powerful advocate for a child's cause than the child, and participating in an advocacy effort can be a great learning process. At 8, Janine was considered too young to attend the meeting at the school, and I don't disagree with that decision, but at 12, it was appropriate that Jarel be there and be given a voice in the discussion, as he was. Jarel was also included along the way in thinking about how he learns best and what would help him learn better, as well as later on in fine-tuning the changes. Jarel's involvement in the process from the beginning was one of the reasons it went so well—he felt some ownership in the new approach and wanted to make sure it worked.

With so many stakeholders and such a complex system of interconnected pieces, school change is usually slow. Start small, go slowly, and be patient. In Jarel's story, the change was remarkably fast and easy, but we benefited from an unusually open-minded and creative principal who was ready to make this kind of change. That is rarely the case. There are usually a lot more meetings involved and a lot more people along the way needing to be convinced. If Janine's family hadn't had another school they could send her to, we would have had to work a lot harder, and it would have taken a lot longer to get to a place where she wouldn't be so frustrated at the first school.

Be appreciative as you enjoy your victory if that's where it goes. If your advocacy efforts fail, however, the best next step might be to accept defeat and work around the situation. In other cases—say with bullying or racism—it's time to go to a higher level, whether the school board or the media. In yet other cases, moving on means changing schools, as Janine's family did, or doing some homeschooling.

Every advocacy experience is unique to the situation and the players, but these general principles will stand you in good stead if you have a cause that matters to you and you want to work collaboratively with others to make a change.

EULOGY VIRTUES ARE MORE IMPORTANT THAN RÉSUMÉ VIRTUES

In a column called "The Moral Bucket List," David Brooks distinguished between résumé virtues and eulogy virtues: "The résumé virtues are the skills you bring to the marketplace. The eulogy virtues are the ones that are talked about at your funeral—whether you were kind, brave, honest, or faithful. Were you capable of deep love?"[3]

Brooks went on to write that, although most of us see the eulogy virtues as more important than the résumé virtues, it is the latter—the attributes that bring wealth, status, recognition, and success in worldly terms—that we put the heaviest focus on in our culture and education. Too often, kids are given more support for developing the skills and strategies they need to get into top universities and make lots of money than for establishing the character strengths that lead to love and fulfillment, the kind of life that creates a meaningful legacy.

What can you do if you want your child to radiate the inner light that reflects the eulogy or legacy virtues? In many ways, that's what this book is all about. From your child's birth through adulthood, encouraging the legacy virtues means slowing your life down enough to be loving and attuned to your child. Too often, parents' patience gets lost in the flurry of their busy lives, but loving attunement is the most powerful tool you have for supporting your child's thriving now and throughout their life. As frequently as you can through the day, make time to listen to your child with love.

Free play is important, too. It nourishes your child's curiosity, self-awareness, and imagination. It also strengthens their self-regulation, autonomy, decision making, conflict resolution, and friendship skills, all contributing to the legacy virtues. A daily dose of outdoor time—preferably in natural settings—reduces your child's stress, increases their optimism, improves health, stimulates the senses, frees the spirit, and enhances creativity. A résumé virtue bonus is that improving attention and focus also increases academic and other kinds of achievement.

Another support you can provide that enhances both legacy and résumé virtues is to look for opportunities for exploration and discovery in the arts, the sciences, architecture, gardening, and more, as widely as possible. Support your child in developing their curiosities into passions.

And as much as it's important for your child to develop their interests, they must also have plenty of downtime. The restful neural processing that occurs in daydreaming is essential to self-discovery and self-actualization. Your child needs a balance of active learning and moving, on the one hand, with do-nothing times, on the other, to replenish their spirits and find their creative wellspring.

As I've mentioned from time to time throughout the book, stress can interfere with a child's healthy development, and kids who learn mindful breathing techniques are better able to manage their stress. They sleep more soundly and are better able to focus their attention on cognitive, emotional, and physical activities. This is great for their character development and also helps with the résumé virtues because it leads to better concentration on tests and exams and better coping with challenging situations.

Holding a growth mindset is another habit you can teach your child that leads to higher measures of well-being, as well as success in every area of life. Reinforce your child's awareness that abilities develop step by step with hard work, persistence, and patience.

In the end, parenting for the eulogy virtues is mostly about love and balance. Although each of these components—free play, outdoor time, exploration, downtime, mindfulness, and mindsets— matters, loving attunement is the most important, the foundation of everything else. And somewhat counterintuitively, by focusing on the legacy virtues of kindness, generosity, wisdom, and integrity, you increase the likelihood your child will create long-term success in academic and professional areas, the résumé virtues. On a larger scale, focusing on the legacy virtues enables you and your child to participate in connecting and collaborating with others to make the world a better place for us all.

THE EARLY YEARS: BIRTH TO 5

I want to come back to the quote I opened this book with: "Somebody's got to be crazy about that kid. That's number one. First, last, and always."[4] Most parents don't realize how powerfully important their loving presence is in their child's life. If your child can trust that you'll be there for them through thick and thin—crazy about them first, last, and always—they have a better chance at health, happiness, and success. If they can trust you to be there for them, they'll be ready to move on and make connections with others. So, in this chapter about reaching out and making connections beyond the family, it all starts with you being crazy about your kid, which includes reliably "showing up" for them.

Showing up is the term that Daniel Siegel and Tina Payne Bryson focus on in *The Power of Showing Up: How Parental Presence Shapes Who Our Kids Become and How Their Brains Get Wired.*[5] They defined it as a way of being present that allows your child to thrive. Like so many of the principles of parenting I discuss through this book, showing up is conceptually simple, practically difficult, and enormously important. Siegel and Bryson described how the four S's (safe, seen, soothed, and secure) apply to all families and situations.

Showing up means helping your child feel safe. You can't protect your child from everything—and you will cripple them if you try—but you can give them a place in the world where they feel safe enough to take the risks they need to take to learn and grow.

Showing up also means helping your child feel seen. When your young (or older) child engages in attention-seeking behavior, override any tendency you might have to irritation and trying to ignore the behavior. Do the opposite. Pay attention to attention-seeking behavior—silly antics, clowning around, acting childish, scrapping with siblings, talking too much or too loudly—as valuable information telling you that your child feels unseen or unvalued. Strive to attune to what's happening underneath the behavior. When asked why people responded well to him around the world when he was president of the United States, Barack Obama wrote about his attempts to listen to others and understand their lives. He said, "To be known. To be heard. To have one's unique identity recognized and seen as worthy. It was a universal human desire."[6] This universal desire to be seen, understood, and valued starts at birth, and you are the person your child most yearns to be seen by.

Showing up means providing the kind of soothing your child needs when they're troubled. That doesn't mean hollow reassurances that they're smart or capable or something else. That will make your little one feel worse. They will know intuitively that you think they are somehow inadequate and need that kind of bolstering. How do you feel when someone gives you a reassuring platitude or pat on the head when you're feeling vulnerable? The kind of soothing your child needs instead is your calm faith in their ability to make it through their problems, with your support as needed.

331

Finally, showing up means giving your child the secure attachment to you that will enable them to thrive and make connections to others. That means showing up, fully present both physically and emotionally, day in and day out. Siegel and Bryson emphasized that quantity of time does matter, no matter how much some parents like to think they can collapse the amount of time they spend with their child if they give them quality time instead. Quality time does matter— time when you're kind, attentive, and patient, not distracted—but so does the quantity of time.

Although I'm including this information on showing up in this section on the early years, these principles continue to apply as your child gets older, too.

CHILDHOOD: 6 TO 10

It's good to strengthen your child's resilience as they grow through the childhood years, so they're in good psychological shape when they encounter the challenges of early adolescence and are prepared to contribute to and benefit from an expanding community as they get older.

Psychologist Dan Keating (who I mentioned in Chapter 7 in connection with creativity) argued that strengthening children's resilience is particularly important at this time of epidemic stress and anxiety, especially in young people, too many of whom are experiencing levels of stress beyond their ability to cope, to the point of undermining their health and development. Keating concluded from the research on this topic that in addition to mindfulness and attention to physical health, the most important resiliency factor for young people is a strong network of social support.[7]

I mentioned psychologist Tracy Dennis-Tiwary in Chapter 9, describing her work on the mindful use of technology to support mental health. She wrote a thoughtful blog post on the nature and definition of mental health, in which she cited Erich Fromm:

> Mental health is characterized by the ability to love and to create ... by a sense of identity based on one's experience of self as the subject and agent of one's powers, [and] by the grasp of reality inside and outside of ourselves, that is, by the development of objectivity and reason.[8]

Thinking about Keating's observations about resiliency factors and Fromm's definition of mental health in the context of other ideas and findings we've considered leads to some practical implications for supporting your child's mental health and general well-being, implications that focus on the importance of human connection. The first of these implications, and probably most important, is to listen to your child, actively, with love. The best way for them to develop the ability to love, which Fromm emphasized as a critical component of mental health, is to experience what it feels like to love and be loved. From there, help your child build and maintain a network of social support. As Keating observed, social support shows up in pretty much every study of people's health and well-being as one of the most important resiliency factors. Support your child in connecting with classmates, as well as extended family, neighbors, your friends, and others you encounter in your daily life.

Another way to encourage your child's resilience and mental health is to support them in finding and expanding their areas of interest. Creativity—Fromm's second component of mental health— is grounded in competence, which nourishes confidence and resilience. Support your child in identifying what they want to do and doing that in safe, guided, age-appropriate ways. As they get older, support them as they experience the consequences—positive and negative—of their decisions. Autonomy and independence are at the root of a sense of agency, of seeing oneself as the subject of one's life rather than as an object for others to respond to and direct.

Remembering that physical health contributes to mental health and resilience, make sure your child gets enough sleep, exercise, fresh air, and intellectual and creative challenges, as well as time for playing and daydreaming, all the dimensions of caring for oneself that I discussed in Chapter 4.

Mindfulness practices (along with social support and physical well-being) are included in Keating's list of the three most powerful ways to support your child's mental health. As I discussed at some length in Chapter 3, mindfulness increases your child's ability to concentrate on tasks, calm their anxieties, and cope with challenging situations.

And finally, there are some circumstances where none of these approaches is enough. Don't hesitate to get help if you think you might need it. If your child isn't thriving—they don't seem to be loving, creating, and becoming the agent of their own life—it's time to reach out into your community for the professional help you need.

ADOLESCENCE: 11 TO 18

Most people feel uncertain and afraid when they experience change that's beyond their control. From the age of 10 or 11 until about 14, that's what's happening to your child: It's a time of change that feels unpredictable and uncontrollable. Through puberty, your child is experiencing major changes everywhere at once, in their hormonal, physical, sexual, social, cognitive, and neurological systems. It's not surprising, then, if early adolescence makes your child moody and unpredictable.

Most teenagers aren't too difficult too often, but if you're the parent of a young teen, it might comfort you to know that challenging one's parents is a healthy part of growing up. At least some of the trouble your kid might be causing you is helping them develop into a successful and resilient adult who knows what matters to them and how to manage their life. Many parents don't realize that it's actually good to argue with your teenager, as long as you're respectful and affectionate. Kids do best in the long run when they grow up in a home that's characterized by lots of heated discussions, as well as lots of love and warmth.[9]

There's a limit to how much challenge is healthy challenge, however. If your teenager is defiant, oppositional, and reliably surly, you may benefit from professional help. However, it could simply be that you need to back off a bit and let them figure things out. In many cases, the situation falls somewhere in the middle, where you'll have to do some hard work to achieve a more harmonious equilibrium with your teenager, but you can do it without professional help.

Sometimes a teen's annoying behavior signifies nothing, but sometimes there's something deeper going on, and the young person needs something from you. In either case, just like when they were a toddler, they feel safe only when they know they can trust you to remain calm and strong, no matter how many of your buttons they push. One of the best things you can do for your out-of-control teenager is to take care of your own mental health. If you know you're about to explode, back off until you've regained your equilibrium and you're strong enough to stay calm.

This is the time for the adolescent-parenting version of showing up. Your caring availability when your adolescent needs you can make all the difference in a volatile moment, helping them choose to behave more wisely and stay out of harm's way. When your teenager wants to talk, do your best to put other activities aside and listen. And try to schedule a regular time you can spend with your teen, a few minutes daily when you can listen to—and hear—anything they want to talk about. Make a weekly date to do something together.

Go for ice cream, take a walk in the neighborhood, take an exercise class together. Your kid might try to get out of your together time, but you should proceed regardless, solo if necessary. Your teenager probably won't let you know it—not until they're all grown up—but this time together might be a lifesaver.

Being a teenager can feel impossibly serious. With a little effort, you can almost always respond to them with gentle humor instead of aggravation. Let them feel they have someone on their side who sees how hard it is and also knows they'll get through it just fine. When your teenager is making you crazy, try completing this sentence in your mind: "It must be hard. . . ." For example, "It must be hard to know that your friends are partying on weeknights, when your parents don't allow that," or "It must be hard wanting to wear the latest styles like some of the kids at school, knowing your family can't afford that."

It's also hard for parents when their child grows into adolescence. Be kind and patient with yourself, too, as you make the rookie errors that rookies make. Your teenager will find your flaws with ruthless efficiency and poke at them like a master of torture. It may seem that they're trying to enrage you, but—just like a toddler—they need you to prove that you're strong enough to resist their provocation and confident enough to stay calm and dependably solid. Stress management techniques such as deep breathing and mindfulness will not only help you cope with your own stress but will also give your teenager a good model for managing the inevitable ups and downs of their life. You get extra points if you pay attention to what your child can teach you about your flaws and learn to do better. (I smile as I write this, thinking about the character flaws my kids so mercilessly uncovered for me.)

Work on learning to trust your teen to figure out the small stuff in their lives. They'll make mistakes, but that's the only way they'll learn. Before puberty, most children are blissfully unaware of the perceptions of others, but teens believe that everyone is looking at them with critical mocking eyes. So, avoid nagging and criticism. Make sure your teen feels your positive gaze. That can make the difference between losing their way in harmful directions and finding and living their strength.

Let your teen know you're always available to listen or do some problem solving with them if they want that, but don't try to solve their problems for them. When they want to talk, be fully present (no distractions, no devices) and positive (no criticism, no judgment). Offer no solutions, just patient attention and acceptance. If your child asks what you think they should do, do your best to avoid giving an answer. Instead, try to ask questions that lead them to identify the solutions. Any solution they feel they've invented will be worth a hundred solutions you give them.

Again, I emphasize the importance of having a strong network of social support. You may need that yourself now as you grapple with the challenges of parenting a teenager. Also, do what you can to encourage your child to have independent relationships with extended family and other adults you trust. Many teens feel dramatically misunderstood by their parents sometimes and therefore lonely in their own homes. Connecting with grandparents, aunts and uncles, friends of the family, teachers, or others can help your child see you and themself through different eyes and provide a safety valve for talking about what's bothering them. Feeling like a member of a closely connected network can help your young person find more confidence and a healing sense of broader connection.

It's part of being a teenager to experience a conflict between the need to be a unique individual and the need to fit in and be "normal." Your child will experience extra pressures on the being-normal side if they have special needs of any kind or they come from a family that seems to them to be different from the mainstream. If you're an immigrant, a member of a cultural or religious minority, or you're in something other than a heterosexual relationship, your child may feel a conflict between their home values and what they see as their peers' values. Kids from minority or unconventional homes do best when their parents are flexible and respect their kids' needs to create their own unique blend of mainstream values and their family's values.

Remind yourself as often as possible that this impossible teenager was once a delightful child and is doing their sticky, imperfect, unconscious best to become that marvelous person again. When one of my now-wonderful adult daughters was a teenage nightmare, I found a photo of her as a sweet 4-year-old. I taped that photo to the fridge. In times of extreme trouble, it helped me stay strong and loving, believing in her essential wonderfulness, which is what it turns out she needed most of all.

If your teenager is seriously troubled (drugs, violence, mental health concerns), it's time to look for professional help. Take advantage of the small parenting window you still have before your teenager is an adult. Follow the recommendations I've already made, but also get the help you need so you can provide them a more solid foundation for moving into independent adulthood.

About a year ago, I heard from a father who had just discovered that his 15-year-old son was using cannabis[10] heavily. Greg told me that Kieran was a great kid—kind, funny, popular with classmates—but had seen a therapist for anxiety and depression when he was 13. Greg asked me how he should respond to this latest problem. Was cannabis as innocuous as Kieran assured him it was?

The short answer is, "Yes and no." Although most adults don't have serious problems related to cannabis use, it's different for teenagers. There are powerfully good reasons that no North American jurisdiction that has, at the time of this writing, legalized cannabis allows it to be sold to or used by people under 19. In *The Origins of You*, Jay Belsky and colleagues reported that those who start using cannabis heavily by age 15 are significantly more likely than others to develop serious mental health problems, including schizophrenia. Persistent cannabis dependence that starts in the mid-teens is also associated with cognitive and academic problems that persist at least into middle adulthood, resulting in financial difficulties, problems in the workplace, and conflicted intimate-partner relationships. The researchers found that the more heavily a teenager used cannabis, the greater the problems they experienced as adults.

The authors also noted that cannabis has become much more potent in the 25 years since their study participants were in their teens and that this almost certainly has implications for mental health, neuropsychological functioning, and work and family life.[11] A 15-year-old today is likely to experience considerably more harm from the same amount of cannabis as their research participants.

On the basis of these findings, as well as many other sources, I told Greg—the dad who had questions about his 15-year-old son's heavy cannabis use—that this was indeed a serious issue and required urgent action. I recommended that he start by making sure Kieran understood the dangers. Many teens think cannabis is harmless. "With patience, love, and no judgment," I told him, "Make sure Kieran knows the serious potential consequences to his brain and mental health, and the long-term, real-world outcomes of heavy cannabis use at his age."

I also recommended that he get professional help as quickly as possible, and if at all possible, it should be from someone who specializes in working with adolescents. Because cannabis (like alcohol and other drugs) is often used as an attempt at self-medication, Kieran needed to be assessed for depression, anxiety, bullying victimization, and other concerns, as well as his cannabis use. This was particularly important in this case because of his prior mental health concerns.

Just as important as my other recommendations was to, as I said, "Spend as much time with Kieran as he will allow. Tell him you love him and are available in any way he needs you. When he is being difficult or nonresponsive, focus your mind and heart on the little boy he used to be. He is still that person." I told him what I'd done with my daughter at that stage (for different problems) and suggested he find a photo of Kieran at his sweetest, most curious, healthiest best, and post it on the refrigerator, so he sees it, and Greg does too.

I suggested to Greg that he read Laurence Steinberg's *Age of Opportunity*[12] and Frances Jensen's *The Teenage Brain: A Neuroscientist's Survival Guide to Raising Adolescents and Young Adults*,[13] two books that are positive, encouraging, and thoughtful, providing straightforward scientific findings and advice for parents who want to understand what's happening with their adolescent and how they can best support their child through the process. I told him what Frances Jensen said about parents' important role in their children's drug use: "Recent research shows that fear of losing their parents' trust and respect is the greatest deterrent to adolescents' drug use."[14] You have to stay connected with your child if you want that desire to retain your trust and respect to deter their drug use.

One of my other recommendations to Greg was to find outlets for Kieran's creative self-expression, whether painting, sculpture, dance, writing, film, photography, or whatever might interest him. As I discussed in Chapter 7, this can literally be a lifesaver in situations like this.

I also recommended to Greg that he do what he could to separate Kieran from his cannabis-using friends. This is where having a network of social support can cut both ways, being highly beneficial when it supports one's strengths but detrimental when it fosters damaging habits such as drug use. Some kids are more vulnerable to peer pressure than others, but if your child is getting involved in dangerous activities such as using drugs, it's time to look for ways to discourage the friendships that enable those activities. That is easier said than done and will require your ingenuity and creativity.

Finally, I told Greg to stay with it. "Yes, this problem is serious," I said. "But in addition to all the scary stuff, the research also shows the power of love and connection and support, which are especially important at this stage of Kieran's life. Your being there for your son now can make all the difference in the life he ends up making for himself."

I spoke to Greg again recently. Things haven't improved. In fact, you might say they've gotten worse, with Kieran's hospitalization for a suicide attempt about 6 months ago. The family is working with a team of therapists, though, and Greg and his wife are continuing to show up for Kieran in every possible way. They are giving him the love and support he needs, and his therapist says Kieran is responding well to therapy. "It will take a while longer before Kieran is out of the woods," the therapist told Greg. "But with your ongoing reliable presence in his life, and your wife's, I'm optimistic that Kieran will pull out of this stronger and wiser. He's one of the lucky ones. He has a family who believes in him."

No parent is ever perfect, but every parent can invest their energy now into building the relationship with your child that will help you both weather as well as possible the storms that life presents you with, whether you find yourself in a deliciously calm moment between storms or the midst of a hurricane.

YOUNG ADULTHOOD: 19 TO 24

By the time your child reaches young adulthood, you'd think you'd be freer than you've been in all the years before that, freer to spend time with your friends and to think about creating your postparenting life. That's only partly true because if you're like most of the people I know and work with, once you become a parent, your kids are never far from your thoughts. If all is going well with them, you are free to live your life and enjoy your adult child as a human being. But

341

if not—and many young adults experience serious bumps in the road when it comes to schooling, jobs, money, relationships, legal problems, substance use, or mental health—you still have critically important work to do.

According to what is now known about the brain's development, it makes a big difference to a young person's long-term development if they continue to have parental support into their mid-20s. I don't mean complete unquestioning financial support (if that's even an option) because you have to be careful not to rob your child of their independence and autonomy. In fact, now's the time to wean your child from financial support, if you haven't already done that, to do whatever you haven't done yet to prepare your young adult for financial self-sufficiency as soon as possible. However, I do mean complete unquestioning acceptance, love, and approval, trusting that your child can get themself out of whatever trouble they get themself into, which they're in a much stronger position to do if they know you believe in them.

At this stage, your child probably has a network of friends and mentors, people they can go to if they want fun, encouragement, conversation, solace, or guidance. With any luck, that network includes you, although that's certainly not always the case. Sometimes parents have to wait until their adult child gets a bit older and more confident before the child feels ready to welcome their parent into their social circle as another adult. Sometimes, however, there's something you need to do as a parent before your adult child is able to enjoy your company.

If you feel your adult child (starting at 19 or so) avoids your company or even dislikes you, ask yourself whether they need you to back off and let them be free to become themself. By this stage, your child should be making all their own decisions about everything unless their behavior directly impacts you. If they're living with you, it's reasonable that you ask for considerate behavior regarding noise, tidiness, and food. If they want to use your car, it's reasonable that they have to follow your rules and schedule. But when it comes to how they're spending their time or money, who they're spending it with, what college courses they're taking (or not), what jobs they're applying for, how they're handling responsibilities, or anything else, things will go better for you both and your relationship if you can find a place of love and trust and work on staying there. Do your best to love the person they are, and trust that you've given them whatever values and skills you can. It's time now to let them find their own way to the life they want to create for themself.

You may remember the story I told about Margaret and Clare in Chapter 7. Margaret provided the support Clare needed to work out how she wanted to use her time at university. By choosing to "waste" her academic year and focus instead on social and emotional skills and writing, Clare was making a choice that many parents would have resisted or even punished. Margaret recognized that her daughter was an independent and responsible young adult and needed to figure things out for herself. She knew that if it proved to be a mistake and at some later time Clare decided she wanted to go back to her studies, Clare would find a way to make that happen. Margaret saw her job as providing the love, respect, and support that helped Clare do what she needed to do at this stage of her development.

In retrospect, Margaret probably made the right decision on this, both for Clare's well-being and her relationship with her daughter. As I mentioned in Chapter 7, Clare went on to make a fulfilling life and career for herself. Margaret and Clare have stayed close, and Margaret is thoroughly enjoying being a grandmother to Clare's daughter, Alix, who I talked about in connection with empathy and bullying.

Clare's father, however—who I haven't mentioned before— wasn't able to accept Clare's decision about not wanting to invest further time and energy in her studies. He and Margaret had divorced when Clare was young, and he had been paying part of her residence fees. When Clare told him about feeling disconnected from her academic work and wanting to study other things instead, he became angry. He told her she was wasting the opportunity that university presented and ruining her life. He also informed her that he would withhold any further residence payments until he saw her getting good grades again. For Clare, this was one more reason not to trust him to listen to her or to have her best interest at heart. It deepened the wedge between them and exacerbated a wound that hasn't yet healed.

TAKING IT INTO THE COMMUNITY: BEING THE VILLAGE

Anthropologist Margaret Mead is believed to have said, "Never doubt that a small group of thoughtful, committed citizens can change the world; indeed, it's the only thing that ever has." That's another way of saying what Helen Keller said in the quote that opens this chapter: "Alone we can do so little, together we can do so much."

These ideas are themes that run through this book, especially in the chapter sections called "Taking It Into the Community." By learning to accept our imperfections as parents while building relationships with our child that can weather any storm, we are developing the strength we need to be part of the village that supports each child, each person, in living the most fulfilled life possible. Each of us has different abilities, challenges, experiences, and values, so our ways of participating in our communities are unique and change over time as our needs, health, interests, and responsibilities change. Each chapter in this book describes some of the ways you might enjoy reaching out, along with your child.

In Chapter 1, I talked about the importance of collective efficacy, the sense of being connected to others in your neighborhood, being able to get and give help as needed. Living in a neighborhood that you experience as friendly enhances your well-being and parenting skills and has many benefits for your child's development. Simply greeting neighbors as you see them and asking about their health or family is a great start to creating a feeling that you live in a friendly neighborhood. You can support local shops and cafes, stopping to spend a few minutes being friendly to the owners, clerks, and servers. You can take the initiative on a fundraiser for a local cause; maybe the school library could use more books, for example, or the park could use a spring cleaning, or you could start up a community garden. If you don't have any ideas, ask your child. You can do some problem solving together and think of something you'll both enjoy that will enhance everyone's sense of collective efficacy.

In Chapter 2, I talked about Angela, whose daughter, Jesse, was helping her friend Marisol by staying with her after school every day, waiting until Marisol's mother came home from work. Angela discovered that Jesse was helping Marisol avoid an abusive step-father and suggested that Jesse bring Marisol home with her, where she could stay until it was safe to go home. Before too long, Angela found a shelter for women and kids where she and Jesse and Marisol could volunteer. Each one of the three benefited from this activity, as did the inhabitants of the shelter. Angela was building her relationship with her daughter at the same time as they were both contributing to the well-being of others in their community.

In Chapter 3, the emphasis was on mindfulness. The community application I discussed there was antiracism and antibullying, learning to pay attention to the small and large violations of equity and inclusion all around us. By teaching your child to be mindful about kindness, diversity, and respect for each other human being, you're building their legacy virtues as you make the world a better place for each of us.

The theme of Chapter 4 was caring for oneself. One dimension of that is good nutrition, and the community application I discussed in that chapter was the garden that Sunnydale Elementary School created. That project had all kinds of benefits for the school, the families that participated, and the neighborhood. Participating in a venture like that is a great way for you and your child to make a big contribution to your community, much larger than you might initially think.

In *Palaces for the People: How Social Infrastructure Can Help Fight Inequality, Polarization, and the Decline of Civic Life*,[15] Eric Klinenberg showed how social infrastructure such as community gardens reduces violent crime as it reduces food inequities. He described a project in Philadelphia where community residents were hired to fix up overgrown vacant lots and abandoned properties to create pocket parks and community gardens in high-crime neighborhoods. There was a 39% reduction in gun violence and substantial net benefits to taxpayers. Klinenberg observed,

> For decades, building prisons for the poor has been our main crime reduction policy, and the social costs have been as great as the economic expense. If we want a better, more equitable, and sustainable solution for the challenges facing our cities and suburbs, we'd be better off building social infrastructure instead.[16]

Residents feel safer and are safer when their neighborhood is well-tended and welcoming.

Klinenberg also described neighborhoods throughout the United States where it used to be impossible to get fresh produce at reasonable prices that are now becoming food destinations through the efforts of small civic organizations. Over 800 community gardens and urban farms have been created in Chicago where vacant lots and burnt-out buildings once stood. The American Public Health Association reported that the benefits of gardens like this go much further than the nutritious food they produce: They reduce the temperature in overheated city centers, reduce social isolation and stress levels in community residents, foster interactions across generations, increase civic participation, and teach children about nature. Growing Home,[17] a Chicago-based organization dedicated to urban farms and community development, has a program for people who have recently left prison, giving them jobs as production assistants and helping them get full-time jobs when they're finished.

In discussing the importance of social infrastructure, Klinenberg also described research showing the steady erosion of outdoor play spaces, which leads to higher levels of stress and obesity, as well as reduced civic skills. Children get more than physical exercise when they play at local playgrounds and participate in team sports. They also learn about collaborative problem solving and how to interact with different kinds of people. And speaking of problem solving, when your child worries about the state of the world, you might want to do some problem solving with them about what you can do to improve the social infrastructure in your neighborhood. You will build your relationship as you work together to make your corner of the world a better, safer, more equitable place for everyone.

National Public Radio named *Palaces for the People* one of the best books of 2018, and a starred review in Booklist concluded, "If America appears fractured at the national level, it can be mended at the local one."[18] This is such an inspiring and timely message and applicable on all levels—oneself, one's child, one's family, one's community, one's country, the world. We are all in this together, and you can make a big difference by starting small in your neighborhood.

In Chapter 5, where the topic was brain building, I talked about how parenting centers can support parents in learning how to encourage their children's healthiest development and responding as well as possible when things aren't going well. By getting active in a neighborhood-based parenting center, you can help be part of the village that it takes to raise our children well.

I discussed an allied idea in Chapter 6, which focused on learning. Getting involved in reading circles that support parents' and kids' literacy can be an enjoyable way for you and your child to build your relationship while you make your community a happier, safer place for everyone.

Creativity was the topic of Chapter 7, and there I discussed again the idea of creative problem solving, this time using the large-scale examples of how Malala Yousafzai and Greta Thunberg noticed local problems (access to schooling and environmental protection), approached the solutions creatively, and then took their efforts global. These are ambitious examples—not every child will identify a problem this big or get international acclaim (and criticism) for their efforts toward solutions—but you and your child can identify problems in your neighborhood, think creatively about possible solutions, and build your relationship as you build your community.

In Chapter 8, I talked about Roots of Empathy and Making Caring Common, two of many programs designed to promote respect, caring, and inclusion at school. Because social and emotional skills are critically important to thriving in every area of life and because some kids don't learn these skills at home, initiatives like these can go a long way to making the world a safer and fairer place, where racism and bullying are not tolerated, and every child gets a chance to make a good life for themself.

In Chapter 9, I talked about some of the many ways you can reach out and make a difference in your community, starting with your own network of social support and moving out from there. Starting with accepting that, like everyone else, you aren't perfect and then taking good care of yourself and nurturing your relationship with your child, you can find the strength and energy to reach out and make a difference for others, which in turn enriches your child and strengthens your relationship with them. It's a circle making a spiral we are all in together, strength building on strength.

Everyone Benefits When the Least Among Us Do Well

There's compelling research illustrating the ways this principle works, of how taking care of yourself, building a strong relationship with your child, and working together to make a difference in your community changes everything and benefits us all.

The Canadian Institute for Advanced Research created a small working group in the late 1990s. The group was composed of widely respected international researchers from disparate fields, and its purpose was to consider how society is affected by individual and community health. Their work led to the Millennium Dialogue for Early Child Development in 2001, cosponsored by the Invest in Kids Foundation and the University of Toronto. You'll be familiar from previous chapters with some of the scientists who participated in the Dialogue: neuroscientist Charles Nelson, who has done innovative work mapping the brain's healthy and atypical development; epidemiologist Thomas Boyce, who (among other things) distinguished between orchid and dandelion children; and developmental psychologist Dan Keating, whose thoughts on creativity I discussed in Chapter 7 and whose work on stress and anxiety I described earlier in this chapter. The other participants in the Dialogue were pediatrician Ronald Barr, child psychologist Megan Gunnar, epidemiologist Clyde Hertzman, clinical child psychologist Alicia Lieberman, developmental psychiatrist Michael Rutter, and child psychologist Richard Tremblay. This cross-disciplinary dialogue of internationally renowned experts resulted in a book edited by Dan Keating, *Nature and Nurture in Early Child Development*,[19] in which each of the experts who participated in the Dialogue described their findings and shared their recommendations for moving forward into a world where every child has a chance to grow up strong, healthy, and productive.

A starting point for discussion among the scientists who participated in the Dialogue was ground-breaking research that showed that the size of the gap between the wealthiest and the poorest citizens in a country has an impact on the outcomes that individuals experience across health, well-being, and longevity.[20] The greater the wealth gap in a given country, the poorer the outcomes for all citizens. Many people are surprised when they learn that countries with large wealth gaps, such as the United States and the United Kingdom, have lower levels of well-being across all indicators compared with countries where social and income differences are less pronounced, such as Norway or Belgium. This means that the wealthiest citizens of large-gap countries don't live as long or do as well as the wealthiest citizens in countries where the gap is smaller, even when those in the large-gap countries, such as the United States, are much wealthier.

Another point of agreement across the participating scientists was the worrying fact that, in spite of many countries' huge wealth-generating capacity, their young people were experiencing increasing levels of alienation, anxiety, and stress-related disorders. The scientists agreed that although families with young children were at high risk and families living in poverty were most vulnerable, this anxiety was having a serious impact even on those who are economically secure.

Three recommendations emerging from the Millennium Dialogue for Early Child Development included that communities should do the following:

1. **Provide early support for high-risk families.** Richard Tremblay and colleagues found that family income, mother's education, single parenthood, and neighborhood are all major influences on children's cognitive and behavioral development and that the roots of delinquency and criminality are in early childhood. They also found that not only can the problems associated with the wealth gap be buffered by family factors but also that these problems are powerfully susceptible to intervention. When communities support their high-risk families

in acquiring and practicing healthy child development habits, children are far less likely to be alienated, aggressive, and violent, which has obvious benefits for society as a whole, as well as for the individuals and families who benefit from the intervention.

2. **Support parents in acquiring parenting skills.** The research of many of the Dialogue experts showed that to develop optimally, infants and young children need to receive certain kinds of stimulation at certain critical periods. One of the recurrent messages of this interdisciplinary gathering was that when parents are given the support they need for learning about their role in how their child develops—the focus of this book— their child's future options change dramatically.

3. **Ensure that schools incorporate social learning processes.** To succeed in the increasingly knowledge-based economy, young people will need more dynamic skills, including knowledge building, question finding, innovation, and collaboration, rather than the facts and static skills required in previous generations. When schools encourage collaborative knowledge-building processes, they give children what they need to be full participants in the rapidly changing world of work in the future.

The multidisciplinary research shared during the Millennium Dialogue for Early Child Development converged in demonstrating the need to invest in the lives of children and families, ensuring that every parent and child has what they need to thrive. It is still the case now, more than 20 years later, that it's in everyone's self-interest that each child has a chance to create a healthy and fulfilling life. This is something we can only do together—it really does take a village.

How to Support Your Community's Optimal Development

The Millennium Dialogue showed that there are good reasons other than altruism to care about what's happening in your community. The healthier your community, your country, and our planet, the greater the chances that you and your child will thrive. I pulled together the recommendations discussed in this chapter, along with many other topics discussed throughout this book, to offer some ideas to encourage.

- **Community-based parenting supports.** Parenting is hard, especially today, in a quickly changing, unpredictable, high-stress world. When parents are supported in learning how children develop and making it through the challenging times, their children are more likely to thrive through childhood and into adulthood.

  Parenting support can help all parents across all income brackets, but it's most urgently needed in high-risk neighborhoods. When parents in these neighborhoods are supported in acquiring strong parenting skills, their children are less likely to experience alienation or participate in aggression or violence and are more likely to succeed at school and beyond.

  There are many ways to provide that support, including drop-in centers, social media groups, and easily accessible networks of professionals. School-based or library-based parenting centers can provide welcoming preschool options and good nutrition, as well as drop-in gathering spots and other parenting support as needed.
- **Universal early education.** Universal prekindergarten starting at age 3 can have an enormous impact on children's long-term outcomes, not only educationally but also on subsequent career choices, income, health, and happiness. Early learning should be play based and include numeracy, literacy, and social–emotional skills. Not only is this a good investment in children's and family's lives, but it also has important economic benefits for society.[21]
- **Public libraries.** A welcoming library staffed by knowledgeable librarians enriches a community. It can be a hub for formal and informal gatherings, children's story hours, information

dissemination, book sharing, and internet access. It can be a place of sanctuary, support, inspiration, encouragement, and expansion.

- **Local parks.** Children and adults do better when they have access to green places for outdoor play and informal gathering: The urban environment improves, people's stress levels go down, crime is reduced, and communities are more likely to thrive. Are there neighborhoods in your community that could be improved by transforming vacant or underused space into pocket parks? Are there neighborhoods where children would benefit from easier access to playgrounds or playground improvements?

- **Community gardens.** Community gardens can be casual meeting places for people from diverse backgrounds across age, race, income, education, and political persuasion. They can also provide great learning opportunities for children and become a source of nutritious food, which is especially important in low-income neighborhoods.

- **Antiracism and antibullying programs at school.** These programs make a difference for every student, both those who might be bystanders, enablers, or perpetrators, as well as those who would otherwise be victims.

- **Universal basic income and universal health care.** Communities with a more equitable distribution of wealth do better across all measures, including education, health, wealth, longevity, and happiness. Even the wealthiest among us benefits when each member of our community has a chance to create a good life and has the necessary supports in place when they need them.[22] I know this issue is highly politicized in the United States, but it's a principle that's generally understood (if not always as well applied as it might be) in Canada and the other G7 countries (France, Italy, Germany, Japan, and the United Kingdom).

353

KEY TAKEAWAYS FOR WEATHERING THE STORMS THAT LIFE
BRINGS

- We are all connected in an ecosystem that includes each person, plant, animal, and body of water.
- Nurture your network of social support. It's one of the most important things you can do for your health, well-being, happiness, and resilience and for that of your family.
- Everyone needs help sometimes. When things get wobbly in your life or your child's—nobody's perfect, and every person and every family has wobbly moments—look for the helpers. They might be extended family members, neighbors, friends, or professionals. You don't need to do this alone.
- You can make a difference. Working with like-minded others, you can become an advocate for making the world a better place in some way that matters to you—fairer, safer, cleaner, kinder, more harmonious.

NOTES

INTRODUCTION

1. The late David MacArthur, Mississauga, Ontario.
2. Belsky, J., Caspi, A., Moffitt, T. E., & Poulton, R. (2020). *The origins of you: How childhood shapes later life.* Harvard University Press.

CHAPTER I

1. HealthyChildren.org
2. Kiff, C. J., Lengua, L. J., & Zalewski, M. (2011). Nature and nurturing: Parenting in the context of child temperament. *Clinical child and family psychology review, 14*(3), 251–301. https://doi.org/10.1007/s10567-011-0093-4
3. Lopez, N. V., Schembre, S., Belcher, B. R., O'Connor, S., Maher, J. P., Arbel, R., Margolin, G., & Dunton, G. F. (2018). Parenting styles, food-related parenting practices, and children's healthy eating: A mediation analysis to examine relationships between parenting and child diet. *Appetite, 128,* 205–213. https://doi.org/10.1016/j.appet.2018.06.021
4. Martinez, I., Garcia, F., Veiga, F., Garcia, O. F., Rodrigues, Y., & Serra, E. (2020). Parenting styles, internalization of values and self-esteem: A cross-cultural study in Spain, Portugal and Brazil. *International Journal of Environmental Research and Public Health, 17*(7), 2370. https://doi.org/10.3390/ijerph17072370

5.   Winnicott, D. W. (1953). *Playing and reality.* Routledge.
6.   Bettelheim, B. (1987). *A good enough parent.* Random House.
7.   Bettelheim (1987), p. xi.
8.   Keltner, D., Oatley, K., & Jenkins, J. (2018). *Understanding emotions* (4th ed.). Wiley. See Chapter 8, "Temperament," p. 222.
9.   Keltner et al. (2018).
10. Sileo, F. J., & Potter, C. S. (2021). *When your child has a chronic medical illness: A guide for the parenting journey.* American Psychological Association.
11. Boyce, W. T. (2020). *The orchid and the dandelion: Why some children struggle and how all can thrive.* Penguin Random House.
12. Boyce (2020), p. 11.
13. Boyce (2020), p. 15.
14. Kurcinka, M. S. (2020). *Raising your spirited child: A guide for parents whose child is more intense, sensitive, perceptive, persistent, and energetic* (3rd ed.). William Morrow.
15. Belsky, J., Caspi, A., Moffitt, T. E., & Poulton, R. (2020). *The origins of you: How childhood shapes later life.* Harvard University Press.
16. Belsky et al. (2020), p. 194.

CHAPTER 2

1.   Dweck, C. S. (2006). *Mindset: The new psychology of success.* Random House.
2.   Yeager, D. S., Hanselman, P., Walton, G. M., Murray, J. S., Crosnoe, R., Muller, C., Tipton, E., Schneider, B., Hulleman, C. S., Hinojosa, C. P., Paunesku, D., Romero, C., Flint, K., Roberts, A., Trott, J., Iachan, R., Buontempo, J., Yang., S. M., Carvalho, C. M., . . . Dweck, C. S. (2019). A national experiment reveals where a growth mindset improves achievement. *Nature, 573,* 364–369. https://doi.org/10.1038/s41586-019-1466-y
3.   Dweck (2006), p. 175.
4.   Kaufman, S. B. (2013). *Ungifted: Intelligence redefined: The truth about talent, practice, creativity, and the many paths to greatness.* Basic Books.
5.   Kaufman (2013), p. 118.
6.   Dweck (2006), p. 170.
7.   Dweck (2006), p. 75.

8. Grogan-Kaylor, A., Ma, J., & Graham-Bermann, S. A. (2018). The case against physical punishment. *Current Opinion in Psychology*, *19*, 22–27. https://doi.org/10.1016/j.copsyc.2017.03.022

9. Meyer, A., Proudfit, G. H., Bufferd, S. J., Kujawa, A. J., Laptook, R. S., Torpey, D. C., & Klein, D. N. (2015). Self-reported and observed punitive parenting prospectively predicts increased error-related brain activity in six-year-old children. *Journal of Abnormal Child Psychology*, *43*, 821–829. https://doi.org/10.1007/s10802-014-9918-1

10. Russell, W. T. (2016). Why you should never use timeouts on your kids. *PBS News Hour.* https://www.pbs.org/newshour/nation/column-12-alternatives-to-timeouts-when-kids-are-at-their-worst

11. Siegel, D., & Bryson, T. P. (2014). 'Time-outs' are hurting your child. *Time.com.* https://time.com/3404701/discipline-time-out-is-not-good/

12. Nelsen, J. (2016). *Positive discipline parenting tools.* Harmony Books.

13. Jensen, F. (2015). *The teenage brain: A neuroscientist's survival guide to raising adolescents and young adults.* Harper.

14. Steinberg, L. (2015). *Age of opportunity: Lessons from the new science of adolescence.* Houghton Mifflin Harcourt.

15. Bleidorn, W. (2015). What accounts for personality maturation in early adulthood? *Current Directions in Psychological Science, 24*(3), 245–252. https://doi.org/10.1177/0963721414568662

16. Eriksson, P. L., Wängqvist, M., Carlsson, J., & Frisén, A. (2020). Identity development in early adulthood. *Developmental Psychology, 56*(10), 1968–1983. https://doi.org/10.1037/dev0001093

17. Pusch, S., Mund, M., Hagemeyer, B., & Finn, C. (2019). Personality development in emerging and young adulthood: A study of age differences. *European Journal of Personality, 33*(3), 245–263. https://doi.org/10.1002/per.2181

CHAPTER 3

1. Brach, T. (2019). *Radical compassion: Learning to love yourself and your world with the practice of RAIN.* Viking.

2. Answers to the Mindfulness Quiz:

    1. **False.** There is a large and growing body of evidence showing the remarkable effectiveness of mindfulness in every dimension of life.

2. **True.** Mindfulness is a great way to find your calm center, which helps you respond wisely to the circumstances with which life presents you.
3. **False.** Meditation is a great way to become mindful, but there are many other pathways, too.
4. All **true.** I talk in this chapter about the research supporting improvements in cognitive functioning, attention, and memory.
5. **False.** As with meditation, yoga can be an excellent entry point to mindfulness but only if you are working with a teacher who focuses on yoga as a mindfulness practice. Most yoga classes are about the physical aspect of yoga, not mindfulness.
6. **False.** Mindfulness has nothing to do with any form of religion. There is no religious component to it. Mindfulness is practiced by Buddhists, but the practice is not exclusive to them.
7. **True.** There is solid evidence that mindfulness reduces anxiety and stress.
8. **False.** Mindfulness doesn't reduce your ability to feel happiness or sadness. It does help you cope with intense feelings and supports your resilience through challenging times, but it doesn't diminish your emotional experiences in any way.
9. **True.** Evidence that mindfulness improves pain management is probably the biggest reason there is so much emphasis on it today, with mindfulness research centers at many of the world's top universities.
10. **False.** Children as young as 2 can learn some basic tools of mindfulness.

3. Lazar, S. (n.d.). *Publications.* https://scholar.harvard.edu/sara_lazar/publications
4. Lazar, S. (2018). *How mindfulness reshapes the brain* [Video]. https://www.youtube.com/watch?v=nZPaQSAy334
5. Ungar, M. (2019). Do happy parents raise healthier kids? *Psychology Today.* https://www.psychologytoday.com/ca/blog/nurturing-resilience/201910/do-happy-parents-raise-healthier-kids
6. Ungar (2019), para. 2.
7. Douglas, A. (2019). *Happy parents happy kids.* Collins.
8. Brown, E. E. (2011). *The complete Tassajara cookbook.* Shambhala.

9. No source available; I heard this simple affirmation a long time ago.
10. No source available; again, something I heard somewhere sometime and retained.
11. Rumi, a 13th-century Persian poet, Islamic scholar, and Sufi mystic.
12. https://www.yogawithcarole.ca/about (Carole Matthews is my sister.)
13. Thich Nhat Hanh, Vietnamese peace activist and Buddhist monk.
14. Keyes, K. (1993). *Handbook to higher consciousness* (5th ed.). Love Line Books.
15. Valdivia, P. (2010). *And so it goes.* Groundwood Books.
16. Valdivia (2010), p. 32.
17. Valdivia (2010), p. 34.
18. Barrett, L. F. (2020). *7½ lessons about the brain.* Mariner Books.
19. Paul, A. M. (2020, November 20). Thinking clearly requires feeling deeply. *BostonGlobe.com.* https://www.bostonglobe.com/2020/11/20/opinion/thinking-clearly-requires-feeling-deeply/ (para. 4).
20. Allen, S. (2018). *The science of gratitude.* John Templeton Foundation, the Greater Good Science Center at UC Berkeley. https://docs.google.com/viewer?url=https%3A%2F%2Fggsc.berkeley.edu%2Fimages%2Fuploads%2FGGSC-JTF_White_Paper-Gratitude-FINAL.pdf
21. Brecher, D. R., & Shaffer, D. K. (n.d.). *Thriving in action.* Thrive RU, Ryerson University. https://www.ryerson.ca/thriveru/tia/
22. Achor, S. (2018). *The happiness advantage: The seven principles of positive psychology.* Crown Business.
23. PRIDE Team. (2019). *Research findings: Children notice race.* Positive Racial Identity Development in Early Education. https://www.racepride.pitt.edu/research-findings-children-notice-race/
24. Ivey-Colson, K., & Turner, L. (2020, September). Ten keys to everyday anti-racism. *Greater Good Magazine.* https://greatergood.berkeley.edu/article/item/ten_keys_to_everyday_anti_racism
25. Ivey-Colson & Turner (2020), para. 9.
26. Alexander, K., & Nelson, K. (2019). *The undefeated.* HMH. https://theundefeated.com/tag/kwame-alexander/
27. Muhammad, I., & Aly, H. (2019). *The proudest blue.* Little, Brown.
28. Johnson, C., Council, L., & Choi, C. (2019). *IntersectionAllies: We make room for all.* Dottir Press. https://www.dottirpress.com/intersection-allies

CHAPTER 4

1. Brooks, J. L. (Director). (2010). *How do you know* [Film]. Columbia Pictures.
2. Casares, W. (2020). *Importance of self-care: Why parents need time out to recharge.* healthychildren.org. https://www.healthychildren.org/English/family-life/family-dynamics/Pages/Importance-of-Self-Care.aspx (para. 3).
3. Piaget, J. (1951). Egocentric thought and sociocentric thought. In L. Smith (Ed. & Trans.), *Sociological studies* (pp. 270–286). Taylor & Francis.
4. Moore, H. (2014). *Why play is the work of childhood.* Fred Rogers Center, St. Vincent's College. https://www.fredrogerscenter.org/2014/09/why-play-is-the-work-of-childhood/ (para. 4).
5. Yogman, M., Garner, A., Hutchinson, J., Hirsh-Pasek, K., & Golinkoff, R. M. (2018). The power of play: A pediatric role in enhancing development in young children. *Pediatrics, 142*(3), e20182058. https://doi.org/10.1542/peds.2018-2058 (p. 1).
6. Charnow, C., & Yogman, M. (2013). *The joy of discovery and the power of play.* Boston Children's Museum. https://docs.google.com/viewer?url=https%3A%2F%2Fwww.bostonchildrensmuseum.org%2Fsites%2Fdefault%2Ffiles%2Fpdfs%2FThe-Power-of-Play.pdf
7. Yogman et al. (2018).
8. Fries, L. R., Martin, N., & van der Horst, K. (2017). Parent–child mealtime interactions associated with toddlers' refusals of novel and familiar foods. *Physiology & Behavior, 176*, 93–100. https://doi.org/10.1016/j.physbeh.2017.03.001
9. Hoban, R., & Hoban, L. (1964). *Bread and jam for Frances.* Harper Collins.
10. National Health Service. (2019). *Physical activity guidelines for children (under 5 years).* National Health Service. https://www.nhs.uk/live-well/exercise/physical-activity-guidelines-children-under-five-years/#:~:text=Toddlers%20should%20be%20physically%20active,the%20day%2C%20including%20playing%20outdoors
11. Cohen, D. (n.d.). *Why kids need to spend time in nature.* Child Mind Institute. https://childmind.org/article/why-kids-need-to-spend-time-in-nature/

12. Dankiw, K. A, Tsiros, M., D., Baldock, K., L., & Kumar, S. (2020). The impacts of unstructured nature play on health in early childhood development: A systematic review. *PLOS ONE, 15*(2), Article e0229006. https://doi.org/10.1371/journal.pone.0229006

13. Tillmann, S., Tobin, D., Avison, W., & Gilliland, J. (2018). Mental health benefits of interactions with nature in children and teenagers: A systematic review. *Journal of Epidemiology & Community Health, 72,* 958–966. https://doi.org/10.1136/jech-2018-210436

14. Dopko, R. L., Capaldi, C. A., & Zelenski, J. M. (2019). The psychological and social benefits of a nature experience for children: A preliminary investigation. *Journal of Environmental Psychology, 63,* 134–138. https://doi.org/10.1016/j.jenvp.2019.05.002

15. Winter, W. C. (2021). *The rested child: Why your tired, wired, or irritable child may have a sleep disorder—and how to help.* Avery.

16. Paruthi, S., Brooks, L. J., D'Ambrosio, C., Hall, W. A., Kotagal, S., Lloyd, R. M., Malow, B. A., Maski, K., Nichols, C., Quan, S. F., Rosen, C. L., Troester, M. M., & Wise, M. S. (2016). Recommended amount of sleep for pediatric populations: A consensus statement of the American Academy of Sleep Medicine. *Journal of Clinical Sleep Medicine, 12*(6), 785–786. https://doi.org/10.5664/jcsm.5866

17. Yogman et al. (2018).

18. Mairs, R., & Nicholls, D. (2016). Assessment and treatment of eating disorders in childhood and adolescence. *Archives of Disease in Childhood, 101*(12), 1168–1175. https://adc.bmj.com/content/101/12/1168.full

19. Haines, J., Haycraft, E., Lytle, L., Nicklaus, S., Kok, F. J., Merdji, M., Fisberg, M., Moreno, L. A., Goulet, O, & Hughes, S. O. (2019). Nurturing children's healthy eating: Position statement. *Appetite, 137,* 124–133. https://doi.org/10.1016/j.appet.2019.02.007 (p. 124).

20. American Heart Association. (2018). *Recommendations for physical activity in adults and kids.* https://www.heart.org/en/healthy-living/fitness/fitness-basics/aha-recs-for-physical-activity-in-adults

21. Walker, T. D. (2014, June). How Finland keeps kids focused through free play. *The Atlantic.* https://www.theatlantic.com/education/archive/2014/06/how-finland-keeps-kids-focused/373544/

22. Chesham, R. A., Booth, J. N., Sweeney, E. L. Ryde, G. C., Gorely, T., Brooks, N. E., & Moran, C. N. (2018). The Daily Mile makes primary

school children more active, less sedentary and improves their fitness and body composition: A quasi-experimental pilot study. *BMC Medicine, 16,* 64. https://doi.org/10.1186/s12916-018-1049-z

23. Dopko et al. (2019).
24. Paruthi et al. (2016), p. 785.
25. Winter (2021), p. xiii.
26. Steinberg, L. (2015). *Age of opportunity: Lessons from the new science of adolescence.* Houghton Mifflin Harcourt.
27. Paruthi et al. (2016), p. 785.
28. Paruthi et al. (2016), p. 785.
29. Jensen, F. (2015). *The teenage brain: A neuroscientist's survival guide to raising adolescents and young adults.* Harper.
30. Jensen (2015), p. 89.
31. Winter (2021), p. 98.
32. American Heart Association (2018).
33. Watson, N. F., Badr, M. S., Belenky, G., Bliwise, D. L., Buxton, O. M., Buysse, D., Dinges, D. F., Gangwisch, J., Grandner, M. A., Kushida, C., Malhotra, R. K., Martin, J. L., Patel, S. R., Quan, S. F., & Tasali, E. (2015). Recommended amount of sleep for a healthy adult: A joint consensus statement of the American Academy of Sleep Medicine and Sleep Research Society. *SLEEP, 38*(6), 843–844. https://doi.org/10.5665/sleep.4716
34. Watson et al. (2015), p. 843.
35. Bryant, E. (2021, April). *Lack of sleep in middle age may increase dementia risk.* National Institutes of Health. https://www.nih.gov/news-events/nih-research-matters/lack-sleep-middle-age-may-increase-dementia-risk
36. Klinenberg, E. (2018). *Palaces for the people: How social infrastructure can help fight inequality, polarization, and the decline of civic life.* Penguin Random House.

CHAPTER 5

1. See, for example, Brazelton, T. B., & Greenspan, S. I. (2000). *The irreducible needs of children: What every child must have to grow, learn, and flourish.* Perseus.

2. Nelson, C. A., de Haan, M., & Thomas, K. M. (2015). *Neuroscience of cognitive development: The role of experience and the developing brain.* Wiley.
3. Cabib, S., Campus, P., Conversi, D., Orsini, C., & Puglisi-Allegra, S. (2020). Functional and dysfunctional neuroplasticity in learning to cope with stress. *Brain Sciences, 10*(2), 127. https://doi.org/10.3390/brainsci10020127
4. Nelson et al. (2015).
5. Nelson et al. (2015).
6. Butcher, K., & Pletcher, J. (2016). *Cognitive development and sensory play.* https://www.canr.msu.edu/news/cognitive_development_and_sensory_play
7. Goodstart Early Learning. (2018). *Exploring the benefits of sensory play.* https://www.goodstart.org.au/news-and-advice/october-2016/exploring-the-benefits-of-sensory-play
8. Frontline. (n.d.). *Inside the teenage brain* [Interview with Jay Giedd]. https://www.pbs.org/wgbh/pages/frontline/shows/teenbrain/interviews/giedd.html
9. Frontline (n.d.)
10. Jensen, F. E. (2015). *The teenage brain: A neuroscientist's survival guide to raising adolescents and young adults.* Harper. (p. 80)
11. Jensen (2015), p. 30.
12. National Institute of Mental Health. (2020). *The teen brain: 7 things to know.* U.S. Department of Health and Human Services. https://www.nimh.nih.gov/health/publications/the-teen-brain-7-things-to-know/
13. Steinberg, L. (2015). *Age of opportunity: Lessons from the new science of adolescence.* Houghton Mifflin Harcourt.
14. Colver A., & Dovey-Pearce G. (2018). The anatomical, hormonal and neurochemical changes that occur during brain development in adolescents and young adults. In A. Hergenroeder & C. Wiemann (Eds.), *Health care transition* (pp. 15–19). Springer. https://doi.org/10.1007/978-3-319-72868-1_2
15. Scott, E., Duell, N., & Steinberg, L. (2018). Brain development, social context, and justice policy. *Washington University Journal of Law and Policy, 57.* https://openscholarship.wustl.edu/law_journal_law_policy/vol57/iss1/8 (p. 20).

16. Hendrickson, E. (2019, May). Failure to launch syndrome. *Scientific American*. https://www.scientificamerican.com/article/failure-to-launch-syndrome/
17. Frontline (n.d.), para. 26.
18. North Shore Child and Family Guidance Center. (2018). *The adolescent brain: An evolving view*. https://www.northshorechildguidance.org/the-adolescent-brain-an-evolving-view/ (para. 6).
19. Delahooke, M. (2019). *Beyond behaviors: Using brain science and compassion to understand children's problem behaviors*. PESI.
20. Delahooke (2019), p. 11.
21. Mount Sinai Parenting Center: https://parenting.mountsinai.org/about/ (para. 1).
22. EarlyON Child and Family Centres, Simcoe North: https://www.nsmhealthline.ca/displayservice.aspx?id=34822
23. See, for example, Carolina Abecedarian Project at the Frank Porter Graham Child Development Institute: https://abc.fpg.unc.edu/abecedarian-project
24. https://nationaldiaperbanknetwork.org/

CHAPTER 6

1. Answers to the true/false quiz:
   1. **False.** This chapter is all about how you can raise your intelligence and support your child in doing the same.
   2. **False.** There's a proven connection between intelligence and physical exercise, good nutrition, time outdoors, and getting enough sleep. (See Chapters 4 and 5 for more on this.)
   3. **True.** A strong network of social support is the most important factor for general well-being, including a healthy brain and longevity.
   4. **False.** A high IQ means you achieve a high score on a test of intelligence. High-scorers on IQ tests can have enormous variability across academic subject area achievement, from well below average to top of the scale.
   5. **False.** IQ score differences by race have nothing to do with actual intelligence differences and quite a lot to do with cultural

differences not taken into account in the tests themselves, as well as big variations in opportunities to learn.

6. **False.** When someone invokes "common sense," they mean it's obvious to them. Sometimes that's because they know so much about the area in question (whether it's auto mechanics, child rearing, or cake baking) that they think everyone else should know that too, or it means they have unquestioned assumptions and misconceptions about that area.

7. **False.** There's no connection between social and emotional problems and intelligence. Some smart people have social or emotional problems, but so do some people who aren't so smart.

8. **False.** Kids who are significantly advanced in their learning often have trouble learning much unless there are special educational accommodations, and some have learning problems in addition to their advancement.

9. **False.** It can be a sign of intelligence to ponder and think and learn things more slowly than others. There's not much connection between the speed of mastery and IQ.

10. **False.** Some kids learn to read early and go on to do just fine but average academically; others don't learn to read until they're 7 and become academic superstars. Like pretty much everything else, it varies.

2. Neisser, U., Boodoo, G., Bouchard, T. J., Jr., Boykin, A. W., Brody, N., Ceci, S. J., Halpern, D. F., Loehlin, J. C., Perloff, R., Sternberg, R. J., & Urbina, S. (1996). Intelligence: Knowns and unknowns. *American Psychologist, 51*(2), 77–101. https://doi.org/10.1037/0003-066X.51.2.77

3. Herrnstein, R. J., & Murray, C. (1994). *The bell curve: Intelligence and class structure in American life*. Free Press.

4. Horowitz, F. D., Subotnik, R. F., & Matthews, D. J. (Eds.). (2009). *The development of giftedness and talent across the life span*. American Psychological Association.

5. Horowitz, Subotnik, & Matthews (2009).

6. Worrell, F. C. (2009). What does gifted mean? Personal and social identity perspectives on giftedness in adolescence. In F. D. Horowitz, R. F. Subotnik, & D. J. Matthews, *The development of giftedness and*

talent across the life span (pp. 131–152). American Psychological Association.

7. Dixson, D., Peters, S. J., Makel, M. C., Jolly, J. L., Matthews, M. S., Miller, E. M., Rambo-Hernandez, K. E., Rinn, A. N., Robins, J. H., & Wilson, H. E. (2020). A call to reframe gifted education as maximizing learning. *Phi Delta Kappan, 102* (4), 22–25. https://doi.org/10.1177/0031721720978057

8. Matthews, D. J., & Foster, J. F. (2021). *Being smart about gifted learning: Empowering parents and kids through challenge and change.* Gifted Unlimited.

9. Matthews, D. J., & Foster, J. F. (2014). *Beyond intelligence: Secrets for raising happily productive kids.* House of Anansi.

10. See Outschool.com for some interesting ideas.

11. Renzulli, J. S. (2021). Assessment for learning: The missing element for identifying high potential in low income and minority groups. *Gifted Education International, 37*(2), 199–208. https://doi.org/10.1177/0261429421998304

12. Reis, S. M., & Peters, P. M. (2021). Research on the Schoolwide Enrichment Model: Four decades of insights, innovation, and evolution. *Gifted Education International, 37*(2), 109–141. https://journals.sagepub.com/doi/pdf/10.1177/0261429420963987

13. Matthews & Foster (2021).

14. Resnick, M. (2018). *Lifelong kindergarten: Cultivating creativity through projects, passion, peers, and play.* MIT Press.

15. Yogman, M., Garner, A., Hutchinson, J., Hirsh-Pasek, K., & Golinkoff, R. M. (2018). The power of play: A pediatric role in enhancing development in young children. *Pediatrics, 142*(3), 2018–2058. https://doi.org/10.1542/peds.2018-2058

16. Hutton, J. S., Horowitz-Krause, T., Mendelsohn, A. L., DeWitt, T., Holland, S. K., & the C-MIND Authorship Consortium. (2015). Home reading environment and brain activation in preschool children listening to stories. *Pediatrics, 136*(3), 466–478. https://doi.org/10.1542/peds.2015-0359

17. O'Keefe, L. (2014). Parents who read to their children nurture more than literary skills. *AAP News, 35*(8), 8.

18. Rinaldi, L., & Karmiloff-Smith, A. (2017). Intelligence as a developing function: A neuroconstructivist approach. *Journal of Intelligence,* 5(2), 18. https://doi.org/10.3390/jintelligence5020018
19. Delahooke, M. (2019). *Beyond behaviors: Using brain science and compassion to understand and solve children's behavioral challenges.* PESI.
20. Yogman et al. (2018).
21. Duke, N. K. (2016). What doesn't work: Literacy practices we should abandon. *Edutopia.* https://www.edutopia.org/blog/literacy-practices-we-should-abandon-nell-k-duke
22. Vatterott, C. (2018). *Rethinking homework: Best practices that support diverse needs* (2nd ed.). ASCD.
23. Desimone, D. (2020). *9 forward-looking colleges that offer gap year programs.* https://www.goabroad.com/articles/gap-year/colleges-that-offer-gap-year-programs
24. https://www.frontiercollege.ca/

CHAPTER 7

1. Keating, D. P. (1980). Four faces of creativity: The continuing plight of the underserved. *Gifted Child Quarterly,* 24(2), 56–61. https://doi.org/10.1177/001698628002400203
2. Sternberg, R. (2002). Encouraging students to decide for creativity. *Research in the Schools,* 9(2), 61–70. https://drive.google.com/file/d/0B6rift-NquGOLWxvSEhSQWtiNGM/view?resourcekey=0-n5dbEpyPkz05QahK5X4F4g
3. Csikszentmihalyi, M. (1991). *Flow: The psychology of optimal experience.* Harper Collins.
4. Csikszentmihalyi, M. (2019). Foreword: The rewards of creativity. In R. Sternberg & J. C. Kaufman (Eds.), *The Cambridge handbook of creativity* (2nd ed., pp. xvii–xviii). Cambridge University Press. https://doi.org/10.1017/9781316979839
5. Csikszentmihalyi, M. (2014). *Flow and the foundations of positive psychology: The collected works of M. Csikszentmihalyi.* Springer.
6. Martin, W. (1999). *The parent's Tao Te Ching: Ancient advice for modern parents.* Perseus Books.

7. Martin (1999), p. 44.
8. Shenk, D., & Saltz, G. (2014). *The genius debate: Identifying the origins of genius.* https://www.learnoutloud.com/Catalog/Social-Sciences/Psychology/The-Genius-Debate-Identifying-the-Origins-of-Genius/82385
9. Martin (1999), p. 59.
10. Malchiodi, C. (2019, August 31). Imagination and expressive arts as antidotes to adversity. *Psychology Today.* https://www.psychologytoday.com/us/blog/arts-and-health/201908/imagination-and-expressive-arts-antidotes-adversity
11. Malchiodi, C. (2015). Creativity as a wellness practice. *Psychology Today.* https://www.psychologytoday.com/ca/blog/arts-and-health/201512/creativity-wellness-practice
12. Barbot, B., & Heuser, B. (2017). Creativity and identity formation in adolescence: A developmental perspective. In M. Karwowski & J. C. Kaufman, *The creative self: Effect of beliefs, self-efficacy, mindset, and identity* (pp. 87–98). Academic Press. https://doi.org/10.1016/B978-0-12-809790-8.00005-4
13. National Organization for Arts in Health. (2017). *Arts, health, and well-being in America.* https://docs.google.com/viewer?url=https%3A%2F%2Fthenoah.net%2Fwp-content%2Fuploads%2F2019%2F01%2FNOAH-2017-White-Paper-Online-Edition.pdf
14. Kim, S., Choe, I., & Kaufman, J. C. (2019). The development and evaluation of the effect of creative problem-solving program on young children's creativity and character. *Thinking Skills and Creativity, 33.* https://doi.org/10.1016/j.tsc.2019.100590
15. Mind Tools Content Team. (n.d.). *Creative problem solving: Finding innovative solutions to challenges.* Mind Tools. https://www.mindtools.com/pages/article/creative-problem-solving.htm
16. UNICEF Australia. (2019). *Five child activists you need to know: They are changing the world.* https://www.unicef.org.au/blog/stories/june-2019/five-child-activists

CHAPTER 8

1. To learn more about the basics of social development, see Goleman, D. (2006). *Social intelligence.* Penguin Random House.

2. To learn more about what's involved in emotional development, see Keltner, D., Oatley, K., & Jenkins, J. (2018). *Understanding emotions* (4th ed.). Wiley.

   Topics range from the historical evolution of emotions through emotion regulation and the brain mechanisms involved in emotions to a final chapter entitled "A Meaningful Life," all illustrated by rich allusions to spiritual traditions, politics, and the arts.

3. Armstrong, K. (2018, January). I feel your pain: The neuroscience of empathy. *Observer.* https://www.psychologicalscience.org/observer/neuroscience-empathy

4. Goleman, D. (2020). *Emotional intelligence: 25th anniversary edition.* Bantam.

5. Decety, J., & Ickes, W. (Eds.). (2011). *The social neuroscience of empathy.* MIT Press.

6. National Scientific Council on the Developing Child. (2004). *Young children develop in an environment of relationships: Working paper 1.* https://developingchild.harvard.edu/wp-content/uploads/2004/04/Young-Children-Develop-in-an-Environment-of-Relationships.pdf

7. Belsky, J., Caspi, A., Moffitt, T. E., & Poulton, R. (2020). *The origins of you: How childhood shapes later life.* Harvard University Press. (p. 53)

8. Lengua, L. (2020). Adversity can affect child self-regulation and resilience. *Psychology Today.* https://www.psychologytoday.com/ca/blog/cultivating-resilience/202003/adversity-can-affect-child-self-regulation-and-resilience

9. Shanker, S. (2016). Self-regulation vs. self-control. *Psychology Today.* https://www.psychologytoday.com/ca/blog/self-reg/201607/self-regulation-vs-self-control

10. Delahooke, M. (2019). *Beyond behaviors: Using brain science and compassion to understand children's problem behaviors.* PESI.

11. Price-Mitchell, M. (2015). Negativity and your child's brain: How to help kids stay positive. *Roots of Action.* https://www.rootsofaction.com/negativity-and-your-childs-brain/

12. Keltner et al. (2018).

13. Keltner et al. (2018), p. 366.

14. Allen, S. (2018). *The science of gratitude.* The Greater Good Science Center, Berkeley. https://docs.google.com/viewer?url=https%3A%2F%2Fggsc.berkeley.edu%2Fimages%2Fuploads%2FGGSC-JTF_White_Paper-Gratitude-FINAL.pdf

15. Keltner et al. (2018).
16. Dweck, C. S. (2006). *Mindset: The new psychology of success.* Random House.
17. Dweck, C. S. (2009). Foreword. In F. D. Horowitz, R. F. Subotnik, & D. J. Matthews (Eds.), *The development of giftedness and talent across the life span* (pp. xi–xiv). American Psychological Association.
18. National Scientific Council on the Developing Child. (2004). *Young children develop in an environment of relationships: Working paper 1.* https://developingchild.harvard.edu/wp-content/uploads/2004/04/Young-Children-Develop-in-an-Environment-of-Relationships.pdf (p. 1).
19. See, for example, Roots of Empathy (https://rootsofempathy.org/) and Making Caring Common (https://mcc.gse.harvard.edu/).
20. Kennedy-Moore, E. (2019). *Kid confidence: Help your child make friends, build resilience, and develop real self-esteem.* New Harbinger.
21. Scarry, R. (1984). *Richard Scarry's Pig Will and Pig Won't.* Penguin Random House.
22. Ungar, M. (2018). More chores, less play: Teaching children self-regulation. *Psychology Today.* https://www.psychologytoday.com/ca/blog/nurturing-resilience/201807/more-chores-less-play-teaching-children-self-regulation
23. Denworth, L. (2020, January). The outsize influence of your middle-school friends. *The Atlantic.* https://www.theatlantic.com/family/archive/2020/01/friendship-crucial-adolescent-brain/605638/
24. Steinberg, L. (2015). *Age of opportunity: Lessons from the new science of adolescence.* Houghton Mifflin Harcourt.
25. Bleidorn, W. (2015). What accounts for personality maturation in early adulthood? *Current Directions in Psychological Science, 24*(3), 245–252. https://doi.org/10.1177/0963721414568662
26. Eriksson, P. L., Wängqvist, M., Carlsson, J., & Frisén, A. (2020). Identity development in early adulthood. *Developmental Psychology, 56*(10), 1968–1983. https://doi.org/10.1037/dev0001093
27. Pusch, S., Mund, M., Hagemeyer, B., & Finn, C. (2019, May). Personality development in emerging and young adulthood: A study of age differences. *European Journal of Personality, 33*(3), 245–263. https://doi.org/10.1002/per.2181
28. https://rootsofempathy.org/school/ ("Who Are We" section).

29. https://mcc.gse.harvard.edu/ ("Our Mission" section).
30. https://mcc.gse.harvard.edu/research-initiatives/tag/Schools (para. 1).

CHAPTER 9

1. Belsky, J., Caspi, A., Moffitt, T. E., & Poulton, R. (2020). *The origins of you: How childhood shapes later life.* Harvard University Press.
2. Belsky et al. (2020), p. 204.
3. https://rootsofempathy.org/
4. https://mcc.gse.harvard.edu/
5. Denizet-Lewis, B. (2017, October 11). Why are more American teenagers than ever suffering from severe anxiety? *The New York Times Magazine.* https://www.nytimes.com/2017/10/11/magazine/why-are-more-american-teenagers-than-ever-suffering-from-severe-anxiety.html (para. 30).
6. Denizet-Lewis (2017), para. 31.
7. Whippman, R. (2016). *America the anxious: How our pursuit of happiness is creating a nation of nervous wrecks.* St. Martin's Press.
8. https://personalzen.com/
9. Dennis-Tiwary, T. A. (2017). Between a cyborg and a hard place. *Garrison Institute Newsletter.* https://www.garrisoninstitute.org/blog/between-a-cyborg-and-a-hard-place/
10. Dennis-Tiwary (2017), para. 3.
11. https://www.commonsensemedia.org/
12. Myruski, S., Gulyayeva, O., Birk, S., Perez-Edgar, K., Buss, K. A., & Dennis-Tiwary, T. A. (2017). Digital disruption? Maternal mobile device use is related to infant social-emotional functioning. *Developmental Science.* https://doi.org/10.1111/desc.12610
13. Hunter College Communications. (2018). *Moms and dads, put down your mobile phones! Hunter study shows that parents' distraction by mobile devices may hinder infant social-emotional development.* http://www.hunter.cuny.edu/communications/pressroom/news/new-moms-put-down-your-mobile-phones-hunter-study-shows-that-parents2019-distraction-by-mobile-devices-may-hinder-infant-social-emotional-development (para. 2).

14. AVG Technologies. (2015). Mobile phones are gaining an increasing share in the battle for parental attention. *AVG Now.* https://now.avg.com/digital-diaries-kids-competing-with-mobile-phones-for-parents-attention

15. UCI News. (2016). *Put the cellphone away! Fragmented baby care can affect brain development.* https://news.uci.edu/2016/01/05/put-the-cellphone-away-fragmented-baby-care-can-affect-brain-development/

16. Neighmond, P. (2014). *For the children's sake, put down that smartphone.* National Public Radio. https://www.npr.org/sections/health-shots/2014/04/21/304196338/for-the-childrens-sake-put-down-that-smartphone

17. Neighmond (2014), para. 5.

18. Steiner-Adair, C. (2014). *The big disconnect.* Harper.

19. Neighmond (2014), para. 8.

20. *Nicky & Vera* is a beautiful illustrated book for young children by Peter Sis. Set in the Holocaust, it underlines the importance of standing up to racism. For my review of that book, see https://www.psychologytoday.com/ca/blog/going-beyond-intelligence/202101/review-children-s-book-the-holocaust-peter-sis

21. Arkowitz, H., & Lilienfeld, S. O. (2013). Is divorce bad for children? *Scientific American Mind.* https://www.scientificamerican.com/index.cfm/_api/render/file/?method=inline&fileID=7BE196F8-CAA3-41E1-BB0D664ACA41364F

22. D'Onofrio, B., & Emery, R. (2019). Parental divorce or separation and children's mental health. *World Psychiatry, 18*(1), 100–101. https://doi.org/10.1002/wps.20590

23. Hetherington, M., & Kelly, J. (2003). *For better or for worse: Divorce reconsidered.* Norton.

24. Hetherington & Kelly (2003).

25. Pew Research Center. (2015, December). *The American family today.* Pew Research Center. https://www.pewresearch.org/social-trends/2015/12/17/1-the-american-family-today/

26. Public Policy Research Portal, Cornell University. (n.d.) *What does the scholarly research say about the well-being of children with gay or lesbian parents?* https://whatweknow.inequality.cornell.edu/topics/lgbt-equality/what-does-the-scholarly-research-say-about-the-wellbeing-of-children-with-gay-or-lesbian-parents/

27. Belsky et al. (2020).
28. Patchin, J. (2021). *New national bullying and cyberbullying data.* Cyberbullying Research Center. https://cyberbullying.org/new-national-bullying-cyberbullying-data
29. Patchin (2021), para. 3.
30. Broadband Search. (2021). *All the latest cyberbullying statistics and what they mean in 2021.* Broadband Search. https://www.broadbandsearch. net/blog/cyber-bullying-statistics
31. National Crime Prevention Council. (2021). *Cyberbullying tips for teens.* National Crime Prevention Council. https://docs.google.com/ viewer?url=https%3A%2F%2Fwww.ncpc.org%2Fwp-content%2F uploads%2F2017%2F11%2FNCPC_Cyberbullying-TipSheet-TipsForTeens.pdf
32. See, for example, Stomp Out Bullying (https://www.stompoutbullying. org/), Cyberbullying Research Center (https://cyberbullying.org/), or Safe at School (https://www.safeatschool.ca/).

CHAPTER 10

1. Webster, A., Cumming, J., & Rowland, S. (2017). Parent advocacy with schools: A success story. In A. Webster, J. Cumming, J., & S. Rowland (Eds.), *Empowering parents of children with autism spectrum disorder* (pp. 189–204). https://doi.org/10.1007/978-981-10-2084-1_11
2. For some experience-based perspectives on effective educational advocacy, see Schlitz, K. L. (2012). The role of educational advocacy. *Psychology Today.* https://www.psychologytoday.com/ca/blog/beyond-the-label/201205/the-role-educational-advocacy or Kidder, A. (2011). *Parent advocacy: The good, the bad, and the ugly.* Edcan Network. https://www.edcan.ca/articles/parent-advocacy-the-good-the-bad-and-the-ugly/
3. Brooks, D. (2015, April 11). The moral bucket list. *The New York Times.* https://www.nytimes.com/2015/04/12/opinion/sunday/david-brooks-the-moral-bucket-list.html (para. 4).
4. Bronfenbrenner, U. (1981). *The ecology of human development: Experiments by nature and design.* Harvard University Press.
5. Siegel, D., & Bryson, T. P. (2020). *The power of showing up: How parental presence shapes who our kids become and how their brains get wired.* Penguin Random House.

6. Obama, B. H. (2020). *A promised land*. Penguin Random House. (p. 448)
7. Keating, D. P. (2017). *Born anxious: The lifelong impact of early life adversity—and how to break the cycle*. St. Martin's Press.
8. Dennis-Tiwary, T. (2018). Digital mental health in the era of techlash: Towards humane health technology. *Psyche's Circuitry*. https://psychescircuitry.com/2018/07/24/digital-mental-health-in-the-era-of-techlash-towards-humane-health-technology/ (para. 2).
9. Steinberg, L. (2015). *Age of opportunity: Lessons from the new science of adolescence*. Houghton Mifflin Harcourt.
10. I use the term *cannabis* here to refer to cannabis products that contain the hallucinogen THC.
11. You might wonder why I'm using findings from 25 years ago and not more current numbers. It's a longitudinal study, so to know about the long-term implications of teenage cannabis use—which is what we're talking about here—we have to go back 25 years to when the now-adults were teenagers.
12. Steinberg (2015).
13. Jensen. F. E. (2015). *The teenage brain: A neuroscientist's survival guide to raising adolescents and young adults*. Harper.
14. Jensen (2015), p. 157.
15. Klinenberg, E. (2018). *Palaces for the people: How social infrastructure can help fight inequality, polarization, and the decline of civic life*. Penguin Random House.
16. Klinenberg (2018), p. 81.
17. growinghomeinc.org
18. Kling, S. (2018). Palaces for the people: How social infrastructure can help fight inequality, polarization, and the decline of civic life. *Booklist*. https://www.booklistonline.com/Palaces-for-the-People-How-Social-Infrastructure-Can-Help-Fight-Inequality-Polarization-and-the-Decline-of-Civic-Life-Eric-Klinenberg/pid=9607925 (para. 1).
19. Keating, D. P. (2011). *Nature and nurture in early child development*. Cambridge University Press.
20. Keating (2011).
21. Hendren, N., & Sprung-Keyser, B. (2020). A unified welfare analysis of government policies. *The Quarterly Journal of Economics, 135*, 3, 1209–1318. https://doi.org/10.1093/qje/qjaa006
22. Keating (2011).

INDEX

ABOUT THE AUTHOR

Dona Matthews, PhD, has worked with children, families, and schools since 1990, in addition to her academic work at several universities in Canada and the United States. She was the executive director of the Millennium Dialogue on Early Child Development, University of Toronto, and founding director of the Hunter College Center for Gifted Studies and Education, City University of New York. She has published widely on child and adolescent development, education, and supporting special needs and frequently shares with parent groups ideas about learning and growing alongside their children. She writes a popular blog for *Psychology Today*, "Going Beyond Intelligence," where she addresses parents' concerns about many aspects of their children's development, and is the coauthor or coeditor of four previous books: *The Development of Giftedness and Talent Across the Life Span* (coeditors Frances Degen Horowitz and Rena F. Subotnik), *The Routledge International Companion to Gifted Education* (coeditors Tom Balchin and Barry Hymer), *Beyond Intelligence: Secrets for Raising Happily Productive Kids* (coauthor Joanne Foster), and *Being Smart About Gifted Learning: Empowering Parents and Kids Through Challenge and Change* (coauthor Joanne Foster). Dr. Matthews's career began with a curiosity about the nature and development of intelligence, including social and emotional intelligences. Her focus now is on sharing the science of gifted development more broadly, encouraging each parent to connect with their child in ways that enhance their relationship, thereby enhancing the opportunities for every child to thrive. Follow Dr. Matthews on Twitter (@donamatthews).